Y0-BSM-936

Broken Bread and
Poured Out Wine

Broken Bread and Poured Out Wine

Spiritual Food
for Hungry Pilgrims

Edith Jackson

Pinecrest Publications
Salisbury Center, NY 13454

BROKEN BREAD AND POURED OUT WINE

Edith Jackson
© 2002

ISBN 0-9718261-0-2

Printed by
Pinecrest Publications
P.O. Box 320
Salisbury Center, NY 13454-0320

First Printing of First Edition, March 2003

Acknowledgements

I desire to briefly acknowledge the individuals who have been instrumental in the bringing forth of this writing.

I dedicate this book to my dear friend and encourager, Joan Patterson. She believed it was in me and called it forth.

I thank my husband, Herbert, for the hours he permitted me to spend in the loft, writing. My daughter, Diane, who unselfishly sacrificed so much of her time to type this manuscript, has my heartfelt thank you. Her husband, Ed, who worked many hours alone to let her have time off, has my thank you too.

I appreciate all those faithful ones who read the manuscript and offered suggestions on the content.

To all those who prayed, and cared, and believed, thank you. Here it is to the glory of God.

His name be praised.

Introduction

I had been in church almost all of my life, as a young child, as a wife and mother, and was moving into middle age when the Lord stirred me and began to draw me after Himself into a deeper walk. I had begun to question why I was on the earth; just to be born, exist, die and go to Heaven? It seemed futile somehow. Oh, I had meaning; I was a wife, mother, career woman, teacher and a leader in my church, but somewhere inside I was dissatisfied, unfulfilled. Middle age was looming ominously before my face, the 'important' phase of my life had passed, so I thought. It has to be down hill from here on! I felt so alone and so unnecessary.

Thanks be to God, it didn't stop there! In my futility, I began to ask questions like, "Who am I and why am I here? Is this all there is?" At this point God blessed me with the answer, Jesus Christ! He wanted a walk with me, a relationship, a friendship, whatever you want to call it. It was more than I could imagine or hope for!

People began to come into my life and cross my path, people who were strange. They talked about Jesus like you would talk about an old, dear friend. He was becoming real. They walked into my Sunday School class, into my business and into my home. At first, they made me uncomfortable. They were not people I would choose, who would know the game plan and the proper thing to do, things like: don't bother me, don't get too close, and for goodness sake, don't be real and say what you mean. There are ways to be friends without costing me anything, aren't there?

From these encounters of the close kind, I began a journey. A journey with Jesus that has taken 20 years. I began a journal in 1977 and journaled my experiences. Last year, my dear friend Joan called and said she had never known me to leave anything unfinished that the Father had asked me to do. Nothing, that is, but finish the book He instructed me to write. I felt so bad when I heard those words. It was evening and before I retired for the night, I told Him I didn't know how, but I was willing if this is what He wanted me to do. Ever so gently in my spirit I heard, "It is already written, it is in the journals, all you have to do is pull it out." This began months of gleaning what I had learned in my 20 year journey. It was finished in the same month in 1997 that it was begun in 1977.

You may ask, another book? There are so many and who has time to read? I asked these questions myself. The reason I give for writing this book: the Father asked me to. There are some thoughts that will hopefully be a help to others who are journeying with Jesus; those who are dissatisfied with the relationship they have and want to go on into the heart of God. It is a tool in the hand of God to be used to stimulate the heart that is searching for more of God.

It is my prayer and desire that you will be fed and encouraged as you prayerfully read these simple thoughts coupled with the scriptures and then make them your prayer and confession on your journey with Jesus. May God richly bless you as you go. Go rejoicing, knowing in your heart that, "He who began a good work in you will finish it" (Phillippians 1:6).

Praise God!

Would you be poured out as wine
upon the altar to me?
Would you be broken as bread to
feed the hungry?

Would you be so one with me
that
I may do just as I will,
To make your life, and light,
and love,
My Word fulfill?

...and if you draw out your soul to the hungry, and satisfy the afflicted soul: then shall your light rise in obscurity and thy darkness be as the noonday." – Isaiah 58:10

GIVE THAT WHICH SUSTAINS YOU

After fulfilling the requirements in verses 6-9, we then go on with the Lord in verse 10 "<u>and</u>..." We sometimes go so far with the Lord, as far as it feels good or brings a good report among our brethren. But God calls us on, to the unlovely, to the unrecognized, to the hard thing.

By the time Jesus came down off the cross, He was unrecognizable as a human being (Isaiah 52:14). He became an object of horror. God has called us by His Spirit to walk the way of Calvary. He spared not His own Son, why should He spare us?

Verse ten says, <u>and</u> you pour out that which sustains your life for the hungry and satisfy the need of the afflicted, <u>then</u>. Yes, oh <u>then</u> shall your light rise in darkness and your obscurity be as the noonday. You may then go on to claim the promises spoken by the mouth of God in verses 11-14.

Father, you who spared not your Son, help me spare not myself. I want in my heart to be poured out for your purposes in this world, but I know I cannot, unless your Spirit enables me.

I love you. I want to love your people.

"Seest thou how faith wrought with his works, and by works was faith made perfect." – James 2:22

GOING ON TO PERFECTION

I see works, not as something you do "for" God, such as a Christian duty or church work, but rather "working out your own salvation with fear and trembling;" to act upon the faith you've been given by God. To believe and sit down is impotent, sterile, bringing forth no fruit. On the other hand, saying, "God said it is so" and acting upon it is faith, as if it has already been done, is working out your salvation.

You have to read the Word to know what He said before you can act on it. Arise, walk, go, come - a command to act on what He said and the results were healing. Your faith has made you well, the acting was the faith.

To believe is to act on faith, or to plant a faith seed. Unbelief is to know the Word of God and refuse to act on it. Is ignorance of the Word an excuse? I think not! Ignorance robs us of all that was provided for us in the cross of Christ. We read the doctor's instructions on our prescriptions and we take the pills, by faith, expecting a change in our condition. Shouldn't we, at least, be that diligent with the Word of God?

Oh Spirit of the Living God, quicken us today to the truth of your Word. You shall <u>know</u> the truth and the truth shall set you free.

I want to know the truth.

"Be not afraid, only believe." – **Mark 5:36b**

BEYOND REASON

In Mark 5:22-24b; 35-43, we have the account of Jairus and Jesus. How much faith did it <u>really</u> take for the ruler of the synagogue, Jairus, to come to Jesus with his need?

His daughter was dying, nothing else had worked. What did he have to lose by coming to Jesus? He had <u>heard</u> from others who had seen Him heal the sick, cure the lame, give sight to the blind. How much faith? He had nothing to lose and everything to gain.

We throw ourselves on the horns of the altar in the "hopeless" situations, the crisis.

But his daughter died before they could <u>do</u> anything. Ah! Here comes the clarion call for faith beyond the reasonable. Jesus, in verse 36, told Jairus, do not be afraid, only believe. You have brought the situation to me, I have followed you, gone with you, willingly stepped into the situation, now, <u>leave it with me</u>. Don't ask me for help and when it seems unreasonable, take it back into your hands. <u>Stand still</u> and see the Glory of God.

We stop short of victory in Jesus when we can't see the logical results. Faith hopes against hope.

Dear Jesus, we want to stand when once we have asked you to come into the situation. We want to stand and see your Glory. Holy Spirit do a work in us to allow this to be.

I want to believe in all things.

"Let the words of my mouth, and the meditation of my heart, be acceptable in thy sight, O Lord, my strength and my redeemer."
Psalm 19:14

SHINE JESUS SHINE !

Life is relationships - I am as close to God as I am to those He has sent my way, for me to minister and witness to. They polish my rough edges and press me into His image (Ephesians 4:13).

I will always react negatively to this polishing, squeezing and forming. I will never be a better person than I am right now! Well, should I just quit and sit down in my miserable self? No, no, a thousand times no! The good news is, my hope is Jesus in me. He is living in me - He's living through me instead of me, to the degree I am surrendered at that moment to Him. It is a matter of exercising my will, a matter of choosing health and happiness, or sickness and death. I choose to allow Jesus to shine out of me today. Discipline and self-control are the actions of the day.

My prayer, Oh Lord, as I deepen and renew my commitment to you, is to give you anew and afresh, more of myself. As I see more, I shall continue to give more. Hallelujah, praise your goodness and your mercy!

Holy Spirit make Jesus big in me today!

*"Because it is given unto you to know the
mysteries of the Kingdom of Heaven."*
Matthew 13:11

STAY IN THE LIGHT

God gives us to know the mysteries of the Kingdom
of Heaven. The spiritual truths by which He deals with
His people.

When others around us are walking in darkness,
we know that we know. According to our faith and dying
to self, we minister these truths to those walking in
darkness.

They do not perceive what we are about, they
misunderstand us, they may even speak evil of good.
What are we to do? Jesus said, 'Father forgive them,
they know not what they do.' No condemnation; rather
continue on, to speak the truth to them in love.

It takes great inner strength and fortitude to stay
in the light God shines on the path when no one seems
to understand.

God gives us a vision of our ministry then withdraws
the reality of it, to strengthen us for the success of it.

*Our prayer must be, with Paul, that God might
strengthen us with might by His Spirit in the inner man.
That we might not become a castaway after showing many
the way.*

I choose not to be a castaway but to go on.

*"Finally, be ye all of one mind, having
compassion one of another; love as brethren,
be pitiful, be courteous:"* – 1 Peter 3:8

COMPASSION

Having compassion is loving people by doing what I
know is best for them, not by doing what is easiest and
most comfortable for me in commiserating with them.
Much of the time, pity is feeding someone's self-pity. We
need to get the patient out of the bed, not climb in with
them!

God is love, love for others. We need to learn to just
be: to relax, enjoy doing whatever we have to do. Just
be a person, yourself, enjoy yourself, like yourself, be
yourself. As you become free to be, others He has for
you to love will seek you out. You don't need to look for
people to minister to, they will find you!

We are a royal priesthood of intercessors. Ordinary
men and women conscious of some special need, of some
special people, royal, having our authority from the
Ascended Christ. Intercessor, the highest of callings, is
taking the place of the one they pray for.

When you want for that person, what you ask more
than your own life, as Moses did, you will indeed have
power before the throne.

*Spirit of intercession come and teach us to pray. Without
your power, we don't know what we should ask.*

I want to make a difference, empower me, oh God.

"Thou openest thine hand, and satisfiest the desire of every living thing." – **Psalm 145:16**

DESIRE SATISFIED

Oh God, purify our desire. In verse 19, the Psalmist follows on to say, He will fulfill the desire of them that fear Him.

Desire creates an image of the thing desired. Psalm 37:4 admonishes us to delight ourselves in the Lord, then He will give us all the desires of our heart. In Hebrew, the word "Meshalah" is used to denote craving from the root for potition

May our petition be as the Psalmist, 'Oh God, my soul pants after you as the hart pants after the water brook,' Psalm 42:1.

Psalm 51:10 should be our prayer - *Create in me a clean heart, Oh God; and renew a right spirit within me.*

The Lord's answer to that prayer in I Peter 1:2 is that the Holy Spirit has been at work in your heart, cleansing you with the blood of Christ Jesus and making you to please Him.

I thank you Lord for creating a clean heart in me.

I expect to see the desire of my heart fulfilled because I fear the Lord my God.

"...happy is that people, that is in such a case: yea, happy is that people whose God is the Lord." – **Psalm 144:15**

HAPPINESS IS

In order to be happy (blessed) you must have the fruit of the Spirit in operation in your life. Your happiness will be in direct proportion to the fullness of the operation of the Spirit of God in your life.

You cannot, you will not, be blessed by your own effort or merit. By choosing to die to self effort and asking the Holy Spirit to come and teach you Jesus indwelling, will you find the fruit active in your life.

We overlook things we must do and rush head on into carrying out God's purposes and plans by our own efforts. He just sits down and, in astonishment, watches us wear ourselves out.

By an act of my will and by faith, I enthrone Jesus as Lord of my house (of me). Holy Spirit, magnify Jesus in me - so that He can come out of the corner He has occupied since I was saved, and take full possession of my house.

Lord, you are not a guest, you own the place. You have free rule and reign. I allow you to place the furnishings and fill the pantry. Everyday, I yield control and ask the Holy Spirit to make Jesus big in me today.

Happiness is Jesus fully occupying my life today.

"For ye were sometimes darkness, but now are ye light in the Lord: walk as children of light." — **Ephesians 5:8**

WALKING IN THE LIGHT

Until I walk in all the light I have been given, I will not be given any more light. The children of Israel were just days away from the promised land, but you know the story - for forty years they went around in circles!

We are sinless in our new spirit - created in the image of God. Controlled by His Spirit, we go forward in the light as He is in the light. When we step forward and are confronted with confusion and uncertainty, we need to step back, get into the Spirit, check things out and get direction.

If we are drawn out and miss the way, should we just keep heading into the darkness? If we were on a trip in a strange place and lost our way, common sense would say to stop and get direction and recover our way. In the Spirit it is the same. Seek forgiveness for missing it and get back on the right track!

Our spirit is the first impression another person has of us! What is your spirit wearing today? Are we clothed in the righteousness, peace, and joy of the Holy Spirit?

Oh Father, I invite your Holy Spirit to dress me today before I walk forth to be Jesus in human form to those around me.

Thank you for my robe of righteousness.

"Behold thou desirest truth in the inward parts and in the hidden part thou shalt make me to know wisdom." – Psalm 51:6

THE 11TH COMMANDMENT - THOU SHALT NOT BE FOUND OUT!

We keep a couple of the commandments and <u>hide</u> the rest. This attitude damns us. Sin does not ultimately damn us - God provides for that. It is refusal to admit it as sin and confess it. It is dishonesty. Follow truth and honesty through the scriptures.

The law says do not steal. My attitude toward that law makes or breaks <u>me</u>. When Adam and Eve sinned, God did not change, they did. They ran and hid. They chose not to commune with God by confessing their act of sin. We break ourselves against the laws of God. They are facts, and facts cannot be changed. The normal operation of a law is a perfectly natural functioning of that thing according to its law, in ease, and spontaneity.

We break ourselves on the law of God — a crisis results — then we seek release in God's love. How can we ever thank Him enough that He loves us? We need to be able to come like little children and throw ourselves in our Fathers arms to receive all that love and acceptance we miss when separated.

The root cause of sin in us is the spirit of error living in us and having total domination.

Oh God, may honesty and truth begin to work in my inward parts, so that Christ Jesus can be in me, to me and through me, all He wants to be.

Come Holy Spirit.

"... the love of Christ constraineth me."
II Corinthians 5:14

SECURE KNOWLEDGE

Nothing but the love of God has remained constant in my life. For all the years I can remember, changes have washed over me: changes in relationships, in age, in location, and in occupation. Always, the love of God overshadowed all the changes and remained changeless. It has charted my course and kept my compass always pointing in the right direction. Nothing can turn you away from the sure fact of the constant love of God (Romans 8:35-39).

God was in Christ, reconciling my world to Himself. This is a pure act of love, an absolute. Draw from this absolute fact in the face of any and all changes that come into your life. Hold your course steady in the goodness of God's love. It will never change or diminish.

Father God, today we need to run into your bosom and smother ourselves in your bountiful goodness. There are many forces trying to get us to run away from you instead of to you. Thank you for proving yourself to us over and over again.

We repent of doubting you.

... whatsoever things are pure ... of good report; if there be any virtue, and if there be any praise, think on these things " – Philippians 4:8

THINKING ABOUT THINGS

Pain is often the only scalpel that will cut through the scar tissue of the heart so that we can get in touch with our feelings. When love cuts away the protective callouses, the actual cause is revealed and healed.

Before hidden bitterness can be exposed and transformed, remembered unforgiveness has to be dealt with honestly. Whatever we cannot forgive, we are doomed one day to live. Whatever a man sows, that shall he also reap. If we sow seeds of unforgiveness, we will reap a life like that.

Could it be, the inability to forgive a frailty in another person indicates that we have the same frailty existing in us?

What we affirm today, we will become tomorrow! I want to affirm that I am one with God and His Son Jesus Christ. His wholeness, power of mind and perfect peace are mine.

Confession clears the mind, when we have nothing in our mind which seems to deserve punishment, then there is no fear of punishment.

Faith sees circumstances as God sees them - whole, beautiful and filled with His love.

Father God, fill us, we pray, today, with your love, your light and your life. Empower us by your Spirit to walk in that love.

I choose to walk in God's love today.

"For out of the abundance of the heart the mouth speaketh." – Matthew 12:34

OUR PERFECT EXAMPLE

If you are to know the strength of God's reliability and integrity, then you must see Him as Jesus saw Him. According to the Amplified Bible, to know means to be intimately acquainted with, through experiential knowledge.

We can only comprehend what a persons inner life and thoughts are by what they say. Seventy times in the gospels, Jesus referred to God as Father.

If Jesus was perfect humanity, He is the perfect example of relationship to God. Instead of confusing our relationship with our earthly father, which may or may not have been good, we need to look at how Jesus conducted Himself in His Father's presence, as well as how He talked to Him.

In John 13:13, we see Jesus secure in the knowledge of who He was, His identity assured. From this knowledge, He was able to serve His disciples in whatever task was required.

From this point of sonship, I too can move out and reach out to others in whatever is needed to help them know sonship.

Thank you Father, you have not asked me to do anything Jesus didn't do successfully first.

I choose to walk where Jesus walked.

January 14

*"See that none render evil for evil unto
any man; but ever follow that which is good,
both among yourselves, and to all men"*
I Thessalonians 5:15

ARE YOU PLUGGED IN?

As I was vacuuming, I noticed I wasn't picking up anything from the carpet. I got my tools and took the vacuum apart. As I did, nothing seemed wrong. I noticed the hose had come unplugged from the vacuum. It seemed funny at the time, but as I thought about it, I saw we can do nothing when we are "unplugged" from our source of power! I could have continued to vacuum, not picking up anything or I could have taken the vacuum to the shop. The simple reality was to plug it in and get back to the source.

When I get unplugged from the Holy Spirit, I get into serious trouble, sometimes even into war, returning evil for evil. Some of Paul's final instructions were for us not to return evil for evil. Stay out of war! I return evil when my heart is not right, when I am unplugged from my source. My river gets clogged and love ceases to flow out of me.

In these serious days, we must diligently seek to stay plugged in. Get into the place you commune with God, and get checked out before you go forth!

We will run to the quiet place, Father. We will run to our source. Thank you for being our supply.

I take Jesus as my source today.

14

"I am the vine, ye are the branches:
He that abideth in me, and I in him, the
same bringeth forth much fruit: for without
me ye can do nothing." – **John 15:5**

THE GREATEST OF THE GRACES

Earnestly desire the fruit of the Spirit to be manifested in your life. Then, the gifts of the Spirit will be in operation at a time when they are needed to express the love of God. Pray that God will, and that He can, (be assured He will if He can) fill you with His love. He can, if you open yourself to receive, by faith, what you asked Him for. As He fills you with His love, the fruit of the Spirit in you will overflow onto everyone with whom you come in contact. It will be a natural thing, not anything you do to make it happen. It is your life reflecting. Your part is to be still and let God work.

Love is called the greatest of the graces, because it is the one in which there is a likeness between the believer and his God. God has no need of faith. He is dependent on no one. There is none superior to Him in whom He must trust. God has no need of hope, for to Him all things are certain.

But God is love, and the more love His people have, the more they are like their Father, in heaven. There will be no faith or hope in heaven. Love will fill all things.

Holy Spirit of God, by whom the Grace gifts operate, thank you for all of them. I need them. But, oh, Spirit of God, perfect love in me, and fit me for heaven.

I want to be pleasing to my Father today.

"Blessed are ye, when men shall revile you,
and persecute you, and shall say all manner
of evil against you falsely, for my sake."
Matthew 5:11

FOR HIS SAKE AND OTHERS

If you are being used of God, you will be misunderstood. To be misunderstood is a form of persecution. Love and pray for those that persecute you for they are enemies of God, not you personally. It is normal to react negatively, but immediately give it to Jesus. Pray as Steven and Jesus, Himself, prayed, "Father, forgive them for they know not what they do".

It's the battle, old as time, but in Psalms 91 and 92 we are told, the battle is the Lords. We are to stand still and see the salvation of the Lord. Was it Steven's prayer of forgiveness that opened Saul's way into salvation (Acts 7:58)? It is also the principle of heaping coals of fire on our enemies' heads. No greater gift can we give than to stand in forgiveness and allow the Holy Spirit to bring conviction.

There is a promise here for those who can go on to Rejoice in persecution. Matthew 5:12 reveals to us the promise of great reward.

Holy Spirit of God, this is an area where we need your help. You must fill us with the knowledge of Jesus and enable us to be as He was on this earth.

I want others to see Jesus in me today.

January 17

"Whereas ye know not what shall be on the morrow. For what is your life? It is even a vapour, that appeareth for a little time, and vanisheth away." – **James 4:14**

LIFE IS FRAGILE

Several years ago, I learned a customer of mine had died. A freak accident on the highway had claimed his life. I wondered how his death would benefit those affected by it. A few years later, my wonderful grandson went to be with Jesus at a very early age. Again, I prayed, "Lord, don't let me miss what you have for me to learn both from his life and now his death." Two valuable lessons came clearer to me than understanding the deaths. One, when God is gracious enough to send someone into my path of life, I am to be thankful for being included in what God is doing, no matter what I'm involved in doing! Number two, store not up for yourself treasures on earth, where rust and moths will destroy them, but store up for yourself treasures in heaven (Matthew 6:19-20). I also saw the certainty of death, the unexpectedness of death, and the necessity of being ready to meet God face to face.

Father, help us remember life is about relationships. Opportunities come and go and never return. May we be aware of the people in our lives. What impartation can I make in their lives?

I'm reminded love never fails.

*"For what man knoweth the things of a man,
save the spirit of man which is in him? even
so the things of God knoweth no man, but the
Spirit of God."* – I Corinthians 2:11

WHO ARE YOU?

This scripture says man's spirit is the only one that knows him. As we get in touch with our spirit and surrender it to the will of God (by faith, we can do this), we give the Spirit of God permission to teach us the things of God in relationship to our humanity. To know yourself is to be free, free indeed. In the knowing we realize, without our union with Him, we can never really know the real us. Our spirit man, in union with God's Spirit, begins to blossom, bloom, grow and yield the fruit of the Holy Spirit.

After the fall of man, Adam still had all his senses. The only thing he lost was communion with God. His senses became perverted through sin and man's true identity was lost to him. We have been restored now, through the death on the cross of God's Son. It is imperative we get reacquainted with the Father now that we have come home. Find the place of communion, take the time to know Him, and you will know who you are.

Holy Spirit, we invite you today to walk into our lives through this prayer. We want you to make Jesus more real to us today and to know the Father more intimately. Come Holy Spirit, we pray.

I yield my will to the Spirit of God.

"And let us not be weary in well doing: for in due season we shall reap, if we faint not."
Galatians 6:9

FAITHFUL IN THE MUNDANE

Faithfulness to the seemingly mundane tasks, that make up the most of life, is of great value to God. How so? It is obedience that frees the Spirit of God to change us in the inner man. As we do the ordinary tasks of a seemingly dull nature, God can transform them into acts of His omnipotence.

We need to call upon the Lord for His grace and mercy in the dull places. It's easy to fly high in moments of ecstasy. It doesn't take nobleness of character to do great exploits, but the simple tasks of living seem to call for special grace. This brings great delight to the Father's heart. He is so quick to hear our cry of, "How long, oh God?" and sends grace and mercy to be our companions.

It's not what assigned paths you walk, it's how you walk them, that honors God. Don't be shoddy in your responsibilities that no one sees, God is watching. It is, after all, His "well done" we are waiting to hear.

Jesus, you called me to love/you and to fellowship with you. I was put here to commune and to fellowship with you. As I live and move and have my being, in you, I am fulfilled.

**Today I will seek opportunities
to fellowship with Jesus.**

**"If the Son therefore shall make you free, ye
shall be free indeed." – John 8:36**

FREE TO BE IN JESUS

Another day, a new beginning. A day to live and
move and have my being in Him. I must lift up Jesus,
and He will do the rest. He said, "If I be lifted up, I will
draw all men to myself." I don't have to go to seminary
or Bible school to lift up Jesus. I don't have to wait until
I know something profound to lift up Jesus. Just go
about holding God's hand, and being in Him, and He
will do the rest. Lift up Jesus by personifying His life,
loving people. Love is the bottom line. You will not fail if
you move in love. You will always be acting for the other
persons best.

*Holy Spirit, I free you, in me, to be all you need to
be today. You have the responsibility for me and all you
bring into my life today, because I give it to you. I am
now free to be me, letting you be who you want to be in
me. Wherever you want to go and whatever you want to
do, I agree.*

Help yourself to me today.

"Therefore if any man be in Christ, he is a new creature: old things are passed away; behold, all things are become new."
II Corinthians 5:17

FREE TO BE

If I am "born-<u>again</u>," a <u>new</u> man, a <u>new</u> creation, I am a brand new being - free to begin all over again, to start something new. We are always trying to finish something we started yesterday or twenty years ago. This can become spiritual bondage. If we are to die daily, then every day I am free to begin again, forgetting, or putting away, those past things and looking forward to the mark of the high calling of God in Christ Jesus. In I Corinthians 13:11, the apostle spoke of this putting away. Putting away is a term used for a funeral or a burying. We're trying often times to be good children and finish what we started. Let each day stand before God as a new thing.

I run the race this day with patience, knowing nothing comes at me, but it has gone through my Heavenly Father and been approved for my good, for my perfecting. Nothing is too big for God and me to handle together, if I play my part, rather than God's. His is to do, mine is to be!

Father God, I believe what your Word says about me. I chose, by my free will, to say with your Word, I am brand new. Old things are indeed passed away. Now I lay them to rest and I remove the grave clothes and put on the garments of praise.

I walk into today free to be.

"When pride cometh, then cometh shame: but with the lowly is wisdom." – **Proverbs 11:2**

KEEP IT LOW

Think with me, of all the analogies of being low: the safe place in a storm; where the roots were stored for keeping in the old days; where the Indians put their ears to the ground to hear the approach of the enemy. The low place is the safe place – rooted and grounded in the Word of God! We go up to the high places, but only to pull the devil's kingdoms down. Stay with your nose in the carpet. God Himself is watching your back! Any time we rise up, we are in a place of danger. The pride of life runs in high color! Jesus Himself was meek and lowly. We are told in this way to learn of Him.

One last comparison; in a fire we are instructed to get to the ground and crawl to safety. The smoke and fumes rise toward the ceiling. We might say, keep it cool, stay in a safe place, where God can instruct us in wisdom and knowledge.

My Precious Lord Jesus, we choose to take your yoke upon us and learn to be lowly. You thought it not robbery to put off your royalty and walk as a man. So much we need to learn of your ways.

Teach us, Holy Spirit, to be like Jesus.

"That he would grant you, according to the riches of his glory, to be strengthened with might by his Spirit in the inner man."
Ephesians 3:16

FILLED AND BAPTIZED

Power, in the inner man, is supplied by the Holy Spirit. His power enables us for service and enables us to fight and resist Satan.

There are requirements to receive this power. Number one, we must yield to the Lord Jesus Christ and obey His will. Secondly, we believe through prayer that He will flood our spirit with His power (Galatians 3:14). Thirdly, this power enables the believer to impart God's life and power to thirsty and dying men.

We are filled with the Spirit for life.

We are baptized in the Spirit for service.

Lord Jesus, we want both! When our spirit man, empowered by the Spirit of God, touches the spirit of another person, they receive life. They can begin to grow in their spirit man and learn of Jesus.

We do pray for the infilling of the Spirit of God, by faith. We also choose to be baptized in the Spirit of God, so that we may go forth and touch those we meet with the life of God.

By faith I believe and receive the Spirit of God.

**"All things that the Father hath are mine:
therefore said I, that he shall take of mine,
and shall shew it unto you." – John 16:15**

CAN YOU BELIEVE?

We see Jesus as comforter. We also see Him as sympathizer, but do we fail to see Him as almighty? We say we don't doubt He can do it, we are just not sure of ourselves. That's an untruth. We know exactly what we're capable of, therefore, we are really doubting God. We need a revelation of the reality that God is almighty.

He brings down from heaven what we need, not up out of ourselves. That's why we wait and rely upon His Spirit to come upon us. This is the empowering of our human spirit by the Spirit of God. In this way, our soul and body manifest the acts of God.

Whatsoever you desire, if you ask believing in your heart, you have it. It shall be yours, not from any action on your part, but as a heavenly gift from the Father.

Father, your Word says if we can only believe, all things are possible. We need the truth about the things we are asking. Your Word is truth. Holy Spirit, make the truth of the Word of God real to us, so that we may believe.

I choose to believe God's Word.

"Sing unto the Lord, bless his name; show forth his salvation from day to day."
Psalm 96:2

ITS A NEW DAY TODAY

In Leviticus 11, we see the principle of doing what God forbids and the resulting uncleanness. It says whosoever eats what God declared unclean was unclean until evening. In Genesis, God clearly reveals days and what each day consisted of. In Exodus, God gave the Israelites manna, a day at a time. In the New Testament, we are admonished, each day is sufficient unto itself - also, to take no thought for tomorrow. In the model prayer, we pray, give us this day our daily bread.

We are called on over and over to live life one day at a time. Each day is a clean, fresh, piece of paper. We have a choice what we write on it.

There is another scripture we need to consider. Let not the sun go down on your anger (Ephesians 4:26). How beautiful and refreshing our days will be if we keep short accounts with God and clean the books every day.

Lord Jesus, we are called to show forth your salvation from day to day. Every day is a day I can "model" you before the world. I want to show you correctly Lord, in all your love, compassion and mercy.

Help me, Holy Spirit, to model Jesus.

"...the light of the knowledge of the glory of God in the face of Jesus Christ."
II Corinthians 4:6b

LOOKING AT JESUS

When we blow it and revert to a spirit of disobedience, the Father accepts our repentance, allowing His mercy to function.

God is merciful. He does not reject us for disobeying, rather he rejects us for refusing His merciful forgiveness. We simply confess our disobedient spirit, allowing Him to show mercy. The Spirit says come before the mercy seat of God.

We must see God as merciful. Often times we are condemning, because we fail to accept God's mercy. We choose to see Him as hard and unapproachable. Therefore, we reflect that image to others. If we see God as He is (loving, merciful, slow to anger), we will reflect that image in our relationships.

It comes back to looking full in the face of Jesus; seeing the character and the nature of God reflected there. We see Jesus as the Spirit reveals Him.

I pray it will always be sweet communion with my Lord - this close fellowship, this assurance that you are sovereign in my life and in the universe. May I be obedient to you through the working of your Spirit. Teach me Father! Use me!

Holy Spirit, I would see Jesus, so that those around me will see Jesus in me.

"But they understood not that saying, and were afraid to ask Him." – **Mark 9:32**

FOLLOWING ON

The discipline of dismay is essential in discipleship. We cannot fathom the Christ that strides before us with face set like flint.

We become dismayed. He is not our comrade, our comforter, as He was, at first, when He bade us come. Our inclination is as the three did on the mount, build a fire and stay there where we've become comfortable, in the service we know, and now enjoy the ritual of it. We look up and see Jesus striding on, not looking back to see if we're following. We'll have to hurry if we want to catch up with Him. Oh, but I'm afraid, I didn't think it would be like this.

I will become dismayed if I do not endure until this darkness of dismay passes. Out of it will come the following of Jesus, which is an unspeakable joy. Fears in the night, joy in the morning!

Holy Spirit, this is where I need your work in my inner man, to build a foundation of faith that can look into the face of the unknown and not freak out. I want to follow on to know Jesus, the power of His might and the fellowship of His suffering.

I choose to follow Jesus today.

*"And go quickly, and tell his disciples
that he is risen from the dead; and, behold,
he goeth before you into Galilee; there shall
ye see him." – Matthew 28:7*

THE FLOW OF GOD

There is no stagnation in the things of God. The flow is ever moving. The disciples stopped only for feeding sessions. Jesus was always on the move.

We must not become ritualized. We must not hasten back to a place we met Jesus at before. He is not there. He has risen and moved on.

There is no power in doing the same thing over and over. God never does the same thing, the same way, twice. We cannot duplicate an act of God. No two sets of circumstances are ever the same, or two individuals ever the same. This disallows duplication or counterfeiting. The work itself is original before the counterfeit can come about. Therefore, any existing thing done again is not of God.

We must determine where the flow of God is and get in it. This takes a deliberate act.

Holy Spirit, we are hearing a lot of talk about the river of God today. It's not a new thing, it is the river that has always flowed from the throne of God. It's not a new river, it's just a fresh call. May we not be afraid of the voice of the Spirit and say yes to the call.

I say yes to the call.

"... Not by might, nor by power, but by my
spirit saith the Lord of hosts."
Zechariah 4:6

NOT BY MIGHT

When a situation seems painful to us personally, we are selfishly concerned about it. As we become less and less (I must decrease so that He may increase) concerned selfishly about situations, we will find it easier to know God's will concerning them.

As you become concerned only with God and His concerns for your fellow man, you will be guided by Jesus in everything. We must get out of the personal (dying to self) and into the impersonal (alive to God), through union with Jesus Christ, to be in His flow. Then any and all service to our fellow man will be Him empowering us to do it.

We get into that flow by loving Him. By loving Him, we enter the life of God which is love. We cannot love Jesus as humans, so the acts of love we do unto others are expressions of our love for Him. Can we stretch ourselves enough to grasp the concept of being Jesus with skin on to others?

By your Spirit, Father, only by your Spirit. Your love is shed abroad in our hearts by your Spirit.

**I choose to walk by the Spirit and
not by my own strength.**

"Let this mind be in you, which was also in Christ Jesus." - Philippians 2:5

BRINGING GOD ON THE SCENE

Prayer is seeking an audience with God. It is not to get gifts, answers, or favors. It is to line ourselves up with the will of God in the matter. God is in action already, the thing has been accomplished eons ago. We merely get into the flow of God's action, which is love. This is what is meant by the river. It is the flow of the life of God washing out from His throne bringing life, giving refreshing to you on earth - God coming on the scene!

Prayer is loving God so much that we seek to please Him in a matter. It is entering into the mind of Christ, becoming one with him. Praying without ceasing is entering into, and abiding in, oneness with Christ Jesus. We will, then, always be seeking to please God by being in the flow (the river) of His love and His will because we are one with Jesus Christ in our thinking, abiding, and obedience.

Father, how wonderful to know we can bring any situation or circumstance in our life to you and come into agreement with you in it. This is a great place of rest.

By faith today, I bring my requests to the place of agreement with God by entering into the mind of Christ. Holy Spirit, you interpret for each of us, bringing us together.

"... O my Lord, I am not eloquent ... I am slow of speech, and of a slow tongue ... O my Lord, send, I pray thee, by the hand of him whom thou wilt send." – Exodus 4:10 & 13

ARE YOU AVAILABLE?

As with Moses, the Father wants only our willingness to be the vessel. He equips us, prepares all the provisions and, also, makes the way. The only thing about Moses that tied God's hands was when he said, "Get someone else. I'm not available." Today, we say with Isaiah in verse 6:8, "Here am I Lord, send me."

We must say "Lord, I am willing to be used, I choose to become available for whatever you choose for me to do. I know nothing. I can do nothing in my own strength that will have any lasting effect. I choose to be empty and available. You are the provider, the maintainer, the furnisher, the equipper and the empowerer. You have full responsibility for everything I do. Therefore, I take no blame when it seems to go wrong and no glory when it seems to go right."

Father, I thank you that you've chosen to let me in on what you're doing. Thank you for being God and for loving me.

The Spirit of God being my helper, I will rouse myself and seek the mind of Christ about everything, especially concerning matters of prayer for others.

February 1

"...I will be with thee: I will not fail thee, nor forsake thee." – Joshua 1:5

COMFORTED IN ALL MY WAYS

In all my years, I have known good and I have known hardship. One overlaying thought has kept me in all my ways. "I will never leave you, nor forsake you." Please think with me a moment about a young man facing a hard time. Joshua has just lost Moses, it's grow up time! I feel sure he was having lots of anxiety about the immediate future. In his distress, he went to God, as he had even when he had Moses as his leader. God spoke these words to him:

1. No one will be able to defeat you as long as you live.
2. I will be with you as I was with Moses.
3. I will be with you always.
4. I will never abandon you.
5. Be determined and confident.
6. Do not neglect any part of the law.
7. Be sure the law is read whenever you worship.
8. Study the law day and night.
9. Make sure you obey the whole law as it is written.
10. Then you will be prosperous and successful.
11. I have commanded you to be determined and confident.
12. Do not be afraid or discouraged, for I the Lord your God, am with you wherever you go. (Joshua 1:5-9)

Father I will be mindful of these promises, you gave me as well as Joshua. Thank You.

I take great comfort in these promises.

"For the upright shall dwell in the land, and the perfect shall remain in it." – Proverbs 2:21

FURTHER INSTRUCTION

Instruction is a wonderful thing if you have a teachable heart and are willing to make adjustments to accommodate new information. Here, in Proverbs 2, we have another example of Godly instruction.

1. Learn what I teach you.
2. Never forget what I tell you to do.
3. Listen to what is wise.
4. Try to understand.
5. Beg for knowledge.
6. Plead for insight.
7. Look for it as hard as you would for silver or hidden treasure.
8. If you do, you will learn to fear the Lord who gives wisdom.
9. If you listen, you will know what is right, what is just, and what is fair.

You will know what you should do. You will become wise. Your knowledge will give you pleasure. Your knowledge and insight will protect you and prevent you from doing wrong. They will keep you away from people who stir up trouble by what they say. Follow the example of good men and live a righteous life.

Father God, I set my heart to be teachable and to learn the ways of the Godly. Then I will dwell in the good land all my days.

I will hear and I will obey.

*"So then faith cometh by hearing, and
hearing by the Word of God."* – **Romans 10:17**

FIRST THINGS FIRST

Faith is the first foundation we must have to build
on. The ground we need to build our foundation on is
the Word of God. God's way of doing everything is to
send His Word. His Word is His promise. Whenever His
Word produces faith, He can keep His promise. Please
read this again and ask the Holy Spirit to work it into
your spirit, so that it belongs to you, this cycle of faith.
God's Word, His never ending Word, creates our faith. It
is the foundation, or the ground, of our faith. Faith
begins where the will of God is known. True faith is not
believing God can, but that He will.

It is God's will for us all to have what He purchased
for us at Calvary. We must not seek His will, but His
path for us individually. God's path involves what you
are to do. God's will is what God wants you to have. To
learn His will for our lives, we simply have to pick it up
and read it. His will: His testament, the Bible.

*Father God, I've asked you so many times to do what
you've already done in your Word. Forgive me for being
lazy and trying to get you to do my part.*

**I will find God's path for me and then read
His Word to know how to walk it.**

"And now for a little space grace hath been shewed from the Lord ..." – Ezra 9:8

LIVING NOW

How can I stop looking over my shoulder at yesterday? It is robbing me of now! My regrets, my failures, my successes - all of them rob me of this moment of life.

I will fail. I will always fail in some way. Satan's great tool is regret; to get my eyes on myself and my failures, and defeat me. When I am living in regret for having missed an opportunity, I lose that moment to be what I was meant to be.

When I fail, and I will, I must carry it straight to God, through the cross of Jesus, by confessing I blew it. Then, I must receive cleansing and go on into the next moment, resting and abiding in Him. Someone has said, "Put the failure in the cup Jesus drank out of!"

This life is not about my perfection or how good I am at being good. It's about living and trying to do the right thing. It's about not being so afraid you'll fail that you never do anything. Get right out there and fall down. Jesus is on the scene. He loves you and picks you up so you can go on.

Oh God, I want to jump out into the flow of life, secure in the knowledge you're here.

I'll be quick to say, "I repent" and mean it.

"I am the true vine, and my Father is the husbandman." – John 15:1

FRUIT PRODUCERS

It's really hard to get good fruit these days! Something is tampering with the vines to destroy the fruit. I see a lot of gifts of the spirit manifesting, but I'm hungry for good fruit. Let's examine the vine that produces good fruit for a moment. God is the tap root, so to speak. Jesus is the vine, and we, the believers, are the branches on which the fruit of the Holy Spirit hangs. It's like jewels or ornaments for the world to see. We do not produce the fruit, the Holy Spirit does, as Jesus abides in us and we in Him.

The fruit of the Spirit is the personality of Jesus, and it comes out of us as we abide in Him. It is not anything we produce. We just abide in Jesus and He is manifested for the whole world to see. We simply keep adoring, loving, relying on Him. We do nothing to produce this fruit. It isn't even ours to partake of. Actually, we are unaware of it. Others see it, for God's glory. He started the whole thing so people could see what He is really like, and want to partake of His life.

Father, I want my fruit to be pleasing to you and good to others. Work on my behalf to bring forth good fruit.

**I allow God to tend my branch
any way He chooses.**

"Every branch in me that beareth not fruit he taketh away: and every branch that beareth fruit, he purgeth it, that it may bring forth more fruit." – John 15:2

NOT FRUIT INSPECTORS

If we become aware of the fruit on our branch, we are looking at ourselves instead of Jesus, and that beautiful fruit falls to the ground before it matures to where it can produce life. When we see the fruit, we become proud. We think we're the vine. Any time we take our eyes off Jesus, growth stops. If we look away long enough, the fruit begins to dry up and look unattractive to others.

We draw others to Christ only when the fruit on our branches is lush, appetizing, whole and unblemished. The degree our fruit manifests Jesus' personality, is the degree we draw others to want to be grafted into the true vine.

We must remain as simple as children not questioning Jesus, just abiding, trusting. Let us be warned not to look inward, not to analyze ourselves. Let the Holy Spirit have free reign to remold, remake us into the image of Christ.

Holy Spirit, you shine the light of truth in the area in my life that needs change. I give you permission to put your finger on that and help me change. I yield to you.

If I am God's, everything must pass through Him before it comes to me. Therefore, I accept it.

*"Have faith in God...that ye may know
the hope of His calling."*
Mark 11:22 and Ephesians 1:18

FAITH THAT WORKS

The Holy Spirit supernaturally empties your spirit of doubt and fills you with an inner knowing. Through this inner knowing, and in spite of doubts that try to creep in, you will not doubt the thing you are to undertake. Every time you have a knowing in your heart and act on it, you take a leap of faith.

The greatest purpose for your struggling is to learn, through your spirit, to see the face of Jesus - to see Him with your inner sight. Through your struggles, you learn to see with your spirit. My mistakes are rungs in the ladder that lead me upward to God. If I believe this, I can grow. I can praise God in all circumstances. I will not spend time in remorse. I will instantly transfer my sin to Jesus and go on my way, rejoicing.

If we have trusted God with our salvation, can we not also trust Him with all our other needs?

Father, so many times we've been disappointed in those we trusted. They were unable to meet our needs, because our trust was misplaced. Help us set our hopes on you and things eternal, to raise our sight to you.

**I choose to see God everywhere and
in everything I need.**

"For we are his workmanship, created in Christ Jesus..." – **Ephesians 2:10**

ABANDONMENT TO GOD

Asking no questions - that's real abandonment! When we pause to question and to try to reason, or to "understand," at that point we have snatched ourselves out of God's hand. Abandonment is total commitment in all things. It is not questioning anything that comes, because it is Christ living His life in you, and it has to be right. He is God!

Our life is hidden in heaven, in Christ Jesus. And the life we live in the flesh is Him living in us. We will be revealed with Him at His coming. This is Him now living in me. When anything comes out that is not Him, I've gotten out of the spirit into the soul realm where the smog is. The Word says it does not yet appear what we will be, but we know when He shall appear we shall be like Him (I John 3:2). Now, what could be more reassuring than to know we're not now what we are going to be? Not only that, but what we really are does not appear as it is. Do you get it? The work is going on inside and being worked from the inside out.

When diamonds are being mined, they aren't what they appear to be as they are coming forth. Take heart, dear one, He is not finished with you!

Holy Spirit, thank you for continuing to work on me.

**Today I say, yes Lord,
chip away, come forth!**

"Judge not, that ye be not judged."
Matthew 7:1

WHAT'S THAT IN YOUR EYE?

Discernment is a call to intercession, not fault finding. A greater love is necessary for me to pray for others. I am sure of God and His goodness and mercy because of what I've experienced in my life. I must be that sure of Him in the life of another, before I can pray for them with the mind of Christ. I know He is working out His good pleasure in their lives, as well as my own. Therefore, I must get beyond pity into compassion. To pray for others with the mind of Christ, I must rid my heart of attitudes like pride, envy and criticism.

I pray right now, Father, and confess these sins and ask you to cover them with the blood of Jesus and replace them with your love. I thank you that you are now doing this.

If we trust God to save our soul, will we not trust him with our sins? The little foxes that trip us up? A few examples: overeating, worry, gossip, self-pity. The power of God slays every element of self-reliance in me. Any time I say I cannot, I have called God a liar!

Father, I want to bring others before your throne in faith, believing you can and will meet their needs, and make a way for them.

As I believe God in my own life, I can
stand and pray for others.

"But what things were gain to me, those I counted loss for Christ." - Philippians 3:7

DETACHING - ATTACHING PROCESS

God uses those in His building program who are "sold out" (Luke 14:26-33). Those who love Him personally, passionately, and devotedly, beyond anything on earth, can expect to be used of God. The faith to love God this way must come from believing that God is holy love. Shipwreck occurs where there is not that mental poise, which comes from being established on the eternal truth that God is holy love (wholly loves also). We must know that God loves us before we can respond to Him. The love of God is shed abroad in our hearts by the Holy Spirit.

God, in Christ Jesus, is forming a new life in us. Old wounds, hurts and habits are being healed. This occurs as we allow the Holy Spirit to have control of our spirit, through prayer and Bible study. Christ in us means a right relationship with God, fellowship restored.

Oh Lord, I pray not to suffer shipwreck. I pray that I will always stay in your Word. Your Word is my schoolmaster, teaching me your ways and your truths, that I may know how to please you and serve you all of my days.

I believe the Word of God is a light unto my path, and will show me how to walk.

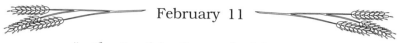

February 11

"...the Lord hath sought him a man
after His own heart..." – I Samuel 13:14

FIRST THE LESSON, THEN THE TEST

Saul was king for two years when his first test came (I Samuel 13). We, too, must have tests. Life is a classroom. We study by ourselves, then we experience the opportunity to put into practice (action) with people what we have read. This is our test, moving from positional truth to experiential truth. If we fail the test, we confess that failure, go on to another study time and try, try again. We aren't to stand still and wring our hands in despair, or lament our sorry state, but to repent and go on!

Saul failed but never repented. God took His hand off of him after giving him ample opportunity to repent. We refer to this as space for repentance. Saul suffered shipwreck. He stopped trusting God for the little things. He took control of the everyday mundane things, and God took His hand off. He can only use us as long as we are dependent on Him, and are pliable, teachable and obedient.

Pride holds us back from acknowledging our mistakes, weaknesses, blunders, sins and errors. Did I catch them all in there? Pride goes before the fall.

My God and my Savior, help me not to be prideful and think too highly of myself.

I will be quick to admit when I blow it.
It's my life insurance policy!

"In him was life; and the life was the light of men. That was the true Light, which lighteth every man that cometh into the world." – **John 1:4, 9**

LOOKING FOR JESUS IN YOU

The only thing I need to have in common with anyone else is Jesus. Every personality and disposition is different. No one is "like" me. Rather than looking for differences or similarities, I must look for Jesus. At that point, we are all alike. I am neither better than nor less than any other child of God. I am the me God made me to be at this point in time. As He moves me, through the power of His Holy Spirit, toward completion, I'll be the me I am meant to be at that point of time.

There is a coming into the rest of God, that is imperative for our well-being, and of our growing and being formed into the image of Jesus Christ, the Son of God. The Holy Spirit must have a cooperative vessel in which to work, to form that image. If I refuse to be still in His hand, He cannot move the work along very quickly.

The admonition to be still and to know that you are God is very real to me at this moment, Father. If I know you are God, I will more freely be still in your hand. Intimate knowledge and awareness of you is critical to my being. Reveal yourself to me as I wait upon you.

I hold myself in the place of waiting for God to reveal Himself to me.

"Casting down imaginations, and every high thing that exalteth itself against the knowledge of God, and bringing into captivity every thought to the obedience of Christ;"
II Corinthians 10:5

PLEASING THE FATHER

The commands of God are given to the life of His son, in us, to our humanity, in which Christ has been formed. His commands are difficult, but immediately, when we obey, they become divinely easy.

Conscience is that faculty in me which attaches itself to the highest I know, and tells me what it demands that I do. Do we see, then, how important, yes critical, it is that we know the truth, as revealed to us by the Holy Spirit? Conscience can only be our guide in matters where we have sought to know the truth about God.

The spirit of man is the candle of the Lord (Proverbs 20:27). It is the eye of the soul. The one thing that keeps the conscience sensitive to God is the continual habit of being open to Him, on the inside. When there is any debate, quit! If you say, "Why shouldn't I do this?" you are on the wrong track. Do not allow anything to obscure your inner communion with God.

Father, I know that only Jesus Christ truly obeyed you in everything He did. I will never be able to obey you if left to my own ways. May your Spirit reveal Jesus to me, in me, and through me.

I will walk in the light today.
Holy Spirit turn on the switch!

February 14

"Why art thou cast down, O my soul? – Psalms 42:5

RX FOR THE BLUES

No sin is worse than self-pity! It obliterates God and puts self-interest on the throne. It opens our mouths to murmurings, and our lives become craving spiritual sponges. There is nothing lovely or generous about them. We must learn the habit of realizing the provision God has made for us.

When God is beginning to become satisfied with us, He impoverishes us until we see He is our fresh wellspring. He is the source of all our supply. He is Alpha and Omega to me, (put your name here).

Think of the sea, the sun, the air, the stars and the moon. What a ministry they have, being what they are. Those who influence us the most are those who live their lives simply and unaffectedly. To be of use to God, I must get rightly related to Jesus. And He will make me unconsciously used every minute I live. I must keep my eyes off of myself and on Jesus.

Look at the rest of Psalm 42 verses 5 and 6, The Psalmist, having a bout of self-pity, begins to talk to himself. He speaks to his soul, and then speaks to God about his soul. What a way to restore good mental health.

Father, I thank you that you are working your divine nature in me, and I don't have to see what you are about in my life. It is enough to know that you are conforming me to the image of Jesus, as I yield myself.

I love you and thank you for loving me.

February 15

"For when for the time ye ought to be teachers, ye have need that one teach you again which be the first principles of the oracles of God:" – **Hebrews 5:12**

PRINCIPLES INSTEAD OF PATTERNS

I awoke a few mornings ago with this thought, "people are trying to make patterns, while I want them to use principles." There are many patterns and designs, but one set of principles - those given to us by God to live and conduct ourselves by. God loves originals. He made everything one of a kind and unique. At the same time, if we all use the same principles, we are all operating on the same standard, so to speak.

I found these words I had written 20 years ago, and feel they are saying the same thing. "Things are moving very swiftly. Those locked into patterns are quenching the Spirit. Today is the day we must flow in the stream of God, or He will move on to others who will. Everything is moving swiftly. Get in the flow of God's will, now! Do not attempt to fix a pattern for God's Spirit to move in. Be open, teachable, alert to the still small voice."

Father, we repent of taking your principles, and trying to make patterns for others to conform to. We want to go into the things you have for us.

I joyfully and gratefully enter into the flow of the move of God.

*"I was in the Spirit on the Lord's day,
and heard behind me a great voice, as of
a trumpet."* – **Revelation 1:10**

IN THE SPIRIT

I was so discouraged at myself yesterday! As I was out of the Spirit, sin entered into my reaction to another's attitude. It carried on into my conversation with another, and then reaped its harvest in a call from yet another. Wow! What a chain reaction and havoc it reaped. It was today before I caught it and confessed it. This left a time of defeat in my life.

When I read I Thessalonians 5:12-24, especially verse 24, I was again encouraged. It is God who calls me and He it is who will do it! Immediately, my eyes were off my failure and onto God. My faith is God in me, believing in Himself.

Then being much encouraged, I went on to Philippians 1:1-11, and saw in verse 6 that I can be sure that God, who began the good work in me, will carry it on until it is finished, on the day of Christ Jesus. In verse 11, we see that our lives will be filled with truly good qualities, which only Jesus can produce, for the praise and glory of God.

God is pleased only with the righteousness of Himself, characterized in us, by Jesus dwelling in us. My part in this is yielding, staying in the Spirit - to choose by an act of my will to do of God's good pleasure.

Father God, we pray with the apostle Paul, from Philippians 1:9-11, that our love may abound yet more and more and that being filled with the fruits of righteousness, we will be to the praise of your Glory.

**I love you Lord Jesus. I yield to your Spirit
to work Philippians 2:13 in me.**

"Then there was a famine in the days of David three years, year after year: and David inquired of the Lord." – II Samuel 21:1

FAMINE IN THE LAND

There was no rain, a famine in Israel. David prayed, and God showed them the reason. They made restitution (verse 14). After they had done all God commanded, it rained. It all sounds so simple. It only gets complicated when you add your name and your circumstances.

God is just and righteous. He forgets not His promises and His covenants with His people. God never lets go of us, even if He has to follow us to hell. He works through circumstances we bring about, as results of our disobedience and forgetfulness of our side of the covenant. He does this to bring us back to the potter's wheel, where we can be molded and made after the image of His Son Jesus.

A thought comes on quenching the Spirit, by refusing to do what you know to be God's will for you. He stops working <u>in</u> you and starts working <u>on</u> you, until you again choose to do His will.

God is pleased with Jesus, and this is the image He wants to see when He looks at us.

Father God, so much of the time I am trying to work a trade off with you by doing something I know you want me to do, so I can do something else I really want to do. Why can't I learn to lay it all down, and embrace your will with all my heart?

I thank you for wanting my highest. Thank you, thank you, thank you!

"And he shall be like a tree planted by the rivers of water..." – **Psalm 1:3**

CONFLICT IS A GOOD THING?

In Psalm 1, we are admonished to draw from the river of grace, so that our fruit will be sweet. Where our roots are is very important. The content of the soil nourishes the tree through the root system. We are to set our affections on things above. Our roots are set and our fruit will be the result of where our roots are.

James 4:6 tells us how to get grace. God "gives grace to the humble." If you can't be humble, get ready to be humiliated. Sometimes, God gives us things as great favors to make us humble. If necessary, He allows us to fall into deep sin, in order to humble us, for nothing is more humbling.

A conflict we cannot solve is humbling, especially when everyone knows about it. When we think of humility, our thoughts turn to Moses. He was called humble by God. He had conflicts in his life that kept him close to the holy of holies. It seems like we could say his life was all about conflict. Jesus was the model of humility for us all. When He was reviled, He reviled not again.

Grace is the desire and power to do God's will. The river of God is the river of God's grace empowering us to be like Jesus.

Father God, when we observe the humility of great men and women in the Bible, when we think of Jesus and His humility, we become embarassed at our own haughtiness. Please forgive us for thinking too highly of ourselves. When we forget who you are and who we are, we lose our humility.

I ask for grace today in all my conflicts.

"Beloved, let us love one another: for love is of God; and every one that loveth, is born of God, and knoweth God." – I John 4:7

FAMILY RELATIONSHIPS

The things that make God so dear to us are not the big blessings, but the little things. The little things show His amazing intimacy with us. It's not that we don't appreciate the big things but, hey, that's God! The small things are usually secret wishes or desires of our heart, and they come unexpectedly.

God guides us by our ordinary choices. And if we are going to choose what He does not want, He will check, and we must heed that check. Whenever there is doubt, stop at once. Never reason it out and say, "I wonder why I shouldn't." God guides our common sense.

When God wants to show you what human nature is like apart from himself, He has to show it to you in yourself. I despair of others to the degree I've forgotten what God has done for me. All I need in order to have hope rekindled in me, for others, is to look and see where I was when the Spirit of God arrested me and began His transformation.

We are looking at relationship here, first myself with God and then with my fellow man. God is very relational. Many verses in His Word refer to the family of God.

Father, we are confused about family at some points. It wasn't always good for us in our earthly families. We want to be family. Teach us.

I want to be a good family member.

"... If any man will come after me, let him deny himself, and take up his cross daily, and follow me." – Luke 9:23

I DIE DAILY

The only thing I can consecrate to God is my right to myself. It is the only thing I have. That's why I grasp it so tightly. It's mine! I must consecrate my right to myself daily, moment by moment, taking up my cross and dying daily to my right to myself. God's gift to me is my right to myself. Therefore, it must be my gift back to God.

I am an original. As I live, move and have my being in Him, I am constantly being an original life. Only in total abandonment to Him does originality flow in and through me. When this is happening, God is sovereign and engineers all things. Therefore, I can rejoice always and in all things give thanks.

In consecrating my right to myself, I hit upon obstinacy at some point. The only way to rid myself of obstinacy is for it to be blown up with dynamite. Obedience to the Holy Spirit is that dynamite. Are we willing to allow the Holy Spirit to blow it all to "smithereens" and rebuild it?

Father, sometimes it seems hard to give up my rights, especially when you gave them to me and they're legitimately mine. Many times, the situation seems unfair, and the other person seems demanding. Help me see it is to you I give up, not to anything else.

I choose to give up my rights to God's will.

"But if we walk in the light, as he is in the light, we have fellowship one with another." – I John 1:7

HOUSE CLEANING

We as Christians are in union with Christ Jesus, because He purchased our redemption with His precious blood. The Father does not deal with me apart from the person of His son, Jesus. As I confess my sin and ask Him to put it under the blood, then Father God can deal with me.

Repentance is seeing how I have loved so many things first, before God. Forgiveness of sin is God washing away my guilt, as expressed in I John 1:9. If we confess our sin to God, He will keep His promise to do what is right. He will forgive us our sins and purify us from all wrong.

Purification comes by applying Christ's blood. There is a fountain that flows from Calvary, a fountain of the righteous blood of Jesus. It has been said, when we step into that flow and look back, it has covered our footprints.

Sin in our lives is darkness. We cannot have fellowship one with another if there is darkness in our lives (I John 1:7). Think for a moment about darkness, how difficult it is to walk in darkness or to find your way. John 1:5 tells us the darkness doesn't comprehend the light. This is enough to cause us to run to the light, to Jesus, the light of the world.

Father God, in reading these verses we are reminded of your awesome love and your patience with us. It takes us so long to make the right turns to bring our lives into line with you and your plans for us. Thank you for the Holy Spirit active in our lives today, making Jesus' redemption real in us.

I will be quick to agree with the Spirit of God about my sin, confess it, and get back into the light of God's love.

*"But ye are a chosen generation, a royal
priesthood, an holy nation, a peculiar people."*
I Peter 2:9

THE WORK OF A SAINT

The real business of my life as a saved person is
intercessory prayer. Whenever God puts you in
circumstances, pray immediately. Pray that His
atonement will be realized in the lives of others as it
has been in yours. Jesus' disciples asked Him to teach
them how to pray. They had been with Him long enough
to realize His life flowed from His prayer relationship
with His Father. They perceived this was what they
needed to have, in order to succeed.

God has told us, in His Word, that we are of the
royal priesthood. Therefore, we have an obligation to
pour ourselves out in the ministry of the interior.
Everything I say and do should be a result of the time I
spend alone, before the throne of grace. I am to relax
(rest) in the knowledge that my redemption is complete
in Christ Jesus. Only at that point can I be right before
God. In Christ I am whole, well, complete and fulfilled. I
must not dig into the interior now. That is the work of
the Holy Spirit. He will bring to mind what needs fixing
and I can then ask for grace and strength to work on
that thing.

*Father, in my time alone before you, I can trust you to
make the necessary adjustments known to me so that I
may please you.*

**I will take action on matters brought to my
attention by the Spirit of God. Yes, Lord!**

"... and the hollow of Jacob's thigh was out of
joint, as he wrestled with him (God) ... it is
better for thee to enter into life halt or
maimed ..." – Genesis 32:25, Matthew 18:8

IN GOD'S INTENSIVE CARE

When God alters a person by regeneration, the
characteristic of that life, to begin with, is that it is
maimed. Unspiritual ones will not understand why you
cannot do as you always have. You cannot explain it,
so don't even attempt it. There never has been a saint
who did not have to live a maimed life to start. It is far
better to enter into life maimed in man's view but lovely
in God's eyes, than to be lovely in man's sight and
maimed in God's. Others may, you cannot when God is
dealing with you about a matter.

Jesus, by the Holy Spirit, has to check you from
doing many things. See that you do not use your
limitations to criticize someone else. We have a great
need for discipline to hold back the snide, biting, critical
remarks that sometimes want to surface. We must ask
God for a better response, for out of the mouth come the
issues of the heart.

*My Lord Jesus, you use others to speak the truth to
us. We are critical of any who do not measure up. Father,
I confess a critical spirit and ask you to forgive me and to
cleanse me from it. I thank you for doing it.*

**Today I will not speak unless I have
something worthwhile and uplifting to say.**

"Herein is love, not that we loved God, but that he loved us, and sent His Son to be the propitiation for our sins." – I John 4:10

A LOVE LETTER TO JESUS

Dearest Lord Jesus,

I am devoted to a cause. I do not serve a doctrine. I am a disciple of yours, given the burning heart of love because your Holy Spirit has shed the love of God abroad, in my heart. It shows me that in my own self, I cannot even love you. This love is the nature of God and I became a partaker of that divine nature through regeneration (what you did for me on Calvary). Now God is free to work in my life, by His Spirit (sanctification).

In this, I can see again that I am worthless apart from you, because you are the door through which all of this is made possible. There is no other way for me to have a relationship with God, my Father, which makes my existence complete. I can now become that person I was created to be, by the power of God working in me, to mold me into that image, by His Holy Spirit. That image is the likeness of Jesus Christ, to become one with Him.

Now Jesus, I want to tell you how much I appreciate what you have done for me and all of mankind who accepts you. Please continue working on me until you can see your image in me.

Thanks a lot, Jesus, for loving me.

*"And Joshua said unto the people, Ye cannot
serve the Lord: for he is an holy God; he is a
jealous God ..." – Joshua 24:19*

CAN I OR CAN'T I?

Is the whole of the Old Testament written to show
us how impossible it is for us to serve God in our
strength? No matter what the determination, without
accepting totally and completely the provision of God
Himself, we can never please Him. In every situation
God brings to bear, the probing of the Holy Spirit comes
to say, "Are you relying on anything or anyone but me?"

All of God's provision has been summed up in Jesus.
All we ever need has been provided in Him. I must choose
to let Jesus make me holy. I can never give up my will.
I must activate it by choosing, as Joshua challenged
the Israelites, "Choose you this day whom ye will serve"
(Joshua 24:15).

My aim is to secure the realization of Jesus Christ
in every set of circumstances. That is why I am to give
thanks and praise in all circumstances that I might
find Jesus in it. Every phase of our actual life has its
counterpart in the life of Jesus (Hebrews 4:15). We are
missing it when we say we cannot do or be what the
Lord requires of us. We're not choosing our inheritance
in Jesus.

*Father, I don't want to make lame excuses to you and
say I cannot. I know I can do all things through Christ
Jesus, my Lord.*

I choose to do what my Father requires.

"But rejoice, inasmuch as ye are partakers of Christ's sufferings..." – I Peter 4:13

TAKING IT FOR JESUS

Every time I insist upon my rights, I hurt the Son of God in me. Whereas, I can prevent Jesus from being hurt, if I take the blow myself. That is the meaning of filling up that which is behind of the afflictions of Christ (Colossians 1:24). The disciple realizes that it is his Lord's honor that is at stake in his life, not his own honor.

Never look for justice. Always give justice. The last part of the verse above is, "...that, when His glory shall be revealed, ye may be glad also with exceeding joy." (I Peter 4:13).

This tells us that in taking the blow for the Son of God, which is foreign to our human nature, the glory of God will be revealed. There is no higher exhilaration than realizing we have gone through a tense time and come out looking like Jesus! Glory, hallelujah! This is truly shouting ground. When I have 'won a battle,' so to speak, I soon realize I have lost the war. This is a time of serious feelings of defeat. When I can learn I don't need to be right, I can give away the life of Christ in that situation.

Lord, we need to be life givers, life sharers, to everyone, especially the hard ones. Please empower us to take it for your sake.

I'll take the blow for Jesus today!

*"I delight to do thy will, O my God:
yea, thy law is within my heart. Teach
me to do thy will: for thou art my God ..."*
Psalm 40:8, Psalm 143:10

CONCERNING THE WILL

If I truly want to know what needs to be pruned, or removed, in my life, so that I am a fruit bearing vine, I must listen to the Holy Spirit's convictions. I can then bring these convictions as questions, to the throne of God. As He answers, the opening is there for truth to drop straight into my innermost being.

Because I asked, my will was turned toward God. If He had merely told me, I would most likely have rejected it as being "imposed" on me against my will. This is why we do not hear when others try to share truths with us. We feel they are "butting in," and we close our will. This is why Jesus said, "blessed are those who hunger and thirst after righteousness, for they shall be filled."

The hunger is the work of the Holy Spirit. The truth is like rain to a desert, when we crave it with all our heart. The Word says, "You have not because you ask not." The having is in the asking. You open your will to Him in the asking.

Father, we are ashamed and even embarrassed at our lack of genuine asking. We hint around and experiment with ways to do it ourselves. All the time, you are waiting. Forgive us.

**I am asking God to give me truth.
I will to hear it and act upon it.**

"For I know the thoughts (plans) that I think toward you, saith the Lord, thoughts of peace, and not of evil, to give you an expected end." – Jeremiah 29:11

ON THE WAY TO PEACE

Journeying with Jesus is just that. From the time of salvation, we begin our pilgrimage and we are on the way to our heavenly Jerusalem. It seems wherever Jesus traveled, He was on the way to Jerusalem. Jerusalem means peace. We are on the way to peace. As feelings surface from the past, ask the Father to please heal them and throw them in the sea of His forgetfulness. If God knew me in my mother's womb, He knew this would happen to me. He has made allowances in His plan for my life to include all the developments of my character. If there are those places in me, because of my reactions that need healing, I pray He will heal them.

I chose to yield my will to the will of God and to rest in confidence in His plan for me. As I remember these simple instructions, I feel I will be free of my past bondages.

God is trying to get us to unlearn something in every cloud, to simplify our belief in Him to that of a child. We must reach the place where there is no one in our cloud but Jesus.

My Father, cloudy days are often times of dissatisfaction. I hear you saying to me, you are in my clouds.

Holy Spirit I don't mind clouds, now that I know Jesus is in my cloud.

**"I will praise thee, for I am fearfully and
wonderfully made..."** – **Psalm 139:14**

ONE OF A KIND

When we are certain of a way God is going to work,
He will never work that way again! Recently I was
sewing, and He showed me why I like to make up a
pattern the second time. I think I can do a better job!
He said if He did things the same way the second time,
we wouldn't need Him so much! Wow, stop and think on
that (selah).

God will not be put in a box or a formula book. He
is God. His ways are past finding out, past our
understanding. Now we can go before Him, and as it
pleases Him, He can reveal Himself to us. It is all at His
good pleasure.

We are to cast ourselves into His hands because He
cares for us. When we abandon ourselves to Him and
His keeping, it matters not how He works. It will always
be right.

To wait on God is not to sit with folded hands, but
to do what we are told to do - to do what our hands find
to do as we live and move and have our being in Him.

*Father, when I forget that I am one of a kind, I get into
all kinds of trouble. So are each and everyone of your
children. I don't relate to them from who I am, but whose
we all are. I love you and want to love others as you do.*

Because He is, I am!

"Blessed (happy) are they which do hunger and thirst after righteousness: for they shall be filled." – Matthew 5:6

GROWING IN GRACE

In II Peter 1:3, Paul admonishes us to do our best to:
    add goodness to our faith;
    knowledge to our goodness;
    self-control to our knowledge;
    endurance to our self-control;
    godliness to our endurance;
    brotherly affection to our godliness;
    love to our brotherly affection.

In Colossians 3:12, he again admonishes us to clothe ourselves with compassion, kindness, humility, gentleness, patience, tolerance, forgiveness and love.

Do these lists sound like the 'best dressed list?' They do to me, and I believe they do to the Father. They also draw a picture of a lifelong journey and a maturing process. How many times do we compare our spiritual growth to a physical workout? We don't start out running a marathon or pressing hundreds of pounds. It is an adding to, and a working out. Many scriptures call us on and upwards in spiritual matters. The result is full stature, grown up and whole.

Father, I want to be on your best dressed list. I give you my will to work within me your truths.

I'm looking good as I exercise my spirit.

"Surely he hath borne our griefs, and carried our sorrows..." – Isaiah 53:4

DIVINE REDEMPTION

We cannot, in ourselves, keep God's commandments. Human nature cannot please God in itself. So God made a way whereby we can be saved. That way was Jesus, God's only Son.

He bore our griefs.

He carried our sorrows.

He was pierced for our transgressions.

He was crushed for our iniquities.

He was chastened for our well-being.

He was scourged for our healing.

My iniquity fell on Him.

He was oppressed, afflicted, and led to the slaughter as a sheep to the shearer.

In this act of Almighty God, I have died and been born again, wholly clean, and free from sin. This same Jesus who died for me will now live for me. As I am kept alive by His act, now He breathes His life into my dead carcass. All the curses are canceled as I appropriate the life of Christ Jesus.

Father, I pray by the revelation of your Word to me, that I will know and appropriate the provisions of the life and death of Jesus. I ask you to have full sway in my life and to fellowship with me continually. I do not want to grieve your Spirit by being unthankful or unthoughtful of you.

I am sensing the life of Jesus in me today.

March 3

"And the Lord said unto Satan, From whence comest thou? And Satan answered the Lord, and said, From going to and fro in the earth, and from walking up and down in it." – Job 2:2

RECLAIMING GROUND

How do I disentangle myself from Satan's root system? Here are some things I learned as I was seeking to take back all the ground my years of rebellion had given to Satan.

1. Desire to be free, dissatisfaction with the status quo, be teachable. [John 8:32 and 36]

2. Recognize your problem, get alone with God. God always speaks to His people alone. Take your Bible. [Psalm 119:30]

3. Believe God can change you. Who would God really like me to be if all the strings were off? [Colossians 3:10 and Luke 1:37]

4. Recognize who is causing you to go wrong. [John 10:10]

5. Ask God to fill you with the Holy Spirit. Don't ask unless you really mean it, for God is faithful. [John 16:23 and I Corinthians 1:9]

6. Repent. You need the power of the Holy Spirit in your life in order to truly repent. [Romans 8:26]

7. Confess: first, who you were; secondly, who Christ is, and thirdly, who you are now. [I John 1:9, I John 4:15 and Philippians 3:9]

8. Recognize yourself as God sees you: a man or woman of great authority, because of who (whose) you are. [Matthew 28:18, 19]

Father, I know I have an enemy who is an accuser, but as I move through these steps, I regain my place of confidence which is knowing who I am in Christ Jesus.

I have been made the righteousness of God in Christ Jesus. That is who I am!

"And be renewed in the spirit of your mind ... But we have the mind of Christ."
Ephesians 4:23 and I Corinthians 2:16

WHERE IS MY MIND?

Let this mind be in you, which was in Christ Jesus. What was the mind of Christ? It was to do His Father's will without asking any questions. It was to be obedient to death. We have a new nature in us because of what Jesus did on Calvary. We died there, we were buried there, and we arose there with Jesus. We have His nature in us, the new nature. Now we no longer have to sin. We do, but the truth is, we don't have to. We don't follow our old nature anymore, we reckon it to be buried 2000 years ago in Jerusalem.

We can now allow the nature of God to rule us, as we have the mind of Christ. Through the Holy Spirit, making the Word of God real to us, we are having our minds renewed to think correctly. God is now in us to will, and to do His good pleasure. What a deal, what a relationship, what a partnership!

Now, the key here is to get our soul and our body to receive this good news. It's not just a ho-hum thing, children, it's a growing process of changing our minds by renewal. This is an ever ongoing process of changing and yielding and growing. It's not hard. The hard part is yielding, then it's such a relief to obey.

Father, I am willing to be made willing to do your will. That is to empty myself of myself by an act of my will.

**I must be conscious of my
Christ consciousness, always.**

**"For God hath not given us the spirit
of fear ..."** – II Timothy 1:7

THE GREAT LIE

All sin is a lie about God. Fear is a breeding ground for sin. It will cause us to lie, and to forsake the Lord. Look at Peter the night he lied and denied Jesus – the longest, saddest night in Peter's life. I believe he remembered it as long as he lived.

Here are some things fear will keep you from:
1. Witnessing
2. Enjoying life
3. Being happy
4. Being well
5. Resting
6. Ability to accept love
7. Ability to give love

Fear criticizes and sits in judgement. Fear believes we will die in poverty and keeps us from enjoying what we have. We could go on naming many other things, but you get the message. Fear is a terrible thief, and causes us to seek to preserve our lives and save ourselves. You see how it is a lie, those who 'give up' their lives save them. We must 'give up' ourselves to God's keeping, and all the above areas of loss, can be restored.

Father, I raise my arms high above my head now as a sign of surrender. I see that, number one, perfect love casts out all fear; and number two, that love covers a multitude of sins – including fear!

**Oh river of God's love, roll over me,
restore me. I want you to, <u>NOW</u>.**

"And I will pray the Father, and he shall give you another Comforter, that he may abide with you for ever." – John 14:16

GOD'S GIFT TO US

God loved us so much, He sent His Son to die for our sins. We must enter into Christ's death with Him to have our sins forgiven. We never have to struggle to die again, but we constantly struggle to stay dead. The Holy Spirit must teach us to stay dead.

I will to stay dead. I choose to stay dead, but the Holy Spirit has to keep me there. I will, and I choose, to keep Christ enthroned in my heart, but the Holy Spirit keeps Him there.

Before we pray and ask the Father to fill us with His Holy Spirit, take a few moments and look in John 16:5-15 and John 14:16-18, to see what the ministry of the Holy Spirit involves. He is the keeping power of God, and Jesus told us just before He returned to the Father, how we must have the Holy Spirit.

Father, I believe I must have the Holy Spirit filling my life, in order to stay in the place you want me to be in. Your Word tells me to ask you to fill me with your Holy Spirit. Now by faith in you and your Word, I ask you to fill me with your Holy Spirit, and I believe you will. I believe you have filled me, and I thank you.

**I choose Christ enthroned in my heart.
And God has filled me with His Spirit,
to keep Him there.**

"I am the vine, ye are the branches: He that abideth in me, and I in him, the same bringeth forth much fruit." – John 15:5

FRUIT MAKING

As I live and move and have my very being in Him, the working of the works of God will be manifested. Blessed are the poor in spirit. Only when I recognize nothing in my hands I bring, simply to thy cross I cling, will the Son of Man be made available in me to others.

I cannot will myself to Him - my will, I will have always! I simply will to yield myself to Him. When I say, 'I wonder if I'm of any use,' I have lost the bloom of the truth of the Lord. In the desert, there are beautiful night blooming flowers that fade at dawn. If you pick them, trying to hold them, they die. They are beautiful just hanging on their vine, so to speak.

He that believeth in me, out of his belly shall flow rivers of living water [John 7:38]. The secret to the flow is believing in Him In questioning my usefulness, or my reason for existing, I have become self centered rather than Christ-centered. Being Christ-centered is knowing that my God can do anything. It is the work of the Holy Spirit to keep me Christ-centered.

Father, today I want to sink down into you, and allow the 'sap' of the Holy Spirit to flow through my life creating fruit.

I deliberately cut back today to enjoy God.

"And they prayed, and said, Thou, Lord, which knowest the hearts of all men, shew whether of these two thou hast chosen." – Acts 1:24

KNOWING AS JESUS KNOWS

Ask Jesus to show you the heart with its needs, so that the dirt, the odor, the sin, or the disease are secondary. With the mind of Christ in us, we can look upon the heart. We will see beyond the offensiveness of the person to the need. Christ meets everyone at the point of their need. If I do look to the need, it is the Lord in me reaching out, and both of us can grow. I am ministering to that point of need, as the hands of Jesus Christ. This is going on to maturity, to servanthood, the place we have been called to by our Father – trained by the Holy Spirit and modeled by Jesus.

Knowing the Will of God and refusing to act on it sends stagnation into the soul and eventually gangrene sets in. The Spirit of God moves as a fresh breeze through our lives. The channels must be open, or we dam up the flow and it begins to stink. We must act (faith it) on the revelatory work of the Spirit as soon as it comes to us.

Father, I know life lived to the fullest is being your hands, feet and mouth to the world around me. I ask you to work in me to change my heart.

**I must keep my eyes on Jesus
and not public opinion.**

"And when he had spoken these things...he was taken up; and a cloud received him out of their sight." – Acts 1:9

JESUS IS EVERYTHING TO ME

We lose sight of Jesus after the ascension. He sat down at the right hand of God to make intercession for us. The redemption of our soul is a finished work of grace. We accept it by faith, simply affirming personally, it has been done for me. I needed it, had to have it, God furnished it, and it is so.

This is not the end of Jesus' work, however. He prayed to the Father to send the Holy Spirit to reveal all truth to me (John 16:13). Then, He ascended on high and sat down to intercede. Every time we ask Him to, He forgives our sins and takes our part when Satan accuses us falsely. "There is therefore now no condemnation to those who are in Christ Jesus" (Romans 8:1).

In the above paragraphs, we see Jesus actively involved as our high priest, our advocate, and our intercessor (Hebrews 4:14, I John 1:9). In closing, we remember He is the head of His church. He is our great shepherd as we journey through this life. We can see Jesus is all we need.

Father, we must keep focused on Jesus. You have promised us a good journey, this is conditioned on Jesus being everything.

Holy Spirit, keep me in Jesus. This is my will and my choice.

"For the weapons of our warfare are not carnal, but mighty through God to the pulling down of strong holds."
II Corinthians 10:4

OUR WEAPONS COME FROM GOD

Forces of evil will flee before you when you walk in the light [James 4:7]. Walking in the light, as Jesus is in the light, is submitting to God. Thy rod and thy staff are a comfort to me. Yes, though I may walk through the shadow of the valley of death, you, oh God, are with me. You ever prepare a table for me, in the very presence of my enemies.

I thank you for allowing me to see, that as I walk in the light (in oneness with Jesus), as He is, I am (in the light). Evil will cry out for mercy as we walk by, for we are more than overcomers, because Jesus overcame the world. He is our life – if we have been crucified with Him. We do not need to fight, but to stand in Him, the armor of God. WE need to stand and to proclaim the power of the Lord.

Let this mind be in you, which was also in Christ Jesus. Cast down these imaginations that exalt themselves above the knowledge of God [II Corinthians 10:5]. As I live and move and have my being in Him, I am more than a conqueror.

I praise you, Lord Jesus. You are the light, the way, the truth. No man cometh to the Father but by you.

I have knowledge of the truth and I will walk in it today.

"Now thanks be unto God, which always causeth us to triumph in Christ, and maketh manifest the savour of his knowledge by us in every place." **– II Corinthians 2:14**

SOMETHING BEAUTIFUL

It is fascinating watching Jesus make our lives over - just standing back and being amazed at His presence doing the changing. We need to ask God to break up the walls of resistance He hits, to be ready and willing to be remolded and remodeled.

We can see our life as Mary's alabaster box. We can bring it to Jesus. It's all we have to bring, a gift given to us by God. I can pour it out for Jesus, because I love Him. I can give Him my life, my all, to be used in His service. It is a fragrant gift, a pleasing savour to God. As it is broken, wonderful aromas waft their way to the throne of God.

In II Corinthians 2:15,16, we are told we are a sweet savour of Christ unto God and to those who are being saved. Here, you also see you are a stench in the nostrils of those that perish. Dear ones, the reality of the Christ life is that it is to be lived unto God, without counting the costs.

Father, I thank you, as I bring my life to you, and do not guard it for myself. You can and will make something beautiful for yourself.

Help yourself Lord!

"I have heard of thee by the hearing of the ear: but now mine eye seeth thee." – Job 42:5

IS ANYTHING BOTHERING YOU?

Brother, are you bothered?
If so...
  We know that
   God sends trouble
   to see if we will trust Him
   so He can make us happy

(Deuteronomy 8:16)

So maybe...
  He is saying
  I made you hungry
             poor
             weak
             unpopular
To see if you would trust me...
  I took away your friends
              family
              health
              savings
              home
              security
To see if you would trust me.

Job had an intellectual belief in God, and he was faithful to the knowledge he had. God chose to take him deeper. It cost him everything he had. Then, stripped of all he had, except God (Job 42), he knew, without a shadow of a doubt, that God is all, in all, with all, working to do His good pleasure.

Father, I thank you that I have seen you with my own eyes. I thank you that you manifest to me in ways that fill all my needs.

**I know, without a shadow of a doubt,
that you are in me, with me, and for me.
You are my all!**

March 13

"For godly sorrow worketh repentance to salvation not to be repented of: but the sorrow of the world worketh death."
II Corinthians 7:10

REAL REPENTANCE

Godly sorrow brings genuine repentance. We must come to the place where we put aside the details, the embarrassment and the humiliation that sin brings. We must go beyond the discovery, the consequences, even the judgement and the punishment. This is the place of repentance where we are concerned only with the sin. When we look at that sin alone, before God, then we are in a position to repent.

King David repented, 'Lord, it was against you and you alone that I have sinned.' We must become sorrowful that our sin sent Jesus to the cross. We are primarily occupied with the consequences of what we've done. We are most often sorry we got caught or found out, but not sorry we have sinned against God Almighty.

Go on to read II Corinthians 7.5-10 to find out how the apostle Paul described an actual situation of Godly sorrow, leading to repentance. We shouldn't live in fear and dread of being 'found out,' but in the realization that God already knows. He not only knows, but has made a way of escape. For the child of God, I John 1:9 is that way.

Father, I want to be quick to repent and to confess my sin. I will to stay tender toward the convicting power of the Holy Spirit.

Repentance is cleansing my conscience.

73

March 14

"... whatsoever things are true ... honest ...
just... pure ... (and) are
of good report ... think on these things."
Philippians 4:8

KINGDOM LIVING NOW

Natural vision devoted to the Holy Spirit becomes the power of perceiving God's will, thus, enabling the whole life to be kept in simplicity.

Thank you, Father, that the whole man, body, soul and spirit can be so yielded to you, that your Spirit can work in it, to bring perfect balance. Perfect balance brings forth health, joy, peace, dominion, power and authority, as sons and daughters of God.

There is stress in living in the world as we know it. Stress is always pushing down:

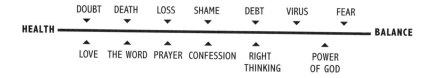

The work of the Holy Spirit is to equalize all things to keep us in balance. Can you begin to grasp the importance, yes the necessity, of staying in the Holy Spirit? The power to counteract the stress we encounter comes from the list below the line.

Father, we know we have been redeemed from the curse. Now we ask you, by your Spirit, to teach us all we need to know to live in your kingdom, now!

I choose to live in balance and in health.

74

March 15

"Wherefore the rather, brethren, give diligence to make your calling and election sure: for if ye do these things, ye shall never fall." – II Peter 1:10

LIVE LIKE GOD

Take a few moments and read through II Peter 1:3-10, to see the full content of the following thoughts:

We are, here, admonished to add to the faith that claims the precious promises of the Father. This is something we are asked to do, giving diligence to them. We need to add virtue, knowledge, self-control, steadfastness, godliness, brotherly affection and love. This seems somewhat like steps or rungs on a ladder. It also seems to be a growth process, as one is attained, we go on to the next. These things, being ours in abundance, make us effective and fruitful in the knowledge of our Lord Jesus Christ.

Our prayer needs to be that the Father, by His Holy Spirit working in our life and on our behalf, will see to it that we accomplish these goals. We don't want to come down to the end, Father, and not have that family resemblance to you. We are aware it is a life long process and comes slower than we would choose. We do pray to become part of the progress rather than being a hindrance to our own growth.

Every day I will ask the Spirit of God to work the graces of God into my life.

"Let this mind be in you, which was also in Christ Jesus." – **Philippians 2:5**

YOU ARE VALUABLE TO GOD

At regeneration, the Son of God is formed in us. Now, in our physical life, He has the same setting He had while on earth. Therefore, we move into a new realm of temptation, the temptation of God as man. The definition most often used for temptation is: the test by an alien power of the possessions held by a personality.

By regeneration, we become of value to be used by God to fill up that which was left of Christ's sufferings. Because of this, the enemy of God, Satan (the thief, robber, destroyer and murderer), tempts us, not that we might sin, but rather lose that value of usefulness to the Father.

Only as Jesus is free to move about in us, accomplishing what He did in His flesh, are we of this value to God. We can only yield our will (renew our mind). The Holy Spirit does the rest. He will do this in us by the same power that raised Jesus from the dead. Therefore, we are to have no fear, for He is greater than anything Satan can throw at His life, in us.

Father, we can see this is true, as we sit and meditate on it, it breaks down in the fire. Thank you for strengthening us in the moment.

I realize Jesus is in me today!

*"Till we all come in the unity of the faith,
and of the knowledge of the Son of God, unto
a perfect [mature] man, unto the measure of
the stature of the fullness of Christ."*
Ephesians 4:13

GOING ON TO MATURITY

Here are four statements that can help us to understand the maturing process in Christ Jesus:

1. We perform FROM position, not FOR position. Another way of stating the above is, I do because I am, not, I am because I do.

2. We reason FROM revelation, not we reason TO revelation. Revelation is the truth about God, His will and His way that has been communicated to us, by Him.

3. We fight FROM victory, not TO victory. Get a good hold on this one before you exhaust yourself in needless battles. Victory is the achievement of mastery or success in a struggle. You see, you start out winning!

4. Relationship must precede fellowship. Union must precede communion. Relationship is a vital connection between two persons. Fellowship is a harmonious, beneficial, reciprocal partnership. Union is the act of making two, one, and communion is intimate fellowship, the act of sharing, mutual participation.

My Lord and my God, meditating on these statements makes me want to be forever and always, in this mature atmosphere, with you. I pray to be kept here, not separated in any way from you.

I am totally fulfilled in this place with God.

"Set a watch, O Lord, before my mouth; keep the door of my lips." – Psalm 141:3

GIVE A GOOD REPORT

The pure in heart shall see God. The pure in heart see everything as pure (Matthew 5:8). Whatsoever a man "thinketh in his heart, so is he" (Proverbs 23:7). "Love covers a multitude of sins" (I Peter 4:8). When asked how "so and so" is, give a good report. God is pleased to hear good things about His children. It was Lucifer who talked against Job to God.

When viewing another's blindness to God, remember it was due only to the grace of God that He allowed you to see the light. Praise Him for allowing you to see light and truth concerning God, intercede at that point for the one that is in darkness.

You see, there is nothing to boast about but Jesus Christ. You have done nothing to earn, or deserve, your position in Him. It is God, both working and willing, in you, to do His good pleasure. It is all of grace. It is to bring honor and glory to Him, or it is not of the Holy Spirit, whose work it is to glorify the unlimited Jesus in you!

Father, help us to remember these two things when speaking of another: Is it for his or her good. And will it bring glory to God? Otherwise, we pray a watch on our mouths.

If I can't say something good today, I chose to keep quiet. Silence can be golden.

"...for he hath said, I will never leave thee, nor forsake thee." – Hebrews 13:5

ALONE BUT NOT LONELY

I am combining two nuggets of truth today, opposite yet alike, both for the married and the single. First of all, at whatever point I'm out of sorts with my mate, I find I am out of sorts with God just there. If I confess it and get it right with God, it automatically gets right with my mate. Then the other areas of my life, children, work or whatever, all line up. We have been given mates as barometers to gauge our relationship to Christ. It is a visual evidence of things unseen.

The second nugget concerns being alone. Aloneness can be from carrying a burden of sin, cut off from fellowship, alienated. Cancer, disease and many sicknesses come as a result of alienation, which is the death process. In John 4, Jesus told the woman at the well He could give her water to drink that was life giving. We see how alienation cuts us off from life. If you are not living, you are dying.

Seek to learn how to abandon yourself more to God's care and keeping, so that He is in all your affairs. This way you need never feel lonely again, even though you may be alone. It is always you and Him in it together.

Father, I know there is truth here for me. By your Holy Spirit, help me to understand how not to be lonely ever again.

I can be alone without being lonely!

"...neither fear ye the people of the land; for they are bread for us..." – **Numbers 14:9**

ADVERSITY

Satan puts a problem in our path, Praise the Lord! It is truly bread for us, the rest of the verse says, and the Lord is with us, fear not. Bread is to strengthen us. God allowed it to mature us, to grow us up.

We don't need to ask God for things but rather to know His Will. We can know His Will by reading His Word. Courage comes from the Word of God. If He said you could say it, then you can say it! Therefore, you must know the Word of God to say it. To know what God said is to know the mind of God. Entering into His thinking is the road to the Spirit filled life.

Steps along this road: 1) Dispossession; emptying myself of who I am, what I know, and what I can do. Even God cannot fill what is already full! 2) Appropriation; walk around, put your foot down and claim those blessings. 3) Progression; every day there is more and more and much more. Never stop growing, don't allow problems in your path to stop your growth. You'll stay green if you are growing, but you will rot if you stay where you were yesterday.

Father, I will not to be frightened into retreat or inactivity by the wiles of the devil. I seek to inherit all the promises that are mine in your Word.

**I will go on and on and on and on
and on with God.**

"...Adam and his wife hid themselves from the presence of the Lord God..." – **Genesis 3:8**

ADAM'S BIG MISTAKE

The sin of Adam was deciding to remove the care and responsibility for himself from God. He decided to take responsibility for himself. The inherited sin of mankind is the disposition of self-realization, I am my own god! In me, this can take the form of moral degradation or moral attainment - there is no difference.

Faith begins as a tiny seed in the heart of a sinner, as sorrow, anxiety, or longing, as a state in which we can no longer endure to live in sin. It gives us boldness (faith) to come to Christ with every sin. Sin does not keep us away from God, no matter how small or gross. It is the failure to confess sin that blocks God's activity in our lives.

Our thanksgiving belongs to God. Being thankful that He doesn't leave us alone in our discomfort, but that He loves us too much to forsake us. He will continue to work to bring us to the end of ourselves, where we just cannot go on in our present state.

Father, we lift up our hearts to you, right now, in gratitude and thankfulness. First of all, for your love displayed in your Son Jesus Christ, then for the keeping, sustaining nurture and guidance of your Holy Spirit.

I will yield the keeping of myself to God today.

"And the Lord thy God will circumcise thine heart, and the heart of thy seed, to love the Lord thy God with all thine heart, and with all thy soul, that thou mayest live."
Deuteronomy 30:6

EXCESS BAGGAGE

Bitter resentment is bred into the heart of a child. As the child matures, it becomes an inner evil. Wild flashes of anger, uncontrollable, will continue to erupt until the hidden resentment is destroyed. The scriptures refer to the stony heart being removed by God, and the heart of flesh coming to man as a gift from God (Ezekiel 36:26).

Hidden resentment can be destroyed by a willingness to turn to Jesus for daily cleansing and strength (Romans 12:1). The emptying of the unconscious mind, of its griefs and wounds and guilts, is greatly speeded by total willingness in the conscious mind to do the Will of the Father.

Praise and thanksgiving are the key. True praise and thanksgiving open the door to absolute willingness. There comes a point where we cannot continue to carry the baggage of the unconscious. It is like a trunk stuffed with things in the basement or the attic. Things we could never rid ourselves of because of the memories attached to them. We steal away, occasionally, and look through them. It is time to clean out the trunks, lighten our loads and be free to go on into the promises of God for each of us.

Father God, I am sick and tired of taking 'sick days' and going to my storage trunk and pulling out memories to brood over and to have 'blue feelings' about. I want to completely empty out my excess, useless, crippling baggage. I want to have a real spring cleaning, so that new life can flood all the dark places, and I can be light as a feather - free to enjoy my life!

Today I'm cleaning house!

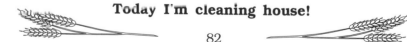

March 23

"And ye shall know the truth, and the truth shall make you free." – John 8:32

WHATEVER HE TELLS YOU, DO IT!

Never allow a truth of God, that is brought home to your soul, to pass without acting on it (not necessarily physically, but in will). His Word, "come unto me," means to transact, or do business with. Everyone who does "come" knows, in that second, the supernatural rush of the life of God invading them, <u>INSTANTLY</u>.

The dominating power of the world, the flesh, and the devil is paralyzed, not by my act, but because my acting linked me to God and His redemptive power. I become plugged in!

Truth is redemptive, only as I act upon that truth by my will, by making a choice. It is always truth. It only becomes experiential, as I act upon it, by choosing to accept it. It becomes reality to me, as I choose to believe it.

Jesus was one with God as He lived on the earth. His will was always to do the Will of His Father. As we seek to be one with Jesus, we must have the same mind in us that was in Him. A pure heart is one that seeks God's Will. To come into oneness with Jesus, our heart must be pure. My prayer, each day, is to come into the oneness more and more (Romans 12:1). Coming into Jesus is a giving up of your whole being into His hands.

Father, I pray to you, asking that you continue to bring me into oneness, by your Holy Spirit. Thank you.

Whatever the Spirit of God reveals to me today, I will do it!

83

"The floods have lifted up, O Lord, the floods have lifted up their voice; the floods lift up their waves." – Psalm 93:3

DISTRACTIONS

The 'temper of the mind' is a dangerous, deadly thing. It creeps into the soul and distracts the mind from God. It cancels out faith in God, at that point, as our confidence in the flesh and human ingenuity rule.

The 'cares of this world' produce a wrong temper of soul. There is enormous power in simple things to distract our attention from God. Refuse (choose) to be swamped with the cares of this temporal life.

The 'lust of vindication' destroys the soul's faith in God. 'I must explain myself, you must understand.' Our Lord never explained anything. He left mistakes to straighten out themselves (not His, but other's mistakes).

Criticism can be distracting. When discernment reveals others are not going on spiritually, discernment can turn into criticism, and it blocks our way to God. Discernment is given, by God, for intercession only.

Father, I can see these road blocks, and detours can keep me out of your presence. They can keep me from fellowship and nourishment in your bosom. I choose, Lord, to set my eyes on the goal ahead. Help me stay focused by your Spirit.

Today I think on God and His ways. I choose not to be distracted (Psalm 93:4).

"Blessed are the poor in spirit; for their's is the kingdom of heaven." – **Matthew 5:3**

BEAUTIFUL ATTITUDES

Jesus gave the <u>be</u>-attitudes, but we cannot hope to maintain them. He knew that, but nevertheless, they are the 'norm' for a long, happy, fulfilled life on the earth.

He also knew He would pray to the Father and He would send the Holy Spirit to indwell us. To the degree that we are yielding to the indwelling Spirit of God, we are living the <u>be</u>autiful attitudes.

To have peace that is continuous, we must keep our minds on what is all important. Vital union with Jesus and the fruit of that union, which is love, is that thing of primary importance. To the degree we are manifesting love, to that degree we are in union with Jesus. When we do the loving thing, in any circumstances, we are in union. If any other attitudes creep in, we have another spirit that must be dealt with.

Father God, your love is the love we must manifest. Since that love is shed in our heart, by your Spirit, we must rely upon and yield to your Spirit, to make that love operable in our lives and circumstances. We do not know how to love. Teach us. Show us, please.

Today, I choose kingdom living.

"And also of the son of the bondwoman will I make a nation, because he is thy seed."
Genesis 21:13

WHO'S IN CHARGE?

Only one overseer can work at a time. Either we are in control of our lives (the natural), or God is (the spiritual). If we insist on managing our own affairs, God will allow it. He doesn't choose to do it this way, but He will allow it.

When we put our natural life in the desert, and by discipline, resolutely keep it under, then God will be with us. He will open up wells and oases, and fulfill all His promises for the natural. He never meant for the natural to have to be sacrificed. His order was for it to be transformed into the spiritual by obedience. It was sin that made it necessary for the natural to be sacrificed.

God designed human nature for Himself. Individuality seeks to counterfeit that, and debases human nature for itself. The continual assertiveness of individuality hinders our spiritual life more than anything. Put it out in the desert, and stop feeding it. God will rescue it and use it as He pleases, if we will abandon it.

Father, I do believe I was created to contain you and to manifest you in the earth. Submission must become my life.

**Today, I submit my will and
choose God's way.**

*"Now faith is the substance of things hoped
for, the evidence of things not seen."*
Hebrews 11:1

TRAVELING BY FAITH

You believe what you read in the Word of God and
then you understand it. We say, "Show me Lord and I'll
believe". He says, "Believe, and I'll show you". God has
prepared a place for us, in His city, the city with the
firm foundation. By faith, we may go there. It is a reality,
it already is, but we won't go there if we don't believe.

Abraham didn't get homesick for Ur. If he had, he
would have had the chance to go back. Rather, he had
his eyes fixed on the God of the new city. In faith, he
was always moving toward that city, always onward.

We, too, can be homesick for 'Ur' or for Egypt's leeks
and onions. Or, we can keep our eyes on God, and
move on, in faith, towards the city not built with hands.

Without faith, it is impossible to please God. Let us
keep our eyes on Jesus, our salvation, the one our faith
depends on from the beginning to the end of the journey
(Isaiah 12:2).

*Father, Abraham lived his life with a view toward the
fulfillment of your covenant with him. I, too, have a
covenant, written in the blood of Jesus. I want to live my
life with a view toward that same city. Thank you. I love
you. I press on.*

Today I travel by faith wherever I go.

March 28

*"... the weeds were wrapped around
my head ... the kingdom of heaven is
like unto ... good seed ..."*
Jonah 2:5, Matthew 13:24

THE WEEDS AND THE SEEDS

We have the resurrection life of Jesus in us as we have accepted salvation and regeneration and yielded to the work of the Holy Spirit. It is a fact, we are one with Jesus Christ.

But, in operation in our body and soul realms are the workings of the old Adam from the seeds we planted there. We are still harvesting crops of the works of the flesh.

As they manifest themselves, we thank God! It makes us aware they are there. We then carry them to the cross, assign them to death by giving them up to Jesus' finished work, and go on in union with Him.

We need not be downcast when the works of Adam appear, but rather, be glad and rejoice that God allows us to see them and know we are harvesting another crop to clear off another field! For a period of time, the wheat and tares (weeds) continue to grow together in our lives. It is by faith we ask the Holy Spirit to identify the tares, so we can take appropriate action to 'purify' that area.

Father, when we see, by the eye of the Spirit, that it is you perfecting what you have begun in us, at salvation, we can rise up with you in agreement.

I say yes, Lord, burn my fields.

March 29

*"And he that was dead came forth,
bound hand and foot with graveclothes:
and his face was bound with a napkin.
Jesus saith unto them ..."* — **John 11:44**

"LOOSE HIM AND LET HIM GO"

In John 11:38-44, Jesus called Lazarus forth from death to life. He commanded those that knew Lazarus to untie him and let him go free. Jesus always calls men forth unto life. Other men often keep them bound to many things: to their own personal experience with Jesus, their own progress in growth, their own beliefs, customs or history.

Man, in the natural, is determined to make man after his own image. This is why Jesus said, 'I, if I be lifted up, I'll draw all men unto myself.' So often we lift up ourselves as the example.

Oh God, forgive us where we have hindered your working in the lives of others. Help us to recognize where we do this, and enable us, by your Holy Spirit, to set them free from ourselves and point them to Jesus. I release everyone, today, that I have bound, by expecting something from them. Something you, Father, have chosen to give of yourself alone. I release pastors, teachers, books, tapes and leaders that I have looked to for that fellowship and understanding, which I can get no where but in God. I release hurts, misunderstandings and disappointments. Fill me with the knowledge of yourself, Lord. You are more than enough.

**I am thankful for leaders and authority
given to me by God.**

*"And all things, whatsoever ye shall ask
in prayer, believing, ye shall receive."*
Matthew 21:22

YOU MUST ASK

This morning, I saw my prayer as a check I send in with my order blank to God. He, in turn, sends my order that I've picked out of the catalog and the Word of promises He has for me concerning my need. These words of promise are for all those who belong to Him and are called children of God. I should be as excited and expectant for the answer (the package) to come daily from God, as I am for the mailman. When I've ordered something, I watch the mailbox for the package to arrive. This is faith in action. Do I have more faith in the mail order store than I do in God?

As I read the catalog (the Bible), I pick out my order (the promise of God I need), and enclose my order blank and my check. Then I wait expectedly and excitedly for God to send the order that I know is coming, because I believe He said it and it is so.

If I doubt the answer is coming, it may be because I didn't fill out the order blank (my request) correctly and enclose my check (my prayer). James 4:2 reminds us we have not because we ask not. John 16:24 tells us to ask, that we might receive.

Father, I do believe everything I need for life and godliness is in you. I also believe I must make my requests known of you.

**I am going to ask God for what I need. I'm
going to write my check!**

"Take my yoke upon you, and learn of me: for I am meek and lowly in heart: and ye shall find rest unto your souls." – Matthew 11:29

CHARACTER — HAVING IT, NOT BEING ONE!

Words are human expressions. Thus, we are given the Bible in order to 'see' Jesus. Jesus told us to learn of Him, for He is meek and lowly. If Jesus was a human image of the invisible God, and He could in fact do nothing on His own, then humility seems to be a characteristic of God's nature. It would seem to be opposite of man's fallen nature - pride.

If God is, Himself, humble and meek, what must we be to please Him? In relationship and fellowship with God, character and disposition are everything. Logical conclusion now shows us these are not ours by natural possession. Jesus exhorted us to learn these from Him in humility.

Of all Christian character, a meek and lowly spirit is the very seed and root. Question: Is my heart in the state my teacher desires it to be in? If not, it is my first task to yield myself to Him to work it in me.

Right now, this instant, Spirit of God, I do yield myself for you to work into the core of my being, a meek and lowly spirit pleasing unto my Father.

Now I want to walk as Jesus walked.

*"But rise, and stand upon thy feet: for
I have appeared unto thee for this purpose,
to make thee a minister and a witness both
of these things which thou hast seen, and
of those things in the which I will appear
unto thee."* – Acts 26:16

A FRESH WORD FOR THE DAY

Jesus did not give Saul a message or a doctrine to proclaim. He told him to tell the people He sent him to, what he had seen on the Damascus road, of Jesus and what He revealed to him later.

Paul saw Jesus, and for the rest of his life he was true to the vision he had that day. He was faithful to proclaim that heavenly message. What he had seen with his own eyes, no one could take away from him. We all need such an encounter.

If we are to be servants of the most high God, we must bring fresh, current messages and revelations from Him, to those He has chosen to hear what He has given us to speak. God will give you each day the manna (Word) you require to serve Him. It will not keep until tomorrow. It must be served up hot and on time or it will be lost. We have the same promise the apostle Paul had. In John 16, we are told that He, the Holy Spirit, will lead you into all truth and reveal to you things to come.

Father, we believe you are the same today as you were when you spoke to Paul. We ask you to empower us, as we believe you and trust you. Give us the words, each day, you would have us share.

Today, I will get plugged in before I go out!

"Jesus said unto her, I am the resurrection, and the life: he that believeth in me, though he were dead, yet shall he live:" – John 11:25

DEAD: WITHOUT LIFE

Lazarus was sick and Jesus loved him. Jesus declared his sickness not unto death, but to the glory of God. Again, in John 11:5, He was said to love them, yet in their time of trial, He tarried. It wasn't time for Jesus to minister life. We have to complete the dying before life can come out of us. We have here an earthly event, with a heavenly teaching.

Between death to self and Christ's life in us, is a sleeping. Unless Jesus withdrew His presence, we would not believe. His coming in the lifeless dead body brings belief to others who witness it. Jesus is the resurrection and the life of those who have died to self. If we believe, we will live. Believe and live! Believe and live!

It grieves Jesus when He offers all of His resurrection self, and we cannot see past the grave. He wants to give us this resurrection life, and when we draw back, He grieves. When Jesus raises us from the dead, He commands those who would hold us to loose us and let us go!

Jesus, Lord, when we go to the tomb looking for you, we find you are not there. Father God has, Himself, raised you to resurrection life. This is your continuous call unto us; to come out from among the dead and live. We want to run and tell everyone, you are risen!

I will go beyond the cross and the tomb to share in Jesus' resurrection power.

"He is not here; for he is risen ..."
Matthew 28:6a

RAISED: TO NEW LIFE

At the resurrection, Jesus moved out of the physical realm, into the spiritual realm. From that point on, it now takes an act of faith to <u>see</u> Him, to <u>see</u> into the spiritual world. It takes an act of faith to obey a spiritual Jesus. The spiritual world is activated by faith. The written Word of God, the Bible, stimulates our faith to the point of acting upon it.

In Luke 24:13-31, there is a very graphic description of those who had been with Jesus before the crucifiction. They were sure it was over and life would return to 'normal.' As they walked along, discussing the events, the risen Lord came up beside them and began to expound the scriptures to them concerning Himself. They recognized Jesus when He sat at meat with them, prayed and broke bread. He was then familiar to them. They began to understand, in verse 32, when their eyes were opened to spiritual things. They recalled how their hearts had burned as He <u>opened</u> the scriptures to them.

Father, we are reminded again, we can go back to the empty tomb and expect to meet Jesus there over and over, or we can go on to the resurrection and see Jesus with spiritual eyes. We chose to be involved with you, in the spiritual world, where you operate in power and signs and wonders. It is the <u>real</u> world. It is where the action really is. You, in your resurrection power, want to shake things up and cause mankind to see and recognize you. You are still limited to your people. Oh God, may we arise!

I want to go forth in resurrection power
and change my world today!

"The entrance of thy words giveth light;
it giveth understanding unto the simple."
Psalm 119:130

FACTS CONCERNING GOD'S WORD

God's Word is the only authentic revelation of God's will. All human statements of Divine truth, however correct, are defective and carry a measure of human authority. In the Word, the voice of God speaks to us directly.

In His Word, God has revealed Himself to each individual. It is a real eye opener to discover that salvation comes from hearing the Word of God. Faith, necessary for receiving of salvation, is in the Word. (See Romans 10:17.)

The Word of God is a living Word. It carries a divine quickening power in it. The faith of it being God's own Word and of the presence and power in it, makes it effectual. The words in which God has chosen to clothe His own Divine thoughts are God breathed, and the life of God dwells in them.

The Holy Spirit must be the interpreter of God's own Word. Divine truth needs a Divine Teacher. The Word, prayerfully read and cherished in the heart, will, through the Holy Spirit, be both light and life. (See John 14:26.)

The Word then brings us into the closest and most intimate fellowship with God, bringing unity of will and life. In His Word. God has revealed His whole heart and His will.

My Father, as I come before you to read your Word, I believe you will quicken it to my heart, by your Spirit.

I yield myself to the working of
God's words in me.

*"And he said to them all, If any man will
come after me, let him deny himself, and
take up his cross daily, and follow me."*
Luke 9:23

OUTSIDE POPULARITY

As we walk on the path of life, we must identify
with Christ's suffering. It doesn't matter about me, Lord,
what do you want? I must be dead to self, dead to the
world, dead to sin, hate my life, lose my life. Jesus
prepared the way. We have to go through it just as He
did, through suffering (denial), to abide in God.

Jesus was an overcomer. He endured the cross
(Hebrews 12:1 and 2). Our goal and our prize is to keep
our eyes focused on Jesus enduring the cross. Our cross
is the flesh condemned and crucified; not my will, but
thine, Father.

In Hebrews 13:11-13, we are called on to follow Jesus
outside the camp. The camp is fellowship with the world.
God is glorified in our willingness to follow Jesus in
such a way. As God is glorified, men are saved.

*Father God, the longer we know you and the closer
we get to you, the more we understand your ways. It has
never been the popular thing to follow Jesus. Here we see
you went outside the camp to crucify our Lord. We get a
glimpse of the narrowing of the way. It is not by your
choice, but few choose to follow you. We also realize the
choice is a daily thing. The opportunity to deny you is ever
present. Help us, oh God, not to deny you.*

**My life is a drama on the stage of time.
How convincing am I in my role?**

"I can do all things through Christ which strengtheneth me." – **Philippians 4:13**

COPING OR CONQUERING?

The scriptures instruct us not to try to 'cope' in our own strength with things, situations, or circumstances, because it's futile. Seek something better than the power to cope. Seek the power of God to overcome (Romans 8:37-39). Our fight is not against flesh and blood, but against sin, carnality and this present world system, controlled by Satan (Ephesians 6:12).

We weary in the battle, only when the flesh is doing the contending (Galatians 6:8,9). The flesh, our own strength, copes. The spirit conquers. We reap what we sow. If we are sowing struggle, stamina and sturdiness out of the flesh, or self efforts, we will reap despair, depression and defeat.

Yield yourself as instruments of righteousness unto God, and be at peace in your situations. By this process, we sense the power of the indwelling Spirit, to bring forth victory and to bear His fruit in us (Galatians 2:22, 23).

Father, I come apart with you in quietness and take inventory of my life and my circumstances, and seek to receive from you the wisdom, direction and ability I need to put myself in a better place. I thank you that you will hear me when I cry unto you.

Today, I will talk it all over with God.

"For the Lord is great, and greatly to be praised: he is to be feared above all gods."
Psalm 96:4

FEAR IS A GOOD THING

Fear and serve the Lord (I Samuel 12:14.) Fear and serve the Lord (Joshua 24:14). What you do in the fear of the Lord you will do faithfully and with a perfect heart (II Chronicles 19:7). The fear of the Lord is wisdom (Job 28:28). The fear of the Lord, the beginning of wisdom (Psalm 111:10). We bless the Lord when we fear Him (Psalm 135:20).

God blesses those that fear Him (Psalm 128:1). The fear of the Lord, the beginning of knowledge (Proverbs 1:7). the fear of the Lord tendeth to life: and he that hath it shall abide satisfied; he shall not be visited with evil (Proverbs 19:23). Those that fear God shall be healed (Malachi 4: 2).

If you fear man, you do not fear God. What a strong statement to make. The Word tells us to fear Him who can destroy the soul. We cannot put man in the place of God. Fear of God is recognizing His authority and power over and in your life. It is recognizing that you belong to Him, and will be obedient to Him, because of that ownership. This is giving to Him His rightful place in your life; seeing Him as God, who He is, sovereign, responsible, in charge. It is humbly assigning your self to its proper place. One day He tenderly showed me, it is wanting to please Him, not wanting to hurt His feelings or disappoint Him. It's sort of like baking Him a pie, just because you want to!

My Father and my God, fear is not at all that we think it is, when in the proper perspective and directed in the right way. Teach us to fear you correctly.

Today, I'll look for opportunities to please God.

"For it is God which worketh in you both to will and to do of his good pleasure."
Philippians 2:13

WHOSE IDEA IS IT, ANYWAY?

When we are discouraged or disappointed over a failure, it is because we fell short of a personal goal, not because we failed to reach the goal God had for us in that situation. We are disappointed because we failed to live up to our expectations, while all along, it is God urging us on to our full potential.

The failure to meet our goals brings suffering until we realize it's what we did, not who we are. We can mess up, or blow it, as some say, and get the 'feeling' our identity was shaken. We falsely attribute what we do or don't do as being who we are. In these times of stress, if we'd learn to take a step back, draw a deep breath and reposition our thinking, we would overcome the temptation to be disappointed. I Peter 5:6-10 says to humble ourselves before or under the hand of God, and He who has called us unto His glory, after we have hurt from failure for awhile, will make us perfect. Now, this perfection is after God's estimation of perfection, not mine.

It's all about growing and maturing and learning to allow God to strengthen and settle us into maturity, by the power of His Holy Spirit.

Father, I choose to come into the rest of being your beloved child; to settle down and stop being disappointed at myself, and accept your estimation of me. I love you!

I go forward today knowing I'm a winner.

"That ye may with one mind and one mouth glorify God, even the Father of our Lord Jesus Christ." – Romans 15:6

WHAT'S BEHIND WHAT I SAY?

Have you known of cases where someone did the right thing but for the wrong reason? This is a very important point to consider. Motive is everything in the final outcome of a thing.

Man was spirit dominated in his original state. At the fall, he sank down, down to soul domination, flesh domination. The spirit is that part of man capable of knowing God. Knowing is to be intimately acquainted with.

The soul is the seat of self-consciousness, the body the seat of sense-consciousness.

In I Corinthians 6:17, we read the spirit that has been redeemed and joined with the Lord, is one spirit with Him. Then, in Hebrews 4:12, we learn as we read the Word of God, the life of God comes through our spirit and into our soul, in resurrection power.

The soul is not destroyed, nor is the individual ability of the believer destroyed. Rather, the soul or personality is animated by the life of God in us. We say the same words, perform the same deeds, but with a different power of animating life behind them. Via the spirit, into the mind, we experience the leading of the Holy Spirit.

Father, we know we are incomplete, unfinished, not at our best, while separated from you. We ask humbly, that Jesus Christ come into our life and change us, through salvation, into the person you created us to be.

Come Holy Spirit, make Jesus real in me today.

**"But we had the sentence of death in
ourselves, that we should not trust in
ourselves, but in God which raiseth the dead:"
II Corinthians 1:9**

NOT MY WAY, BUT HIS

Jesus did not trust Himself to men because He knew what was in their heart (Matthew 9:4). Jesus cannot trust Himself to me because He knows what is in my heart. The heart of man is deceitfully wicked (Jeremiah 17:9). This puts things in perspective, doesn't it?

To each of us has been given a measure of faith. We are saved by faith, but that faith is apart from us. It is the gift of God. We have nothing of which to boast. Nothing, nothing, nothing!

God made us in His own image – we rebelled. God made a way to reconcile us. His very own Son, Jesus, is that way of reconciliation. God ultimately saves us by drawing us, through the power of His Spirit, back to Himself.

Then we choose to die to our self life and to sin, in order to live life, or to continue as we are, only existing. God has a plan to allow us to fulfill our destiny, to be reconciled (brought back to the image of Himself). It's a plan for us to be the best of all He created us to be. We can thwart that plan at any point (retard our growth) by saying, "no" to God and "yes" to self. At every turn, we have to assign the self life to the place of death that Jesus assigned it to when He died on the cross.

As I behold Jesus, I see myself and all my faults. As I pray and believe, I see myself cleansed by His blood and clothed in His righteousness, by His Spirit.

I say, "yes" to God's plan and "no" to my own way.

**"I am crucified with Christ: nevertheless I
live: yet not I, but Christ liveth in me..."
Galatians 2:20a**

CRUCIFIED WITH CHRIST

Jesus bore my sins and was God's perfect lamb of sacrifice for those sins. I was crucified with Christ, not for my sins, but rather to die in my sinful nature, my Adam ancestry. Jesus died for my sins (my acts of wrong doing). I died to my sinful nature. Jesus arose the first of the new creation. God's new world order, the Kingdom of God now has a king, Jesus.

I arose with Him into newness of life. I was baptized into His death and raised with His nature in me. My spirit and God's Spirit fused as one. I ascended with Jesus, where He is seated on the right hand of the Father, making intercession, praying, for me.

Jesus asked His Father, God, to send the Holy Spirit to keep me in this new life. As we walk in light of this truth, His blood cleanses us from all unrighteousness.

Father God, my natural mind would reject this as a complicated thing. It is only as the gift of faith, you imparted into me, is activated, by your Word, that this becomes yes and amen to my heart. By the eye of faith I see it is the plan you've always had to bring me back to yourself.

**As I read the Word today, I will ask the
Holy Spirit to help me understand.**

*"And God is able to make all grace abound
toward you: that ye, always having all
sufficiency in all things, may abound to
every good work:"* – **II Corinthians 9:8**

ALL SUFFICIENCY

If you will bear with me for a moment, I would like to share a clear teaching from God's Word that can and will set the tone, or quality, of our life here on earth. It's found in II Corinthians 9:6-15, and I ask you to read it, so what I say is clearly not my thoughts, but direction from the Father.

Sufficiency means having enough resources to retain one's economic independence from others. Because of God's power, it is possible for the Christian, always and in all things, to be independent of all but God.

God's servants never need to worry about exhausting their resources by giving. God has seen to it that they will always be productive. Through God's provision, the believer remains financially capable of doing good deeds of every kind for others. Giving enables others to glorify God because of you. They, in turn, bless you by their prayers on your behalf. It is another cycle originating from God, back to God. God gets the Glory. You get the blessing.

Father, this concept doesn't come naturally to us, for we are creatures of getting for ourselves. Even when your Word says it is more blessed to give than to receive, we often stumble or balk. Release in us the spirit of hilarious giving so we may be perfected in this area.

**I choose to cooperate with the
spirit of giving today.**

*"Let us therefore fear, lest, a promise being
left us of entering into his rest, any of you
should seem to come short of it."*
Hebrews 4:1

ENTERING REST TODAY

When God rested on the Sabbath, He had finished the creation of the world. Everything was made. God invites His children to enter into that Sabbath rest. Those that hear His voice may enter in.

The Hebrews did not enter into the rest prepared for them by God. They were stubborn, rebellious, disloyal and disobedient. Being deceived by sin leads to stubbornness [Hebrews 3:13]. Here we are admonished to help one another, as long as the today applies to us. There will come a time when our today is no more, see entire third chapter of Hebrews.

We hear the good news preached. Our part is to accept it. We, who hear and accept, do enter into the rest of God. God's spirit will not always strive with man, so we need to take advantage of the today of God's call. This rest is likened unto God's seventh day rest because He had finished creating everything and it was good. If we enter into the rest prepared for us, everything is finished and it is good.

Father, we hear the voice of your Spirit telling us if we hear your voice, not to harden our hearts. We do not want to harden our hearts to your voice, but rather to open our hearts and receive your Word to us.

I am listening to hear God's Word to me.

*"Then Joseph, being raised from sleep, did
as the angel of the Lord had bidden him,
and took unto him his wife." – Matthew 1:24*

GUIDANCE

When Christ is being formed in a person, God gives them obedient believers to walk with. Joseph was obedient to protect and keep Mary, as Jesus was formed in her. Let us be careful to give thanks to God for His supplying of these saints to our lives. We also need to be aware that they are God sent, and avail ourselves of the wisdom and instruction they bring.

When we are earnestly desiring to be obedient unto the Word of God, He often visits us with dreams, to direct our paths. If Christ is formed in us, dreams take a less prominent place in our guidance. As we go here and there, it will be Christ in us obeying the commands and wishes of His Father.

We are in the age of the Church, led by the Holy Spirit. If God can "get through" to us in our conscious realm, then He doesn't need the use of the sub-conscious via dreams. As we have our channels open to Him, He can communicate with us openly and freely. The final check point is always the Word of God.

Father, we can see and understand, in your love, you ever seek opportunities and ways to communicate with us. We desire to open up unto you and grow in trust and knowledge and maturity.

I will listen for the voice of God today.

April 15

*"My little children, of whom I travail in birth
again until Christ be formed in you."*
Galatians 4:19

JESUS OUR EXAMPLE

In these few minutes today, I would ask you to focus on the earthly life of Jesus, as a picture of the Christian life we all live. Every new birth is a living example of Jesus being born in Mary. She was overshadowed by the Spirit of God, and that life that came forth was born of God, not man.

After a period of time, known only to God, that child matures and becomes a young man. He goes about his Father's business, and is a member of a family with responsibilities and assignments.

As he proved capable and willing in these family matters, he is matured and launches out in a full time pursuit of his Father's purposes. He is enabled and empowered by the Spirit of God, to carry out these pursuits and plans.

The Holy Spirit dwells in me like radar, scanning my inward parts, seeking to permeate my being with His presence. At the point He finds "hidden blockages," He shines the light, and I must yield or break. The hurting comes when I refuse to yield.

My Lord and My God, I know what you have just revealed to me is true. I know it's the way it works, the way it was meant to be. Its just those unconverted areas of my life where I resist you that hurt. I repent. I want your way more than anything.

I will yield where I sense the Spirit working on me.

"And saying, Repent ye: for the kingdom of heaven is at hand." – Matthew 3:2

JESUS CAN DO IT

Before Christ is revealed, God sends a messenger, such as John, who lifts up Jesus and preaches repentance. We respond to that message, not to the messenger. John was faithful to do that thing he was born to do - to introduce Jesus and then get out of the way.

Preaching repentance, and identifying Jesus as the Son of God, brings Him on the scene. Jesus can work where He is lifted up. In our zealousness, we sometimes overlook our part in the general scheme of events. We are just messengers. Our part is to bring an introductive message of Jesus. Then, He shows up and does the rest!

For myself, I have struggled more in this area over my years as a Christian, than any other. For years, I kept a note on my mirror, "Let God be God." It has been a life long goal to decrease, so that He might continue to increase [John 3:30]. There is a wonderful verse that says as we gaze into the Word, we become more like the image we see revealed there [II Corinthians 3:18]. That image is Jesus.

Father, we want our priorities straight. We want to be aware that we are the messenger, sent by you, to take the knowledge of the light of the world into all the dark places. Jesus, when presented, is always enough.

I want to look like Jesus today.

"Then was Jesus led up of the Spirit into the
wilderness, to be tempted of the devil."
Matthew 4:1

TEMPTATION

Jesus was tempted, just as Adam was. Satan isn't very original, he only has one plan. He uses it over and over again, on every person. Jesus was the only person who never fell for Satan's line. This was because He thought nothing of Himself, but rather thought always of His Father's will. He sought, out of His love for His Father, always to please Him.

Where Adam accepted temptation by eating, Jesus fasted. He denied Himself and did not rely on common sense. He relied on God, instead, through the strength of His Word [Matthew 4:4]. This reveals an area of obedience required of us, in walking with God. It 'seems' like it's okay and since everyone else seems to be doing it, why shouldn't I? If we are walking in covenant relationship with God, He requires things of us from time to time that really do defy our reason. These are exercises in hearing and doing the will of God. These are times of great blessing and satisfaction, if we can bring ourselves to walk this way.

Father, we know it is you that draws us and calls us forth. We also know that unless we yield ourselves to these overtures, they will pass us right by. We want to hasten to answer your call. Help us by your Spirit (Song of Solomon 1:4).

As I feel God drawing me today,
I will run after Him.

*"For in that he himself hath suffered
being tempted, he is able to succour them
that are tempted."* – Hebrews 2:18

SATAN'S STRATEGIES EXPOSED

The three areas of temptation are: the pride of life - good to make one wise, the lust of the eyes - good to look at, and the lust of the flesh - good to eat. Satan tempted Jesus twice to <u>prove</u> He was the Son of God. To defend Himself, would be to have the sin of pride. Jesus never defended Himself, which is the pride of life. It would be good to do a study of the strategy of Satan in Jesus' temptation, found in Matthew 4.

Satan used up his plan on Jesus, and it failed. How encouraging to realize it was all tested by Jesus, all exposed. There aren't any new weapons Satan can surprise you with to trip you up. Jesus dealt with the whole plan and defeated Satan.

After his plan failed on Jesus, Satan withdrew and decided to work on the other end of the deal - to attack Jesus through the nature of those Jesus would come in contact with. Hebrews 4:15 tells us this still didn't work. Jesus, being tempted in all points, remained without sin.

It was the Spirit that led Jesus into the wilderness to be tested. Once you belong to God, He leads, controls and directs your life.

Father, my stubbornness, doubt, and unbelief slow down and hinder my progress. Forgive me for these sins. Cleanse me and use me, I pray.

I am encouraged to know Satan has been exposed!

**"Yea, the darkness hideth not from thee: but
the night shineth as the day; the darkness
and the light are both alike to thee."
Psalm 139:12**

BUMPS IN THE ROAD

As long as life moves smoothly, full of blessings, we don't have a chance to see how much faith we truly have. It really isn't a matter of "how much" faith we have. It is a matter of where our faith is.

A crisis is our high water mark. It is a way we can measure, so to speak, our faith. Is it real? Is it intact? Is it working? Was it faith in God, or in what God can give me or has done for me? My thoughts turn to Job. He was able to say, "Though he slays me, yet will I trust Him" [Job 13:15].

This is why we need to be so thankful for a crisis or a hard place. It is a time to be still and to see the salvation of God! It is a time to rest in trust, and to settle into what we believe to be the truth of God. He doesn't always reveal to us the whys and wherefores of life. Is He God? Does He mean what He has told us in His Word? It is a time to yield yourself to God and to His will, that we may be pleasing unto Him, and bring joy to His heart.

Father, most of my life I've sought to bring you into my life, and ask you to protect me from anything I wasn't comfortable with. Please forgive me for my selfishness. Have your way.

I'd rather have Jesus, than anything.

**"But let your communication be, Yea, yea;
Nay, nay: for whatsoever is more than these
cometh of evil." – Matthew 5:37**

YOUR WORD STANDS

It is not necessary to swear by anything. A Christian's yes means yes and his no means no. His Word is his bond. This, of course, is a Spirit controlled, Spirit led Christian.

When we begin to 'explain' what we meant when we said what we said, we get into trouble. If indeed we spoke true, it will bear witness that it was true. Matthew 5:37 could be paraphrased, 'drop the truth and run'! We seem, so much of the time, to want to be understood, that we talk a thing to death.

There is also a Word that says to guard your heart, for out of it come the issues of life [Proverbs 4:23]. We always come back to examining our heart, our motive, in saying or doing a thing.

Father, we are convicted that our words are not true much of the time. We say what we think someone wants to hear or what is expected of us, to be politically correct. Our peace with you and those around us will be ultimately in speaking true words, in an attitude of love. We will be on firm ground, even if misunderstood. Help us to be brave enough to allow the Spirit of truth to work in our life.

**What I say today can, and will,
change tomorrow.**

April 21

"That ye may be the children of your Father which is in heaven: for he maketh his sun to rise on the evil and on the good, and sendeth rain on the just and on the unjust."
Matthew 5:45

EMULATING GOD

The children of God must have the same character as God the Father. Here, we see God treating the good and the evil alike in this world. He is a loving God, and His love is manifested alike to the just and the unjust. If we are to be His children, we must treat the evil and the good with the same loving consideration.

In verse 44, we are admonished to love our enemies, to bless those who curse us, and do good to those who hate us. Also, we are to pray for those that despitefully use us and persecute us. This is contrary to what we hear of worldly thought (verse 43).

In verse 48, we see 'like father like son,' taught by Jesus, as acceptable behavior for a child of God. Our children emulate our actions because they are with us all the time. They are fully acquainted with our ways by association. If we are closely associated with our heavenly Father, because we are with Him continually, how can we help but emulate Him? We are like that which our heart is stayed upon.

Father God, this doesn't seem to be a suggestion to us, but rather an expected manner of behavior. We are to be so closely related to you, we begin to take on your very attitudes and actions towards all others. This is a divine work of grace you alone can accomplish in us. Thank you.

I want to treat others as God does.

*"And whatsoever ye do, do it heartily, as to
the Lord, and not unto men;"*
Colossians 3:23

SECRET DEEDS

Continuing on, as we have for several days, in the teachings of Jesus on the mountain, we look at two subjects found in Matthew 6:1-8. The first is concerned with giving alms; the second, with prayer. God is the one we are serving with our alms and with our prayers. It is doing business with Him that counts, not earning a reputation among men.

We are to be so closely related to our Father that we have no need to please anyone else in our giving and praying. We do alms and we pray because of our relationship with God, as a natural outcome of our fellowship with Him. Alms is referred to in scriptures as righteousness. Could we paraphrase this and say, when we do the 'right thing' in the situation or circumstance?

We are to be as Jesus was, when He washed the disciples' feet - so sure of who we are in our relationship to the Father, that we have nothing to prove and no need to impress.

Father God, what freeing and revolutionary concepts are taught here. Help us, by your Holy Spirit, to develop this kind of relationship with you, that gives, does, and prays spontaneously, from a heart filled with love for you. We desire to be perfect, as you are, in this world.

**I'll do something today,
just because I love God.**

April 23

Now be ye not stiffnecked, as your fathers were,
but yield yourselves unto the Lord..."
II Chronicles 30:8

I GIVE UP

You can't do it.
Entrust your will to Jesus.
Instantly release His Holy Spirit.
Let Him supernaturally work in you.
Do it now, without delay!

We cannot decide for Jesus. Today, we decide yes. Tomorrow, we decide no. Our will is affected by both our emotions and our intellect. Whichever is in the driver's seat at the time, affects our decisions.

The reason there are so few lasting transactions for Christ in our meetings and in our churches, is that we call on man to decide. What we must do is ask man to yield to Jesus - to allow, permit, grant authority, move over, relinquish our will, to yield our choice to Jesus.

'It is God that is at work in us to will and to do His good pleasure' (Philippians 2:13). What is His good pleasure? It is to come to Him, through Jesus Christ; to accept the fact, by faith, that Jesus made a way of reconciliation to God.

When we yield to this fact, we set in motion the power that raised Jesus from the dead, the power of the Holy Spirit unleashed to bring us to salvation and regeneration.

Father, I see that choosing still keeps me in charge. Yielding releases you to bring me to yourself. I yield my will to Jesus.

Nothing in my hand I bring.
Simply to thy cross I cling.

114

"After this manner therefore pray ye..."
Matthew 6:9

PRAYER

Our Father - We recognize God's relationship to others. He's not our private property. Which art in heaven - we identify which God we are addressing and where He lives. Hallowed be thy name - we establish God's character, recognizing His authority and position. Thy kingdom come, thy will be done - we give God permission, as far as we are concerned, to have His own way, yielding ourselves to His authority. In earth as it is in heaven - we want the perfection of heaven to be on earth, recognizing that in heaven there is no conflict of wills. God's will is always done. Give us this day our daily bread - we know all good gifts come down from the Father, knowing He will supply bread tomorrow as well as today, trusting Him to meet our needs (Matthew 6:9-11).

Father God, we pause here in meditating on the model prayer. The only thing the disciples asked Jesus to teach them was how to pray. We stand in the same place Lord. Teach us to pray. Trust and faith arise in our hearts as we speak out these truths, in communication with you, through your Holy Spirit.

**I will sink down in the knowledge that I
have a heavenly Father, who sees and knows
and will meet my every need. Thank you.**

"And it came to pass, that as he was praying in a certain place, when he ceased, one of his disciples said unto him, Lord, teach us to pray, as John also taught his disciples."
Luke 11:1

MORE PRAYER

<u>And forgive us our debts as we forgive our debtors</u> - because we forgive our debtors, we know that God will forgive us. As we are in right relationship to God, we recognize His sovereignty. We revere His name and abide in His love. Therefore, our attitude is right toward our debtors. If everything we have comes from the Father, no man owes us anything. Because of this right relationship, we can be assured that He forgives our debts.

<u>And lead us not into temptation, but deliver us from evil</u> - if these previous things are true, God won't need to discipline us, through temptations. We'll already be in line with His will. He won't need to turn us over to the evil one, the tempter, to test us.

<u>For thine is the kingdom, and the power, and the Glory forever</u> - we recognize God has the power and the glory because the kingdom is His. We are partakers of His heavenly kingdom, through the death, burial and resurrection of Jesus (Matthew 6:12-13). Amen - we know who you are! Recognizing God as omnipresent, omnipotent and omniscient.

Father, our heart leaps in our bosom in paeans of praise and thanksgiving, as this prayer crashes to an ending, recognizing your all-consuming majesty. To think we are your children humbles us at the same time, filling us with gratefulness.

I stand amazed in the presence of God.

"Behold, I send an Angel before thee, to keep thee in the way, and to bring thee into the place which I have prepared." — **Exodus 23:20**

POSSESSING OUR PROMISES

In Exodus 23: 20-33, we see a picture of the spirit-led Christian going on to maturity and finding their fulfillment in God. In verse 23, we see the angel, as the Holy Spirit, leading them into the promises. He is instructing and guiding them not to bow down to foreign gods, nor serve them, nor do the works of them. As the spirit leads into the place God has prepared for you and you are obedient to that leading, God will bless your bread and your water and will take sickness from among you (verse 25).

The key to waiting on God is found in verse 29. If He drove out all the hindrances (I refer to it as garbage) before the Holy Spirit has been able to teach us truths to replace the garbage, it would be like the parable of the unclean spirits (Matthew 12:43-45). In verse 30, we see it is little by little that God will drive out garbage, until we are full of the knowledge of the truth, and inherit the land that God prepared for us before the foundation of the world. The promise in verse 31 is that then God will give you power over the enemy, and you will drive them out of the land.

Father, I'm beginning to understand it is a journey we are on with you. Your Holy Spirit has been sent to bring us home to you. Obeying you brings us there so much faster.

I choose to obey what I hear God say today.

*"...by strength of hand the Lord brought you
out from this place..." – Exodus 13:3*

A PEOPLE WITH A HERITAGE

God chose a people in the Hebrews, an insignificant people by world standards. God loved the whole world. He needed a people to demonstrate what it is supposed to be like between God and people. People respond to what they see in other people. We relate to people - human relates to human.

God took the lowly servant people of the Egyptians and said, "this is my people, so all the people of the earth may know that the hand of the Lord is powerful." We see God powerful in nature and things around us, but we respond to God in another person.

Today, I saw it was the hand of God that led them into the wilderness, and in the fullness of time, He led them out the same way He led them in. They could not get into the wilderness without the Red Sea parting, and they couldn't get out without the Jordan River parting.

God was in control! He called them, gave them instructions - what to do and how to do it. God was in charge that 40 years, preparing a people for the place He had prepared for them.

My Lord and My God, you are the same yesterday, today and forever. How you worked with Israel, you work with me. I yield to you.

My steps are ordered of the Lord.

**"But God hath chosen the foolish things of
the world to confound the wise; and God
hath chosen the weak things of the world to
confound...(the) mighty."** – I Corinthians 1:27

A PEOPLE WITH A PURPOSE

Just as God chose an insignificant people, in the Israelites, to demonstrate His power to the peoples of all the earth, so He has chosen the insignificant ones of the world in His plan to present Jesus to the world. Again, we see the pattern of being led into the wilderness for proving, as modeled by Jesus in His own wilderness experience. As He is, so are we in this world (I John 4:17).

When you are in the wilderness, know that God will let you out in the fullness of time, when the reasons for being there have been accomplished and the rule of God established in that matter. It is in His time and if you are there, know it will pass when God chooses to let you out.

It is preparation. And you spend not one day longer in the wilderness than is necessary for the perfecting of a vessel, that the world will know the power of the hand of God (I Peter 5:6).

Father, we can take great comfort in knowing there are procedures necessary for living and growing and maturing. They are not 'punishments,' doled out to us indiscriminately. Rather, they are classrooms for instructions to life and godliness.

I bless God today for 'child training' me!

*"Ye call me Master and Lord: and
ye say well; for so I am." – John 13:13*

WRESTLING WITH GOD

We want someone or something to be stronger and bigger than we are. We want to find someone to master us. We don't want to have to make choices, but to be mastered. We want to find that one that brings us, by force, to our knees. That's why we are always wanting miracles from God. They show us His power!

Instead of that thing we wrestle against, we find a meek and lowly Jesus of Nazareth standing before us; Showing us He knows us and still accepts us, and gives us an opportunity to be reconciled to the God we are wrestling with. Jesus, who says, "if you have seen me, you have seen the Father," knows us better than we know ourselves and still wants us, still loves us.

Mastership in experience is love. A master is one who has brought me into the secure sense that he has met and solved every perplexity and problem of my mind. It is not ruling over me, but making me feel secure and safe. This is true mastership, and always operates by love.

Father, this is truly finding a master - one in whom I can place my heart with safety, one in whom I can find all my answers as 'yes' and 'amen.' I truly bow my knee to Jesus, my Master and my Lord.

**I am secure today in the knowledge that I
am connected to the master of the
universe!**

"And I will pray the Father, and he shall give you another Comforter, that he may abide with you for ever:" – John 14:16

NEVER ALONE

In the 16th chapter of John, we see Jesus preparing His disciples for the arrival of the Holy Spirit, in the new dimension of the Church age. God walked with Adam in the Spirit, before sin entered. After that, God withdrew His spiritual presence from Adam, and dealt with him in his intellect (all Adam could now understand).

When the second Adam, Jesus, came, He canceled out the first Adam's sin. This made communion possible again between God and His new creations (born again men).

In the 16th chapter of John, Jesus outlined the ministry of the Holy Spirit (what the disciples could expect). The first 'job' of the Holy Spirit is to convict of sin. It is sin that separates us from fellowship, or communion, with God. In His love for us and His hunger for fellowship with us, God allows His Spirit to convict us of any and all sin, so we can repent and be cleansed and have fellowship restored.

My Father, I do not want sin and rebelliousness and foolishness to stand in my way of open and free communication with you. I gladly receive the ministry of the Holy Spirit in conviction of sin. Thank you for making the way to yourself for me.

I refuse to let sin keep me from my Father!

*"Thus saith the Lord of hosts; Consider
your ways."* – **Haggai 1:7**

DON'T BOTHER ME LORD, I'M BUSY

In Haggai, chapter 1, we see the people of God looking every man to his own affairs. God had a work that needed to be done, but they were unaware of it because they were so busy 'trying to make ends meet' (verse 6). The harder they worked, the less they had, because they were neglecting the kingdom of God (Matthew 6:33).

In verse 9, even what they managed to scrape up, God blew away. Verse 2 shows their total unconcern for God's work. When the prophet of God pointed out their problem (verse 12), they all responded by obeying the Word of the Lord. Verse 14 shows that when God spoke they obeyed.

God stirred up their spirits. (It is God at work in you both to will and to do His good pleasure. - Philippians 2:13) God gave them the will to obey and then the power to complete the task.

Look back to where Haggai spoke the Word of the Lord to the people (verse 1). The hearing of the Word brought forth faith in the hearer to respond to God.

Father, I pray for a thirsting and hungering in my heart, to hear your Word. I ask for your Holy Spirit to make your Word real to me, so I will respond as they did.

**I determine to spend time
reading my Bible.**

*"So shall my word be that goeth forth out of
my mouth: it shall not return unto me void,
but it shall accomplish that which I please,
and it shall prosper in the thing whereto I
sent it." — Isaiah 55:11*

FAITH FILLED WORDS

It is reassuring to know that God will not allow His
Word to depend on us. He sends His Word (*Rhema*) forth,
and faith comes with that Word. Within the Word spoken
by God is the power for its fulfillment. It does not depend
on you to accomplish that for which it was sent forth.

God's business is serious! He does all the working
out of His own business. He uses available vessels, and
they are blessed to be in on what God is doing. He knows
we, as humans, are incapable of supernatural things,
so He does it all, including furnishing the faith necessary
to accomplish whatever He wants done.

All He needs from us is availability, a yielded vessel,
awaiting the assignment. If every minute of every day
we are committed, yielded, empty vessels, as God needs
something done, He will use us. If we're unyielded, He
flows on until He finds a yielded vessel.

*Father, it doesn't seem hard to be available. Yet, we
keep ourselves so busy we ask you to wait or come some
other time. We are like Martha, encumbered with many
things. Please forgive us, use us.*

God knows my address. I want to be home.

"Jesus Christ the same yesterday, and today, and forever." – Hebrews 13:8

FAMILY

If we study the Bible purely as a history book, we can see the character of God never changes. There is no shadow of turning with Him. The way He dealt with Israel in forming a nation, a heredity for Jesus to be born out of, He will and does deal with us.

God has a plan to create a family of His own with Jesus as the elder brother. Throughout eternity, we, who have Christ formed in us, will be in this family.

We must read the Bible, especially the New Testament with this thought. It is written to the Christ nature in us. It will be enmity to our old nature which cannot bear it. But the new nature in us, the Christ nature, is willing and eager to hear and to do as it requires. The only food the new nature receives is the Word of God. It is meat and drink to the Christ nature in us. It grows and thrives on hearing the Word.

Father, it has been said if I feed my body no more than I feed my spirit, I'd soon die of malnutrition. Help me to feed more often on the living bread, your Word.

I determine to feed my spirit man by reading the Bible so he can grow and mature.

"Jesus said unto him, Thou shalt love the Lord thy God with all thy heart, and with all thy soul, and with all thy mind."
Matthew 22:37

THE LAW OF LOVE

God has always attempted to get man to recognize this law of love in order to bring him into the place of relationship, or son-ship, that God desires to have with man. We aren't listening to God. This commandment was His way of telling us how to arrive at this relationship.

God is love. Love made all things, and holds all things together. Love redeemed all things. Anything less than love would have given up on us a long time ago. *Agape* love is not an emotion, but aggressive, benevolent, sacrificial, outgoing good will.

Oh, kind acts may bring temporary relief for a period of time, but no permanent healing takes place. Only what we do as a result of *agape* love will benefit anyone. Love puts the welfare of the other above our own.

Only what has been done in love will bring reward. Everything else will burn up when confronted by the love of God. The love of God will destroy all that is not love, by the force it manifests. Only love will remain.

Father, I believe you are a consuming fire and what is not love in me will be judged and destroyed. I pray for the Holy Spirit to shed your love in my heart and to perfect it in me.

In love is my safety and my salvation.

 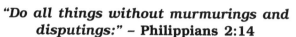
"Do all things without murmurings and disputings:" – **Philippians 2:14**

SHINING LIGHTS

Do <u>all</u> things, that includes everything that comes our way in the course of our day, without murmurings (resentment) and complaining. Our words express the true condition of our heart. When we do this, we learn to do whatever our hand finds to do, and to do it without resentment, eagerly, to the glory of God.

Then we will be blameless children of God, shining as lights in the world, transparent, so all can see God. I first discovered these verses (Philippians 2:12-16) at Christmas time when everyone was putting out luminaries for decorations. They were first put out in the desert to light the way to the Christ child. The Word, "lights," as expressed in Philippians 2:15, translates "luminaries" in the center reference of the American Standard Bible. I was so excited to see we can be as lights, pointing the way to Christ.

Father, this is a goal I believe you have set before us; to be lights in the world, to point those we meet to the Christ child. Jesus came as a child, to grow among men and die to reconcile mankind to you. We are to be witnesses to that fact.

**For my light to be seen,
I must be transparent.**

**"Therefore if any man be in Christ, he is a
new creature: old things are passed away;
behold, all things are become new."**
II Corinthians 5:17

LIFE BEGINS HERE

It has been said, "He who is most holy, has the most of Jesus inside of him." Jesus was made the holiness and the righteousness of God (I Corinthians 1:30).

God pays no respect to anything we bring to Him. There is only one thing God wants of us and that is our unconditional surrender.

When we are born again, the Holy Spirit begins to work His new creation in us. There comes a time when there is not a bit of the old order left and all things are of God. Let me tell you child of God, it doesn't happen in five minutes!

How do we get to this life that has no lusts, no self-interests, no sensitivity to wrongs - This love that is not provoked, that thinks no evil and is always kind? We get this by not allowing a bit of the old life to survive - by only, simply, perfectly trusting in God! Such trust that no longer seeks God's blessings, but only wants God Himself.

It requires supernatural grace from God to live 24 hours every day as a saint, to go through drudgery as a disciple, and to live an ordinary, unobserved, ignored existence.

Father, we sense, in our born again spirit, a drawing to this kind of relationship with you. We sense it will fill the need of our soul with satisfaction. We believe there is a God-sized hole in the midst of each of us, that is filled and satisfied only by your presence. You have told us to ask and we will receive. We ask to be filled again with your Holy Spirit.

**I do believe I have received the gift of the
Holy Spirit, because I asked God for it.**

"For bodily exercise profiteth little: but godliness is profitable unto all things, having promise of the life that now is, and of that which is to come." – I Timothy 4:8

SPIRITUAL EXERCISE

It seems to me, as I study Proverbs, the teachings of Jesus and the epistles, the continuous admonition of all the Word of God, is for us to do something concerning our spiritual growth. It seems to require a great effort to heed, to put on, to cast off, to hear, to follow, seek and find - all activity in a positive way. All seem to be acts of faith toward the faithfulness of God.

We read in the Word, and 'faith it'. ("Faith cometh by hearing and hearing by the Word of God." Romans 10:17) When we 'faith it', we act in a positive way on the instructions we receive as we read. It is sort of like a treasure hunt. We apply ourselves diligently to read the road map (the Bible) and follow the directions to locate the treasure. It is foolishness to read the Bible and not act upon it.

We get fat, fat, fat, but no muscle. Muscle comes in the exercising. Only a long distance runner will finish the race of life. The fat will sit and be satisfied with themselves. Some will fall asleep at the starting post. Jesus is holding the crown of life at the finish line.

Dear Lord, all of life is an example for us of how to best live and grow and finish our course. We are aware if we do not exercise ourselves to godliness, we will not make the long haul. We pray for the desire to read your Word and obey. It is by your Spirit that we will overcome laziness.

I will run my course today.

"Be not deceived; God is not mocked: for whatsoever a man soweth, that shall he also reap." – Galatians 6:7

LIVING FOR ETERNITY

When life as we know it now comes to an end, we shall see as Jesus sees and know as God knows. When we see as He sees, we will see how life was meant to be lived, how far short we fell, and what blessings we missed because of it.

There will be tears in heaven because the Word tells us they will be wiped away. What a painful moment when we see what should have been.

Oh Spirit of God, live the life of Christ in and through us as you choose, according to your great wisdom and knowledge. May we be but empty vessels, emptied of the self life to be filled with all the fullness of God - just to be your instruments of peace to a lost and dying world, to be obedient to go and do those seemingly foolish things that we don't understand; to fulfill your will among men.

Father, help us to see that these few, short earthly years are only a time of training, that this life is just the seedtime for eternity. May we become more and more far sighted as we stretch the borders to include all of eternity. Life will become so much richer and fuller with the awareness that it isn't going to end soon.

I walk out toward my exciting future with God.

"Now faith is the substance of things hoped
for, the evidence of things not seen."
Hebrews 11:1

BY FAITH

In the 11th chapter of Hebrews, we read how great men and women of God responded to His call on their lives. Abraham was promised by God, that through Isaac his seed would be called (Hebrews 11:18). Yet, God called for Isaac to be placed on the altar. Abraham was obedient, believing God would fulfill His promises, through Isaac, even if it required raising him from the dead.

Like his father, Isaac, too, looked far into the future and believed God. We see here the importance of the spiritual influence of the father. Jacob and Joseph also believed the promises of God.

Moses gave up all the wealth, power and pleasures of Egypt, to identify himself with God's purposes. We cannot ride mid stream of mammon and God. We must choose, as all God's servants have been called to choose. "As for me and my house, we will serve the Lord" (Joshua 24:15).

God speaks. We hear. Then, we must act on what we hear, in faith. We must believe God for what we cannot see, not troubling our minds (verse 8).

Father, in reading and meditating on this roll call of faith, we get a picture of what it means to believe you. Many times, we will have to deny our reason and blindly go forth in trust. We ask now for this gift of trust, that we may launch out with you.

I will not let fear pull me back
from following God's call. I will
trust Him with all of my life.

"But without faith it is impossible to please Him (God) ..." – Hebrews 11:6a

ONLY BELIEVE

In reading the eleventh chapter of Hebrews, it seems the only thing God asks of us is to believe Him - to have faith in His promises.

The roll call begins with Abel. He took God at His Word and brought the kind of gift God commanded.

Enoch walked with God, by faith, in fellowship. He did not taste death.

There are two areas of faith necessary. First is to believe that God is. And secondly, to believe that He rewards those who earnestly and diligently seek Him out (verse 6).

Noah listened and believed, and then acted in faith.

Sarah received physical power by her faith. She considered God reliable and trustworthy and true to His Word.

God's people look off into the distance, knowing what they work for may not become reality to them now, knowing they are strangers, temporary residents and exiles upon the earth. They are in search of their homeland, their own country.

Verse 40 gives us cause for rejoicing, that even these things did not move God's hand to fulfill His promise, but rather gave us time to be included!

How we praise you, Father, and give you thanks for your excellent greatness; your steadfast faithfulness not to be moved from your plans.

I give thanks that God's plan included me!

 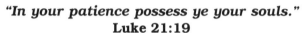

"In your patience possess ye your souls."
Luke 21:19

CLEAN UP YOUR ACT

Joshua's strategy for clearing the land of Canaan can be the same you use for clearing the land of your soul. Our souls are cluttered with sin patterns, habits and compulsions. Uncontrolled thoughts and actions have become strongholds and fortresses of resistance. Here are some guidelines for battle. II Chronicles 20:15 tells us to depend on the Lord's strength and guidance. It says the battle is the Lord's, not ours. Exodus 23:29 shows how they fall one by one. Lust, fear, worry, gluttony, lying, all enemies of our new nature, fall one at a time.

We are also told to take possession of the land and be fruitful in it. As we possess our soul, we clear it of sin and allow God's Spirit to produce fruit. Look at the verses in Exodus 23:20-33 to learn of the angel of God's covenant. We are God's covenant people in this church age, because we believe and have received Jesus Christ's finished work on Calvary.

Father, these scriptures and these thoughts bring such hope and comfort to us. It's encouraging to know you love us so much that you continue your work of grace in us, to bring us on to maturity, that perfection you have called us to. We realize it is a life long work, and we know we are on a journey.

Today, I walk by faith in the finished work of Calvary and call on God's Spirit to help me grow.

"Seeing ye have purified your souls in obeying the truth through the Spirit unto unfeigned love of the brethren, see that ye love one another with a pure heart fervently:"
I Peter 1:22

WHY STRONGHOLDS?

We have an enemy. His name is Satan and he loves to be worshiped. His goal is to keep us from knowing God as He is. Strongholds develop by yielding to the sins of the flesh. The area in which we are a slave to sin is called a stronghold (Romans 6:12-16).

It will be helpful to see what a stronghold cycle is. Thoughts lead to emotions, which lead to actions, which develop into habits, if continued. Habits, in turn, become strongholds, or a way of life. Look at it in Proverbs 5:22 — thought, emotion, action, habit, stronghold.

Some steps in removing strongholds: First of all, be sure you are a Christian. Ask Jesus to be Lord over every area of your life. Then, we must realize that only God, in His power, can remove strongholds (Psalm 124:7&8). Our part is to yield to God and follow His ways. He must see we mean business. It is necessary to identify strongholds in our lives. Ask God to reveal, by His Spirit, what strongholds are in your life.

Father, we begin to see in our lifelong journey with you, that we clean up our lives as you reveal the needs. We thank you that you don't overwhelm us with thoughts of how bad we are. Rather, you put your finger on an area of unacceptable behavior and in our yielding to your diagnosis of the problem, your Spirit goes to work.

Whatever the Holy Spirit shines the light on in my life today, I give permission for Him to fix.

"I beseech you therefore, brethren, by the
mercies of God, that ye present your bodies a
living sacrifice, holy, acceptable unto God ..."
Romans 12:1

SELF DEDICATION

In verse 1 of Romans 12, we are told to make a special act of dedicating ourselves totally to God. All our members and faculties are to be a living sacrifice (devoted, consecrated) to God. This act pleases Him. A living sacrifice is to be done while there is life in our body. This is not something extraordinary. It is instead our reasonable [rational, intelligent] service.

Then we read the opposite in verse 2, what we are not to do. Do not be conformed to this world (present system). Rather, be transformed, or changed, by the renewing of your mind, to have new ideas and attitudes. Our spirit is reborn, brand new. The old man dies and Jesus is born in us. We are made new creations.

At the same time, our soul is transformed, changed, by the renewing of our mind. Our born again spirit grows under the leadership of the Holy Spirit, as we read the Word, and our mind is changed by what we read. We want to know the will of God for us. We learn it by reading the Word.

Father, we thank you we have the Holy Spirit to reveal the truth of your Word to our spirit man. We know we must apply ourselves to read.

Today, I will read the 'Will of God' for myself.

"While the earth remaineth, seedtime and harvest, and cold and heat, and summer and winter, and day and night, shall not cease."
Genesis 8:22

SEEDTIME AND HARVEST

It is a principle of God. He set the universe up to yield only after a seed had been planted. It is God's nature to give first.

He gave us the earth.

He gave us dominion.

He gave Israel freedom.

He gave Israel Canaan.

God has always been true to His nature and given first. That's why He can rightfully expect something in return from us. When we don't give back, we break ourselves against the law, or nature, of God.

Since we are human (finite) and God is not, we cannot give directly to Him. We must give as we 'know' to give to beings like ourselves. In giving to 'others' (beings like us), especially the household of faith, we are honoring God. We are giving back to Him.

In giving us Jesus, God demonstrated the greatest giving possible. Jesus voluntarily laid down His own life when He stepped down from Glory and ultimately to Calvary. It stands then that NO ONE LOVES US LIKE GOD LOVES US!

Father God, to be loved with the constant, pure, unselfish love that You pour out on us is beyond our ability to understand. That is why we must accept it, by faith.

I choose to receive the love of God for me.

"My sheep hear my voice, and I know them,
and they follow me:" – John 10:27

RELATIONSHIP

We can never refuse to obey God's commands with the excuse 'He doesn't understand.' God knows us intimately, totally. He knows even the environmental influences that have shaped us. We have no excuses to keep us from doing the will of God concerning us. He does not ask us to do the impossible, but only that which is hard, so He can stretch us - bring us out of ourselves and into Him.

In calling His sheep, He calls them out of the sheepfold, out into green pastures and still water, out where we've never been before. He calls them into the rich, nourishing pastures of His Word, into new relationships with other sheep of His flock. If we are to benefit from hearing His voice, we must step out to do what He calls us to do. It is by an action or decision of our will. This is faith in action - the agreement of our will to God's will through obedience, and glad cooperation. Not until this takes place do we move toward the shepherd. Then we begin to experience the benefits of His care and management.

Father God, more and more I realize we are in relationship. Sheep and shepherd, father and child, are all used to reveal that relationship. The more I understand this, the more I trust you and move closer to you. Thank you for loving and caring for me.

**I rejoice today in realizing I am family with
the creator of the universe. This is not
abstract, it is reality.**

"And said, Verily I say unto you, Except ye be converted, and become as little children, ye shall not enter into the kingdom of heaven."
Matthew 18:3

CONVERSION

Conversion is to change over, to adapt to another way. One can convert a piece of machinery so it functions a different way, to use it for another purpose. To be converted from worldly adults to little children is the hard thing God asks of us.

As we are brought into new circumstances, we are to be converted in them; changed from our selfish desires to the will of God. We are to be as little children, content because our parent is with us, assured everything will be fine.

Continuously, we are brought into new situations and circumstances, and our obstinate will lashes out and refuses to accept the changes. As we are converted in them, we are 'changed over' to the mind of Christ, to think on it as He did. He was totally abandoned to God's will.

As we become as little children, in abiding in God's will, we are His responsibility. If we trust our wits, we produce consequences for which God will hold us responsible.

Dear Heavenly Father, we are reminded to 'put on the new man,' through this process of conversion. We can claim more and more territory (of our lives) and become free indeed. We realize the hindrances in our spiritual lives are areas where we are not converted.

I am more interested in changing than I am in being comfortable. Help yourself, Lord.

"And the earth was without form, and void; and darkness was upon the face of the deep. And the Spirit of God moved upon the face of the waters." – Genesis 1:2

IS ANYTHING TOO HARD FOR GOD?

The same Spirit of God who brooded over the earth, active in carrying out God's commands to create, is likewise in me creating life, new life, Christ's life in me.

Without the Holy Spirit following God the Father's commands, the new life of Christ cannot be formed in me. This is why blasphemy against the Holy Spirit is the unpardonable sin (Matthew 12:31).

When Christ is formed in me, by the mighty working of the Holy Spirit, then God the Father can use me, as He did Jesus, to bring about the redemption of mankind.

Nothing is impossible for the Spirit of God. He makes God's commands realities. It was His power that raised Jesus from the dead (Romans 8:11). Can He make God's commands a reality in me? What would hinder this happening? I must cooperate with Him and give my permission for Him to work in me.

Spirit of God, I do want you to work in my life and to change my thinking and to cause me to be like Jesus. I quickly give you permission, and I ask you to bless me with your presence and power. Thank you, Jesus, for asking Father God to send His Spirit to abide in and with me.

I will be quick to say, Yes Lord, here am I. Use me.

"If thou doest well, shalt thou not be accepted? and if thou doest not well, sin lieth at the door. And unto thee shall be his desire, and thou shalt rule over him."
Genesis 4:7

WHO AM I MAD AT?

As children of God, we seek to please Him, but not everything we do is pleasing to God's nature. He cannot compromise or give us the edge, so to speak. When we have tried, according to our human nature, to please God, He has to reject us - not us actually, but our offering. Look with me at the pattern. We seek in our strength to please God, yet in our own strength nothing is pleasing to God. We then become angry when God rejects our efforts, angry and indignant as Cain was in Genesis 4:1-10. (Please read for better understanding.) Anger is followed by sadness and depression (self-pity) for failing. This is God's likeness distorted by sin.

The progression is anger, indignation, sadness and depression - now we're out of fellowship with God. We have the choice of repenting or refusing. If we refuse, sin stands now at the door, waiting to claim us. Here, God gives the command, 'You must master it.' How? By confessing you were wrong and restoring your fellowship with God.

The result of anger against God is turned toward other people. Cain slew Abel because he never mastered the sin.

Father, I realize I am often obstinate, seeking to do it my way, and expecting you to bear with me and let me slide by. As I read your Word and listen to your Holy Spirit, I know this is wrong. I want to be quick to repent and quick to move to restored fellowship with you. I cannot survive long, following my own ways. Thank you for forgiving my sins when I call upon you.

I will watch to see why I am irritable with others. Am I out of sorts with God?

**"And God remembered Noah, and every living
thing, and all the cattle that was with him
in the ark; and God made a wind to pass
over the earth, and the waters asswaged;"**
Genesis 8:1

LIFE IS AN ARK

God earnestly remembered Noah. God never forgets us. Scripture tells us that our names are engraved in the palms of His hands (Isaiah 49:16). When He told Noah to build and furnish the ark, He told him how to build it and what to take in the ark. He provided, through Noah's obedience, extra animals for the sacrifices He would require of him when the flood was over.

When we belong to God, He furnishes us with everything He will require of us for service and stewardship. He gives us our offerings, that will be suitable to Him. It is absolutely true that we have nothing to give God but ourselves.

Noah was in that ark, shut up from everything, for 1 year and 10 days. His faith in God was all he had to sustain him. If he had attempted to do anything on his own, it would have brought death to all of them. Death comes to us when we attempt to do anything on our own.

Father, there is a real graphic lesson for us in this story. Our life, so to speak, is an ark experience. From the time we begin to obey you and follow you, you close us into an ark with you - an ark of faith living. May we grow in obedience and faith.

**I choose to wait for God's voice telling me
when it is time to make a move.**

"And Abraham said, My son, God will provide himself a lamb for a burnt offering: so they went both of them together." – Genesis 22:8

GOD MAKES PROVISION

When God and man make a covenant (salvation), God requires certain things of that man:

Obedience

Loyalty

Single-mindedness

Separation

Complete allegiance to serve the one God.

Man cannot do these things. These attitudes are not in him naturally.

But God, through the covenant (new birth) of man, supernaturally gives the obedience and all the rest. This is through the power of the Holy Spirit of God working in us to bring it about.

Abraham was an ordinary man. God's call on his life made him extraordinary. God called Abraham to be a father to many nations. God never gives a call unless He provides all that is needed to answer the call. He not only calls and gives the provision, He also cares for whatever we have to give up for Him.

Father God, as we look at this story of Abraham and Isaac again, we are called into a deeper level of trust. We fall so far short of moving out to meet you and your call because we lack the necessary trust. We pray and ask for the gift of trust to be ours. Thank you for providing all we need to follow you.

I choose to trust God with the details and follow Him.

May 21

"And the thing was very grievous in Abraham's sight—because of his son."
Genesis 21:11

WHAT DO YOU NEED?

Sarah told Abraham to get rid of Ishmael and his mother Hagar. Isaac was the seed God intended to use to fulfill the covenant He had made with Abraham. God told him to do as Sarah asked. God didn't want anything in Abraham's life to distract from the covenant. It is comforting to learn that God made provision for that which He required Abraham to give up. It was a hard thing for Abraham (Genesis 21:9-13).

Often, in the midst of our happiness and contentment, God calls on us to give up something precious to us. It is always hard to give up something for God, until we die to whatever the need is, to hang onto it. It's that need that separates us from God, not the thing itself, but the need for it.

We are to need nothing but God, in Jesus Christ, our Lord. God has made provision for all our needs, in Jesus. The name of Jesus is the power of attorney.

Father God, we are not talking about losses here. Rather, we are talking about our relationship with you and our recognizing it is first place in our life. Our <u>need</u> for something other than you displaces you as primary in our lives. Help us, oh Spirit of God, to see this in proper perspective and release the care and keeping of our lives to you.

**I <u>know</u> all my needs are met in Christ
Jesus. I want to <u>remember</u> it more.**

"Then Isaac sowed in that land, and received in the same year an hundredfold: and the Lord blessed him." –Genesis 26:12

SOIL TESTING

God promised Isaac blessings and numerous descendants, if he would obey as Abraham had (Genesis 26:5). He was to obey God's voice, keep God's charge, keep God's commands, statutes and laws. In verse 12, Isaac sowed seed and God gave increase.

In Mark 4:20, Jesus said those who receive the Word, bear 30, 60 and 100 fold fruit. The Word is God's seed. Those who faithfully receive it will reap fruitfulness. Mark 4:22-25 tells us that what is hidden is to be revealed. If we have spiritual ears, we are to be listening, perceiving and comprehending. Then Jesus gave a warning: be careful! The thought and study you give to what you are hearing will be the measure of knowledge and virtue that comes back to you. The end of that verse (verse 24), and more besides will be given to you.

Father, we can see that your Word, when heard, listened to and comprehended, brings knowledge and virtue. We also see it is in proportion to our time spent in the Word, that we benefit. Now it is up to us to apply ourselves to what we have heard. Create in us, oh God, a hunger for more of your truth, as revealed by your Spirit.

The Bible is God's seed. I am the soil it is sowed in. I want to be fertile soil.

"And he builded an altar there, and called upon the name of the Lord, and pitched his tent there: and there Isaac's servants digged a well." – Genesis 26:25

PEACE, A WORTHY GOAL

Isaac is a good example of a Godly man. When he moved, he had his priorities straight. God first; he built an altar and waited on the Lord. Family second; he pitched his tent. Business third; he dug a well.

In Genesis 27:41, we see a quarrel between brothers which began centuries of death and destruction. Let's look at some of the carnage from Esau's descendants toward those of Jacob. In Exodus 17:8, it was the Amalekites that obstructed their flight from Egypt. Numbers 20:17-20 shows the Edomites refusing Jacob's children passage. I Samuel 22:22 has Doeg nearly causing David's death.

In the New Testament, Herod had the male babies in Bethlehem slain. Herod Agrippa cut off John the Baptist's head. Herod Antipas jailed Peter and killed James.

Satan needs no better medium than a family feud. This causes us to see God's wisdom, when He instructed us not to let the sun go down on our anger (Ephesians 4:26). As much as possible, live in peace with all men (Hebrews 12:14). Christians are to be peacemakers.

Father we know we have been reconciled, made to be at peace with you, through Jesus. How can we not seek to be at peace with our fellow man? Peace is to be our goal. Send the Spirit of peace to reign in our hearts, whereby we can make peace a reality in our lives.

I choose to seek peace, to live in peace and to take peace wherever I go.

May 24

"And so it is written, The first man Adam was made a living soul; the last Adam was made a quickening spirit." – **I Corinthians 15:45**

TWICE MADE

<u>Generation</u>: firing up, beginning to work, a build up of energy.

<u>De-generation</u>: running down, losing momentum, gradual loss of energy. Becoming something less than the intended purpose.

<u>Re-generation</u>: a new source of energy applied, motor rewound, new work installed.

<u>Generation</u>: created by God to live in fellowship with Him, dependent on Him for life.

<u>De-generation</u>: breaking loose by disobedience Adam and Eve and their descendants knowing better than God about themselves.

<u>Re-generation</u>: God providing a way back to fellowship with Himself.

Twice made, twice born, twice created. After regeneration, the life I live is not my life, but the life of Christ Jesus now living in me. I was blessed with life and then blessed with new life, that the quality of life now on earth, is elevated to the highest possibility. Of all men, those who know and have received this truth are the happiest. Not only do they have better quality of life now, but security of eternity, where it continues to get better and better.

Father God, how can I help but to bless you and sing forth your praises forevermore? You so perfectly care for and provide all we need to come out of the curse of de-generation - the slowing down, decaying and dying process, into the life of regeneration, where all things are energized by you and your Spirit, where we can live in life and productivity throughout eternity, beginning now. Thank you. Bless you. Praise be to you.

I am alive in God, with wonderful prospects of a bright future!

145

*"For this cause I bow my knees unto the
Father of our Lord Jesus Christ, of whom the
whole family in heaven and earth is named."*
Ephesians 3:14, 15

EL SHADDAI

This is the name of God as strengthener and satisfier of His people, all-sufficient, enriches, makes fruitful. It is Father-mother God, <u>all</u> sufficient.

Allow me to break down in some measure the offices or duties of the God Family; Father, Spirit and Son. We see <u>Father God</u> protects, cares for, sustains, guards, saves from enemies, and provides for. We can then see <u>Mother Spirit</u> teaches, guides, leads, stands by the side of and wipes our tears. <u>Son Jesus Christ</u> paid the price so we could have both of the above, a complete family. He now intercedes for us, always at God's throne, as the enemy accuses us. He is preparing our place to be with Him forever. He is coming again to receive us unto Himself, that where He is, we can be also.

In these troubled days, the family is receiving a real beating. There are fewer and fewer family units standing. We can be comforted and encouraged to know as we lift our eyes and our hearts toward our heavenly family, we will be healed and made whole.

Father, we were made to function in an ever increasingly productive way. We are to be a blessing and a delight to your heart, but also join in your purposes for the earth and the millions of people on it. Oh God, as I lift my eyes, I see I am not dysfunctional because of negative influences and weaknesses of my earthly family. Instead, I am whole and created in your image and empowered by the Spirit's training, to be a positive influence where I am.

**I feel good in sensing I have a destiny, and
that God and I are a majority.**

"And thus shall ye eat it; with your loins girded, your shoes on your feet, and your staff in your hand; and ye shall eat it in haste: it is the Lord's passover."
Exodus 12:11

READY TO GO

God's dealings in the Old Testament, with Israel are an example of how God deals with the church today. He redeemed a people (Israel) out of bondage (Egypt) to a cruel ruler (Pharaoh). He redeemed them through a man (Moses).

We were in bondage to sin and we worked for Satan. God sent Jesus to lead us out, redeem us, free us. Man sees in Word pictures. We comprehend through the communication of words. The Bible is a compilation of words, demonstrating God's dealings with men.

What is expected of us now that we have been lead out (saved by faith in Jesus' death for our sins)? We are expected to get up and go! We are to follow Him and obey His teachings.

In Exodus 8:25, Pharaoh says, don't go far, don't go for good and leave your children behind. When Satan sees we will follow Jesus, he works on the wedge system. Just don't go getting crazy, fanatical, don't go all the way to discipleship.

Jesus said, "if ye love me..." - a picture of the church on the way to the kingdom at the end of the age, full of converted members. He calls on us to follow on, to gird up our loins, put our shoes on, and get going.

Father, your Word continues to reveal to us that it's going somewhere, every day, on the way. By your power, and by your Spirit strengthening us, we will make it all the way. Thank you for never leaving nor forsaking us on the trail.

I will dress myself spiritually for the journey. I sure can't travel in pajamas!

"That they all may be one; as thou, Father, art in me, and I in thee, that they also may be one in us: ..." – John 17:21

DIVERSITY IN UNITY

God the Father - giver of life, Jesus the Son - redeemer of life, Holy Spirit - dispenser of life.

God, in Jesus, bought me back from Satan, to whom Adam had sold his birthright. Jesus came, dwelt among men, died, was buried, resurrected and ascended back to the Father. All acts of a redeeming nature originate from God, go through man, and back to God for completion.

We are bought back, but green as gourds! Jesus couldn't leave his disciples alone for a minute without a problem arising. So the teacher, instructor, keeper of God's truth, the Holy Spirit, was sent from God, by Jesus' request, on our behalf. He had walked among us and knew our weaknesses. He knew we couldn't make it alone in an unconverted world.

The Holy Spirit is Jesus' attorney and executor of His estate. He reads the will and tells us about the inheritance. Until Jesus returns to claim all that belongs to Him, the Holy Spirit is in charge, to keep safe what is God's, in Christ Jesus.

Father, as we see this perfect working together of the Godhead, each functioning in your areas of leadership, how can we help but see how effective it would be for us, in the church, to function in this same way? Diversity in unity, the strength magnified and never weakened through strife. Jesus prayed for us to be one, as you and He are one. Spirit of Grace, move on us, as you did on creation, and bring order to our chaos!

I want to cooperate and add to the body of Christ.

**"And the children of Israel stripped themselves
of their ornaments by the mount Horeb."
Exodus 33:6**

DIVINE INITIATIVE

The people of God had sinned seriously while Moses was on the mountain receiving the Ten Commandments from God. They had sought to make a god of their own choosing. God said, "you have not chosen me, but I have chosen you" (John 15:16). This turns it around and makes us the receiver and not the instigator.

God cannot because of His holiness, abide with sin. So God, in His mercy, withdrew from the people and sent an angel to lead them. The people got down to serious business when God withdrew His presence. Verse 6 tells us they took off their ornaments. The party was over! They realized a relationship with God was most important in their lives. It was preparation for what God would require of them a little later.

Exodus 35:21-22 tells us the Lord asked everyone who was ready to give an offering of their ornaments. You see, they were ready because they had laid them down in their hearts previously. The actual giving could then be done in joy, with thanksgiving, from a <u>willing</u> heart.

Father, we know you still seek cheerful givers. Thank you that even in this, you prepare our hearts and make us ready to give. As we seek you with all our hearts, the desire for other things falls away.

**I will to give cheerfully, freely, and quickly
what the Lord requires.**

"Then saith he unto them, My soul is
exceeding sorrowful, even unto death:
tarry ye here, and watch with me."
Matthew 26:38

DESPAIR

We are prone to despair when we have slept through an opportunity given to us by the Lord to watch with Him. That opportunity has passed, never to be experienced again. Yet, He comes to us again and says, "go on to the next thing." Arise, another opportunity has presented itself.

In Matthew 26:38, the disciples were presented with their first opportunity to watch. In verse 40, Jesus gave gentle rebuke. In verse 41, He admonishes them now to "watch and pray, so that you enter not into temptation." As we follow on, we see in verse 43, He did not rebuke them for again being asleep.

The words we all dread to hear are spoken in verse 45, "you missed your opportunity to watch with me." We can either enter into His service or sleep through it. There is no rebuke here, just sleep on, rest. You're going to need the rest, for you'll soon have another opportunity.

Look with me at verses 31 and 32 of this chapter and see great consolation given by Jesus. He told the disciples they would all 'blow it,' because He was going to be smitten, but that after He was resurrected, He'd see them in Galilee. These words have lifted me from despair over failures and set my feet to running toward Galilee numerous times.

My Lord and my God, when I see your tender mercies so graphically displayed in your Word and then turn those words to my own heart personally, I gasp with amazement. You have love so divine, so magnificent; love that anticipated all my needs, through all my life, and provided grace sufficient to meet all those needs. My heart cannot but swell in love and adoration towards you.

I am so glad God knows me so intimately. I
will not try to hide anything from Him today.

"Ye lust, and have not: ye kill, and desire to have, and cannot obtain: ye fight and war, yet ye have not, because ye ask not." – James 4:2

ASK AND RECEIVE

In Exodus 17:6, the Israelites had a need. They were thirsty. God told Moses to <u>smite</u> the rock. That rock represented Christ. Water gushed forth to meet their physical needs, representing the Holy Spirit. We have a need. We are lost, alienated from God. Jesus was crucified, and out of His death came the Holy Spirit, to meet our spiritual needs.

Numbers 20:11-24 gives the story of another time Israel had a need. They were thirsty. God told Moses to <u>speak</u> to the rock. Moses disobeyed. Under stress, he reverted to the "old" way and struck the rock. He took credit to himself for what God did. Verse 10, "Must we fetch you water?" He lost his temper and smote the rock. He even called the Israelites names. In verse 10, he referred to them as rebels. He was provoked by their need and resented them.

At this point, God once again spoke to Moses and told him because he was acting in unbelief, God was not being glorified among His people. The sadness of this continues to the end of the story, in verse 24, when Moses was unable to go into the promised land, because of his unbelief.

Father, Jesus was crucified once and for all. We have no further need for an act of force to receive any need we have. May we be enlightened to see that all we need is to <u>ask</u> Jesus, who in turn prays to the Father, and the answer comes, as the Holy Spirit gushes out to deliver the answer, through Jesus, from the Father.

Today, I will spend quality time asking God specifically for that thing I've been wrestling with.

"But, as it is written, Eye hath not seen, nor ear heard, neither have entered into the heart of man, the things which God hath prepared for them that love him."
I Corinthians 2:9

ENTERING OUR INHERITANCE

In Numbers 33:51-56, God told the Israelites, "When you have passed over Jordan into the land, then you shall: drive out all the inhabitants, destroy all their idols and completely demolish their high places. Take possession of the land and dwell in it, for God has given this land to you to possess it".

You cannot pass over Jordan until you are surrendered, totally, to the Lord Jesus Christ. The promised land is the Kingdom of God. When we have surrendered to Jesus, as Lord, we are to drive out of our lives all the previous things that have occupied our lives.

We are to demolish, do away with, anything in our lives we gave allegiance to (home, job, children, spouse, parents, possessions). We are to tear down our prideful positions. Any and all things we do now, we do in the power of the Holy Spirit. We are to take charge of our lives, take authority over circumstances, events and relationships that had us captive.

Then we can dwell in our land, live our lives as unto the Lord Jesus Christ. It is not sufficient to be saved. We must go on to possess the land, to live richly, abundantly, after the knowledge of the Lord. It is our birthright as redeemed, born again children of God.

Holy Spirit, I ask you to make these truths live in me.

I make Jesus Lord of me and my domain again today.

*"And in the fourth watch of the night
Jesus went unto them, walking on the sea."*
Matthew 14:25

DO I DROWN OR DARE I TRUST JESUS?

As long as we can use common sense to work out our problems, we are not abandoned to Jesus Christ. We are still tied to the shore. Jesus says, "Launch out into the deep, ask me for help from there. When you are trusting in me alone, I will hear you and supernaturally release you from your problems."

We are showing unbelief when we hang on to common sense, when we see something as impossible. Yes, it is so, but it is at that point that Jesus comes to us, walking on the water.

When we are redeemed, we are part of God's family. Our refusal to enter into God's rest because of unbelief causes Him much grief. In Israel, God chose a nation of no reputation and asked them to obey Him and to listen to His commands. Then He would bless them above all the nations on the earth. As Christians, we are spiritual Israelites, God's family. We belong to Him, called out, chosen and delivered from all our enemies. We have the same deal Israel did, "Trust me, and I'll take care of you," God said.

Father God, why are we so obstinate and take so long to walk into the place of rest, the place of safety, security and well-being? We are like children wanting to prove how big we are! Help us, oh God, to release the feelings of figuring it all out, and being so smart and independent. It's so counter-productive. Thank you for the place of rest and peace.

**I'm so glad I can lay it all down and rely,
today, on God's provisions.**

"And preached, saying, There cometh one mightier than I after me, the latchet of whose shoes I am not worthy to stoop down and unloose." – Mark 1:7

REAL LEADERSHIP

Deuteronomy 17:14-20 tells of God's instruction to Israel on choosing a king. When a king was to be chosen to rule over them, he was to have a written copy of the Word. He was to read it all the days of his life, so he would not be lifted up and think he was better than his brothers.

All we ever do will be through the power of the Holy Spirit, because God ordained it to be so. We can never be successful in any endeavor for God or His kingdom, on our own initiative. Only through the power of the Holy Spirit can we be the servants we've been called to be.

By God's mercy, He sets us free from our pride, so that we may lovingly serve Him. We have no claim on His mercy. He blesses us because He loves us. Our good works flow from that mercy. They, like everything else good, originate from God.

In the present world system, we have the wrong conception of what a king or ruler is. We see them high and lifted up, favored among men and sought out for what they can offer. In the kingdom of God, the ruler is the servant of all. Our example should be Jesus, who suffered the loss of all reputation, to fulfill the will of God for mankind.

My Lord and my God, until I have learned that I must continually decrease that Jesus might continue to increase, I have learned nothing. Serving in the kingdom of God is the greatest honor we can rise to. We are then being your hands and your feet in reality. We are doing, in the earth, what you desire to do, but cannot because you are infinite.

I choose to be abased, that I may abound to all good works, in Christ Jesus.

*"And thou shalt remember all the way which
the Lord thy God led thee these forty years in
the wilderness, to humble thee, and to prove
thee, to know what was in thine heart, whether
thou wouldest keep his commandments, or no."*
Deuteronomy 8:2

WILDERNESS: DAYS OF PREPARATION

The wilderness experience is to teach us total reliance on God; no country, no home, no material possessions and no store of provisions, only total reliance on the God of the universe. Before we can cross over the Jordan, we have to totally trust in and rely upon God's provision, in Jesus Christ.

Total abandonment to Jesus Christ is believing that God is meeting all our needs, according to His riches in glory, in Christ Jesus. We have to be stripped down to nothing to cross the Jordan. We have to enter in miraculously. God takes us into the wilderness through the Red Sea. He brings us out of the wilderness through the Jordan River. Both are miracles!

Equipped with the presence of God, the Word of God and the leadership of Joshua, Israel cleansed, repentant and sanctified, entered Canaan. The book of Joshua illustrates the principle that the child of God will be involved in conflict, if he earnestly undertakes to possess all God has promised to him on this earth. (See also Ephesians 6:10-18 for instructions on how to accomplish this.)

Father God, why can we see your hand with Israel and others in history, and be so blind to your dealing with us? If we truly know you never change, we must come to accept your ways and your dealings with us as normal and natural, as progressive steps, or stages, in the development of our relationship. We must move on and become the testimony you have ordained for us to be among men. Thank you for developing the fruit of the Spirit in our lives.

**I believe the way into the abundant life is
through the wilderness. I won't sit down, but
go on, until I come out the other side.**

"It is a fearful thing to fall into the hands of the living God." – **Hebrews 10:31**

SHOUTING GROUND

Looking in Joshua chapters 4-6, we again see a lesson for ourselves. The people of Israel spied out the land and agreed to God's terms and went into the promised land.

1. The ark went before them.
2. God miraculously made the way.
3. They were to set up a place of worship
4. They were to be circumcised.

In Egypt and the wilderness, no one had been circumcised. This is a picture of world conformity. Before any act was committed, they had to be circumcised, depicting their hearts turned fully to God, in the righteousness of Jesus. This was taking our place in death and resurrection; putting to death, once and for all, the deeds of the body, through the Spirit.

The first battle for the conquest of the land was Jericho. The armed men were to go first, and then the ark. They marched around the fortress six days. On the 7th day, seven times around - no cries, no works of their own, just obedience. After this total obedience, they were told to give a great shout <u>before</u> the wall fell. The shout was for victory. It was calling into being the things that were not as if they were (Romans 4:17).

Father, it is a stretching of our faith and trust to give the victory shout before our walls go down. In this we can see what honor we can give to you, recognizing who you are and your power to accomplish all that you have promised.

I will joyfully shout unto the Lord today.

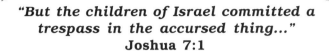

"But the children of Israel committed a trespass in the accursed thing..."
Joshua 7:1

CITIZENSHIP

Because of obedience, the children of God conquered Jericho. Rather, God gave them Jericho. The next step, after riding high on victory, was to fall into sin. Our most dangerous time is immediately after a victory. The sweet smell of success leaves us vulnerable.

Looking in Joshua 7, we see the threefold sin. That is the deliberate disobedience of Achan, the decision to send a few men (depending on human strength) and no communication with God for directions. When God gives a victory, we must not touch the Glory. We must rely totally on God and seek His instructions.

Joshua had to search out the sin and destroy it, before God took them another step in victory. You can live in the promised land and not possess it because of sin. God tested them, in the first encounter, with instructions to take nothing. They needed to know their hearts. The second time, He allowed them to take the spoils, because their hearts were right (Joshua 8). However the instruction comes, be obedient. Walking in covenant with God assures continual success.

Father God, what a shock to realize that entering into the promised land is not the end. It is only the beginning. We have just opened up a whole new realm of learning and growing. We are on the threshold of success, but we have to learn how to live here. Thank you for your Holy Spirit.

I need to learn my rights as a citizen of heaven and take my responsibility seriously.

 June 6

"And the men took of their victuals, and
asked not counsel at the mouth of the Lord."
Joshua 9:14

IN THE SMALL THINGS

Continuing to follow Joshua and the Israelites, we see they had learned obedience in the big things like Jericho and Ai, yet they failed to see the need for guidance in everything, even the small things (Joshua 9). By making rash promises before consulting God, sin abode right down the middle of the land, causing division. Any decision made without divine guidance leads to division.

Chapter 10 shows Joshua and Israel as a fragment of the army of God. Israel was the hand of God in judgement, for the time was full of the iniquity of the people in the land. Israel asked for divine sanction, knowing the battle was not theirs, but the Lord's. Joshua 5:13,14 shows the Lord was not for or against Israel. He was the commander and chief of God's host.

The responsibility of life in the promised land is shown here. When Israel entered Canaan, they entered the battle of the Lord. The battle was going to happen. By being obedient, Israel received the blessing of joining in what God was doing.

My Lord, seeking guidance in even the small issues concerning us is as important as anything we do. We are living in the promised land and we want to be productive.

**I need to find what God is doing, where the
Spirit is flowing, and enter in.**

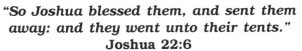

**"So Joshua blessed them, and sent them
away: and they went unto their tents."
Joshua 22:6**

WHAT GOD HAS BLESSED, DON'T CURSE

In Joshua chapters 21 and 22, we find that 2 1/2 tribes of Israel chose to settle on the opposite side of the Jordan. God agreed and told Moses to let them have the land. Nevertheless, they united in common effort to help their brethren conquer their land and inhabit it. When it was done, Joshua told them they could go home, charging them to keep faithful (Joshua 22:4-5).

They did a "different" thing and the children of Israel rose up to punish them (Joshua 22:12). By giving them an opportunity to explain their way, peace was wonderfully restored, and what they had done blessed the others (Joshua 22:30-33).

We need to listen to our brothers who do a different thing, to see if it is of God before we judge it. God would have us be united in Him, in seeking and serving, but able to do a different thing, as He commands. We sometimes seek to destroy all that is not like we are. We fear a new thing. We feel threatened by it.

Man sought to destroy Jesus because He sought to do a new thing.

Father God, we are aware that the worst enemy to the new move of God is the last move of God. Why are we so insecure and fearful? Or is it pride and prejudice? Help us, oh God, not to judge from our bias, but seek to follow your Spirit.

**I want to have ears to hear what the Spirit
is saying about things I don't understand.**

"Now we have received, not the spirit of the world, but the Spirit which is of God; that we might know the things that are freely given to us of God." – I Corinthians 2:12

THAT WE MAY KNOW

Acts 1:8 says, "ye shall be witnesses...," samples, living examples. Everything we do is to be a witness. 'How would the Lord handle this if He were standing here in my shoes?' If we are living a dedicated life, our every act is a rebuke to the sin in the lives of others. The life of God in us is a tangible force, a compelling or repelling force emanating from every child of God. This force, is a rebuke and a reprimand to every child of the world when they encounter it.

John 14:20 expresses, "that ye may know: I am in the Father, you shall know you are in me and I in you." To know is surety, certainty and knowledge of God, His plan and His way. Once we have had heart surgery (been born again), God's Spirit becomes our mentor, our leader and our comforter.

When will we know? We will know in that day. In what day? We'll know in the day in which you ask the Father, in Jesus' name (John 16:23). In that day, ask, and you shall know.

Lord, here I am. I want everything you feel I need to lead a maximized Christian life. I believe your Word tells me I need the Holy Spirit, to lead and guide me, into all truth. So I am asking for the baptism in the Holy Spirit, and I believe that what I ask you for, I receive.

I have received the baptism in the Holy Spirit. I want to walk and live in the Spirit.

June 9

"Ye are my friends, if ye do whatsoever I command you." – John 15:14

COMMANDS AND PROMISES

Psalm 37

Command: "Trust in the Lord (wholly rely upon, cleave to, put yourself in His hands) and do good."

Promise: "Thou shalt dwell in the land and be fed."

Command: "Delight thyself also in the Lord" (enjoy fellowship with, romp, be happy).

Promise: "He shall give thee the desires of thy heart."

Command: "Commit thy way unto the Lord" (count yourself on His side, cast your lot with Him).

Promise: "and He shall bring forth thy righteousness as the light. And thy justice as the noonday."

Command: "Rest in the Lord; wait patiently; fret not thyself; cease from anger; forsake wrath; fret not thyself of evil doers."

Promise. "The meek shall inherit the earth, shall delight themselves in peace."

Command: "Wait on the Lord, keep His way."

Promise: "He shall exalt thee to inherit the land."

No longing, no desire of my heart, will be unsatisfied if, and when, I delight myself in Him. We are His, in order to live as His.

Dear Lord, as we reflect on Psalm 37, we get a picture of a satisfied life, lived within the covenant we have with you. How could we want anything more – or settle for anything less?

I see God's commands as easy to be entreated. They are only for good.

"And the Lord said unto Gideon, The people that are with thee are too many for me to give the Midianites into their hands, lest Israel vaunt themselves against me, saying, Mine own hand hath saved me." – Judges 7:2

INABILITY RELEASES GOD'S ABILITY

In Judges, the 7th chapter, we see God using weakness to accomplish great and mighty things. God can only use us in a mighty way as we acknowledge our weaknesses. In Judges, we see Him using an ax goad (3:31), a nail (4:21), trumpets, pitchers and lamps (7:20), a millstone, (9:53) and a jawbone (15:15). Deliverance always came when they were relying on God. Defeat always came when they relied on their own abilities.

We see, in the story of Gideon, how God increased his faith for the task at hand. You see, God understood Gideon and what steps to take to bring him along. God had their hands full of useless weapons, so they could not rely on weapons of their own choosing (7:20). It required complete dependence on God and trust in His methods.

God's arithmetic is different form ours. Suffering is God's division, making it possible for us to become simple enough to relate to Him. It is His means of separating us from ourselves. Unless we become as little children, we cannot see the kingdom of God.

Father God, we are prone to increase, thinking the more we have and the bigger we get, the better it will be. You continually strive to reduce us, to bring us down to a size you can use. May we decrease more and more.

I see less is better. Less of me but more of Him - more Lord!

*"Is there not an appointed time to
man upon earth?" – Job 7:1a*

IN TIMES OF DARKNESS, HOLD ON

There is a time appointed to man to learn obedience to the will of God, before He can be trusted with authority in the kingdom of God. Months, perhaps years, of weary waiting, instead of happy service.

Our faith after salvation is real, but it may not be at work in actual things. In our studies and devotions, our faith is real. Then we leave the classroom, so to speak, and enter the "real world," and we fail the test. We find ourselves reacting rather than acting by faith. We become scattered, dead internally to the blessings of God. Until God engineers circumstances to bring us to the place of inner desolation, our faith operates by feelings and blessings.

After this experience, we can praise God that all is well, no matter what the circumstances, or where God places us. Darkness comes by the sovereignty of God. He wants to, yes. He means to bring us to a place of wanting God, Himself, only, not His blessings. He would have us make our bed in the darkness, lie down in the dark, and rest in His faithfulness.

Father, we are reminded of Job, the story of every man's journey into knowing you for himself. We know we pass through many places and seasons in our quest to know you. Darkness is one of them. Thank you for never leaving us.

**In the dark, I will walk forward in faith, for
I am assured the Lord is with me.**

"For we are his workmanship, created in
Christ Jesus unto good works, which God hath
before ordained that we should walk in them."
Ephesians 2:10

UNDER CONSTRUCTION

I work from the outside in. God works from the inside out. I have attempted to build an edifice and ask God to dwell in it, to fill the beautiful structure with His Spirit.

God says, "As the bricks lie in disarray, all torn down, completely in shambles, I will send my Holy Spirit to inhabit the torn down places. Then, from the inside, I will lay the foundations and it will be immovable. I will place the bricks in the order in which I know they will stand against any strain that comes against them."

In Hebrews 13:5, God said, "...I will never leave you nor forsake you." "Lo, I am with you even to the end of the world." (Matthew 28:20). I have total and complete freedom from any responsibility for myself or any others in this relationship.

I am God's.

I am free.

God demands one thing from me in return for all He is to me: my complete and total obedience. Is this asking too much of me? God arranging me and making me a lasting workmanship and then filling me with Himself in exchange for my eternal "yes, Lord?" You decide for yourself!

Father, as for me, it is not even up for discussion. I love you, trust you and I want you to rearrange me to please yourself.

I know whatever God does to me, in me,
and through me today is right. I accept it.

"Be still, and know that I am God: I will be exalted among the heathen, I will be exalted in the earth." – Psalm 46:10

CURIOSITY

I want to "glimpse" God at work. I intrude, therefore, into what He is about, so I might "get in on it." Curiosity got Eve in the garden. Satan will always test us at our curiosity level.

We check into what God is doing in the lives of our family, friends and neighbors. It is curiosity that keeps checking our line of prayer, to see how the answer is coming. It is curiosity that causes us to stick our noses into everyone else's business.

Curiosity is no part spirit. It is a desire to know about anything, especially unusual or novel things. It is a quality of the human mind. A curious person has not come under the law of obedience. He wants to open the Holy of Holies, to see what's in there. He reads the Word to get an unknown glimpse of God. Curiosity would destroy faith, make it of no avail.

Curiosity earns its living by the sweat of the brow. Spirituality accepts the good, from God's hand, under the law of obedience. Obedience is the complete giving over of the human thought to the divine will.

Be still and know! How? Why? When? Where? - all of curiosity.

Father God, curiosity leads us into avenues and areas that are not helpful or necessary. We can enter into things that will lead us away from your guidance in our search for the unknown factors. We submit ourselves to the law of obedience, thus entering into the harbor of safety. We desire to instantly obey your voice, taking no thought to ourselves, concerning the outcome - believing you will do all you said you would do and bring us to a good end.

The command and the outcome are God's. I will find out that I'm right where I need to be.

> *"For I know the thoughts that I think toward you, saith the Lord, thoughts of peace, and not of evil, to give you an expected end."*
> **Jeremiah 29:11**

GOD DOESN'T NEED ANY HELP!

Moses was promised, by God, to be Israel's deliverer. He had to help God out by killing an Egyptian. God promised Abraham he would be the father of many nations. He and Sarah decided to help God out. God kept His promise to Abraham. He always keeps His promises to man. It just takes Him longer when we help Him out.

God promised to make Jacob ruler over Esau. He and Rebekah decided to help God out. God kept His promise. It just took Him longer because Jacob always had to help Him out.

God promised Joseph an elevated place of rulership. Joseph had to help God out by telling his family. God anointed David king of Israel. Saul sought to kill him and he ran to the Philistines. God let David go, until he wore himself out and recognized his helplessness.

Moses had to spend 40 years in the desert alone. Abraham had to put Isaac on the altar, trusting God. Jacob wrestled all night with God's angel. Joseph had to go through the pit, to slavery, to prison, because he helped God out. David had to repent in tears and anguish.

I wonder how much sooner God's plans could have been fulfilled, if His chosen people were not always helping Him out?

Father God, ruler over all things. To realize you think thoughts toward me, thoughts that are always of peace, to know that you want only good for me and that you are continually working toward that end brings me to my knees before you. To give you thanks always and in all things is requiring very little from me, in return for all you are to me. I have to begin somewhere, though, and I begin by saying thank you, from the bottom of my heart.

Today is a perfect day to realize the goodness of my God.

*"And the king was much moved, and went up
to the chamber over the gate, and wept: and
as he went, thus he said, O my son Absalom,
my son, my son Absalom! would God I had
died for thee, O Absalom, my son, my son!"*
II Samuel 18:33

ASSUMING RESPONSIBILITY

David was anointed king over all of Israel, by God's command. He was a man after God's own heart and yet he sinned greatly. He took another man's wife and then had him killed to cover up his own sin. God forgave David when he repented (Psalm 51), but the consequences of his sin lasted all his life, in the sins of his children.

David never ceased longing after his children, and he never sought revenge or even justice, no matter how grave their sins against him. I believe David assumed responsibility for his part in the sins of his children. He would have preferred to suffer in their place. II Samuel 18:33 is a type of the deep, abiding love God has for us when we perish in our sins.

When David's children, in rebellion, turned and sought his life, he made no defense, he moved and let them rail on against him. He humbly hung his head and remained silent.

My Lord and my God. In David we see an example of a godly man living with the consequences of his past failures. May we, as parents, realize our role in the forming of our children's lives, and thus, set them free to find their own peace with you. Even in our deep contrition, there are prices to be paid, but thank you for being a comfort to us as we pray and intercede and believe for the salvation of our loved ones.

**I accept my responsibility before God,
and seek to overcome my past failures,
by His grace.**

"He saved others; himself he cannot save. If he be the King of Israel, let him now come down from the cross, and we will believe him."
Matthew 27:42

CALVARY TRUTH

In the wilderness, the law of the life of Jesus was revealed. He fed not Himself, but later He fed others. He could draw on the power of the Godhead to bless, feed, heal and save others; concerning Himself, nothing! To have the power to save yourself, and refuse to use it because others could not be saved, is the life of Jesus manifested to those He redeemed.

To pour out your life for others who misjudge you, this is Calvary. To have the power to save yourself, and not use it because it means loss to others, this is Calvary. To be used to deliver souls from the power of Satan, and then to be at the apparent mercy of the hour and power of darkness yourself, as Christ was, this is Calvary truth. Life, power, blessing, deliverance for others and nothing for yourself, except to lie in the Will of the Father, and accept whatever He permits to come to you; the voluntary choice to suffer and to die, rather than save yourself, is higher even than faith to conquer and subdue!

Father, to be broken to this point is a worthy goal; to be your life, poured out through a human vessel, to touch other lives. This is a goal we wish to attain. To forget about ourselves, and allow Calvary love to be the life force emanating from us. Oh God, please bring it about.

I would be broken and poured out for Christ's sake to the world.

**"And hath raised us up together, and made us
sit together in heavenly places in Christ Jesus:"
Ephesians 2:6**

THE PRICE OF THE THRONE

The way up is down! Cease to struggle and resist. The preparation for reigning is now! To learn never to stand for your "rights" - now is the time: this present year, this present circumstance. God has placed you exactly where He can fulfill your prayer and prepare you for the future.

Everything is upside down. That is God's highest vote of confidence in you! How far can you trust God in the dark?

There are no second causes to the soul hidden in God. Misunderstandings, sorrows, trials, everything here is the Will of God, to His child. If the things around us fret us, the enemy has succeeded in pulling us down enough to do it. As we go in and out among the things that try us, we must trust and praise our God, that He is keeping us "far above all" (Galatians 5:1). Jesus can keep us "far above all," as we learn to live in His faithfulness, and cease to struggle and resist. We just need to lie down in His Will day by day and say, "Yes Lord," to all that comes (Ephesians 1:20,21).

Father God, I see that I have wasted so much time and strength in wrestling with my life's circumstances, trying to get them to go away or to cease being. Rather, I should embrace them as opportunities, filters, so to speak, through which I am being perfected.

**I want to agree with Colossians 2:12 and
have faith in the working of God, who
raised Jesus from the dead!**

June 18

"He shall see of the travail of his soul, and shall be satisfied: by his knowledge shall my righteous servant justify many; for he shall bear their iniquities." – **Isaiah 53:11**

AT-ONE-MENT

Cleansing and covering:
<u>Cleansing</u> - removing the filthiness that sin brought into the life of a man or woman.

<u>Covering</u> - protecting from the consequences of that sin.

Cleansing, covering, and removal of sin brings restoration of fellowship to God.

Isaiah 53:6, "All we, like sheep, have gone astray; we have turned every one to his own way; and the Lord hath laid on him the iniquity of us all."

John 1:29, "...Behold the lamb of God which taketh away the sin of the world."

I John 1:9, "If we confess our sins, he is faithful and just to forgive us our sins, and to cleanse us from all unrighteousness."

Forgiveness, cleansing, covering, and removal of sin brings restoration of the presence of God.

Hebrews 10:1, "For the law, having a shadow of good things to come, and not the very image of the things, can never with those sacrifices which they offered year by year continually make the comers thereunto perfect."

Our Lord and God, we can see by these scriptural truths what you relieved us of, by offering Jesus, as the sacrificial lamb, for the sins of mankind. We personally realize this and we partake of this sacrifice by our faith in Jesus Christ and His atoning work on the cross. We are so thankful to have been saved, cleansed and restored.

**I walk free today, joyously knowing that
I am redeemed and restored
to relationship with God.**

*"Whereupon, O king Agrippa, I was not
disobedient unto the heavenly vision:"*
Acts 26:19

THROUGH A GLASS DARKLY

When John was banished to the Isle of Patmos, it must have seemed like the end of his service to God. What seemed to be the end was but the beginning of a far greater work of glory than John could have imagined.

The 40 years, on the back side of the desert, took the "I am" out of Moses and gave him "who am I?" Bringing God on the scene always takes the "I am" out of us. Moses endured as seeing <u>Him</u>. His whole life seemed one long wilderness wandering. He had to endure on the sole ground of God's Word.

There may be momentary desolation. God may withdraw from our consciousness, that our faith may rest in Him alone. We get our mountain by way of the cross and the long trail of endurance. Caleb had vision to gain his mountain. Therefore, he measured his granite by the vision he gained, through the promise he had received (Joshua 14:6-9). If the way seems mysterious, we must enter deeper into the vision of God and His purposes and desires.

Father, we all could say with the saints and patriarchs throughout the ages, "I don't quite see what this is all about." We also understand it is by faith we live in relationship with you. Help us, oh Lord, to know that without vision, we will perish. We will also turn and sorrowfully walk away. Vision will keep us focused on the finish line. For vision to remain, we pray today.

I choose to see by the eye of faith.

"And thine ears shall hear a Word behind thee, saying, This is the way, walk ye in it, when ye turn to the right hand, and when ye turn to the left." – Isaiah 30:21

20/20 VISION

All the revelation needed to bring our will to the Will of God is in the pages of the Bible. Hagar did not get a river from God. All He did was open her eyes to what was already there. We have great need of eye salve (Revelation 3:18). There are steps and stops of discipline and endurance in God directed lives. The trail begins at Calvary. Mountains are only accessible by zigzag trails, over chains of foothills, and wearying ups and downs.

Vision can make a man so certain of the future, he can walk unwaveringly through all circumstances and conditions that would seem to convey the exact opposite to what he has seen by faith. Vision steeled Peter in the face of bitterest opposition (Acts 12:1-4). Stephen had vision before the attack of the Sanhedrin (Acts 7:54-56). We also see Elisha surrounded by the armies of the Syrians (II Kings 6:13-18).

Beware of impressions, emotions, physical thrills, voices or anything that is not according to Bible standard and to our own highest reason. Paul operated on the revealed will of God.

Father God, without clear knowledge of your Word, as revealed to us by your Holy Spirit, we easily get caught up in the confusing den of noises and voices around us. Everyone seems to have an opinion, but we clearly will perish without vision of you.

To see clearly, I must apply the ointment of God's Word to my eyes.

June 21

*"The Lord of hosts hath sworn, saying, Surely
as I have thought, so shall it come to pass;
and as I have purposed, so shall it stand:"*
Isaiah 14:24

DIVINE DESTINY

The law of purpose is a determining factor in all things in the whole universe. Every person has a working principle of action (purpose). This is their philosophy of life. Unconsciously, this underlying basis is responsible for all motivation and response.

Paul, on the Damascus road, had a purpose of life, but there he met the divine purpose and it changed the world. It is as necessary to be saved from a wrong philosophy of life, as it is to be saved from sin and error.

The world will never be saved until it has been brought back to the realization of Divine Destiny. Man must know the world is a workshop where God is working a great purpose. He must know, also, that his first duty to God and himself is to discover that purpose, and dedicate his life to its realization. Only in the discovery of God's desire and its perfect realization will man attain his greatest satisfaction and reach his true destiny.

Father, we understand that we are so directly and intimately related to you and your desire, that we will never be satisfied or fulfilled, apart from realization of your purposes. Everything you are about involves us. We must move into a deeper intimacy with you.

I will spend time today, alone, in God's presence.

June 22

"Truly God is good to Israel, even to such as are of a clean heart." – Psalm 73:1

THE END OF THE MATTER

In Psalm 73:1-10, the child of God is shown questioning, perhaps envying, the easy lifestyle of the rich, ungodly man, which seems so much easier than their own life. Verse 10 even tells of the children of God returning to the wicked and blindly drinking from the full cup they offer. Following on, in verses 11-15, the godly man, now full from the cup of the wicked, begins to justify his actions, until he wearies, in verse 16, of trying to reason it all out.

The solution to this all too common quandary is then given in verse 17; "until I went into the sanctuary of God; then understood I their end." It had been too great an effort and too painful a process to figure it all out, but when he entered God's sanctuary, it became clear.

Jesus Christ is God's sanctuary for Christians. He has been made the fullness of God's wisdom. In Him, we know all things. Take time now to go on and read the rest of the story, as the child of God now communes with his heavenly Father and, in verse 28, sees how good it is for him to draw near to God.

Father God, I want to say, with the Psalmist of old, "It is good for me to draw near to you." It is good for me to realize all the riches and successes in this world, apart from knowing you, will only bring temporary pleasure and ultimately end in death and separation.

I have put my trust in the Lord God, that I may declare all His works.

June 23

*"Through God we shall do valiantly: for
He it is that shall tread down our enemies."*
Psalm 108:13

A CRY FOR HELP

Today, we are concentrating on seven verses in Psalm 108 (verses 7-13). We want to see God's holiness, in His sanctuary. He speaks, in His holiness, in His sanctuary, and when we enter in, He speaks to us. It is here that things become clear to us. In verse 12, we are reminded that deliverance comes from God. Man's help is in vain. Verse 13 declares it is God who treads down our adversaries.

We are washed by the reading of the Word (Ephesians 5:26). We are made holy by being cleansed in the reading and doing of the Word of God. When we are holy, we hear from God. Like attracts like. We must be like God to commune with Him. We must seek to be like Him, as a child imitates its parent.

God is holy. We must be holy (I Peter 1:16). Let this mind be in you, that was in Christ Jesus (Philippians 5:2). He had a mind to be obedient to His heavenly father. God has a divine purpose and, by obedience, Jesus fit into that purpose. We can only fit into our place by obedience; cheerfully, willingly, freely following the blueprint.

My Father God, verse 13 tells us it is you who treads down our adversaries. I am but to follow you, trusting you with the details. I will not do this unless my mind is renewed by reading your Word. Faith will come by hearing your Word.

**I want to hear, receive, and obey the
Word of God.**

"I cried unto thee, O Lord: I said, Thou art my refuge, and my portion in the land of the living." – Psalm 142:5

DELIVERANCE THROUGH FAITH

The entire Psalm 142 can be used as a personal prayer for deliverance. Deliverance is found in faith. Romans 10:8-15 brings us into faith. "Faith cometh by hearing and hearing by the Word of God."

Get into the Word of God. Saturate yourself with the Word. Bathe in it. Dwell in it. Live in it. The Word of faith is near you, even in your mouth. Look back over these words and see a pattern of life. We have rituals, or routines, in the living process. Can we draw a parallel with the Word of God? Can we have the same ritual or routine in making the Word a part of our living process?

Speak the Word. Confess the Word. Read it to find out what God is saying, and then agree with Him, by saying the same thing He says. For with the mouth confession is made unto salvation. Psalm 142:2 & 3 says, "when I complained, my spirit was overwhelmed." Goodness, we don't need to overwhelm ourselves with our complaining, do we? When we say what God says, we have a hold on solutions instead of problems.

My Lord, it is all so clear and so easy to see. Why do we read and come away and fall back into the same old negative thinking? Help us, Oh Lord, to be changed. If you change us, by your power, we will be changed. We are humbly asking you to work a miracle of renewing our mind, as we determine to make reading your Word part of our life process!

Praise God, Praise God, Praise God!

"Set a watch, O Lord, before my mouth; keep the door of my lips." – Psalm 141:3

GOOD ORAL HYGIENE

Proverbs 21:23 says, "Who so keepeth his mouth and his tongue keepeth his soul from troubles." God has called His people to prayer. Jesus told His disciples that the house of God was to be a house of prayer. In prayer and communication with God, as He shares His heart with His pray-er, things are revealed that are to be kept, meditated on and turned into intercession. We can easily see the necessity of keeping our mouths and our tongues.

The Lord wants to heal and unite His church. The knowledge received for prayer could split and divide and hurt if handled in the wrong manner. Psalm 141 is very helpful for instruction on keeping our hearts right before God. It is a prayer for preservation from evil. Why are we always concerned with evil coming towards us and seldom aware of evil preceding from us, through our words?

Psalm 51:15 is also a wonderful prayer for us all to pray:

"Oh Lord, open thou my lips; and my mouth shall show forth thy praise." If only our lips were sealed so that they opened only to allow praises to God and helpful words for others.

Father, we need a cleansing in our hearts of wrong attitudes and thoughts about others, so that our hearts can be pure.

I thank the Lord for a purifying of my thoughts and the intents of my heart today.

June 26

"And, behold, I am with thee, and will keep thee in all places whither thou goest ... for I will not leave thee ..."
Genesis 28:15

NEVER ALONE

God said it. It is so. When He was making Himself and His character known unto man, in Deuteronomy 31:6, He said, "I will never leave <u>you</u> nor forsake you." God is steadfast, never changing, without shadow of turning. He is not subject to, or ruled by His emotions, but by what He said. God is bound by His words and He said, "I will never leave you."

Who moves? We in our selfishness, make up our minds to be our own master, and we turn from God in discontent and rebellion. In Hebrews 13, verse 5, God said to be content with your lot in life, with who you are; for God made you, you. Verse 6 tells us God is with us, forming our character.

It is God who is with us and in us, helping us overcome our situations. Overcoming is having victory, being on top of the situation. We must not fear what man can do to us. We relate on the wrong level. It is our relationship to God that sets the standard for relating to man.

Our Heavenly Father, we always come back to relating. Everything in proper order brings balance and peace in all our dealings, both with you and others. When we see you as first, we settle into correct responses to everything around us.

**I know I am never alone.
I have no need of fear.**

"Hear my prayer, O Lord, give ear to my supplications: in thy faithfulness answer me, and in thy righteousness." – Psalm 143:1

A CRY FOR HELP

Psalm 143 shows us the character of Jehovah. He is steadfast, righteous and faithful. We can count on Him at all times. Verse 3 shows Satan as the enemy of our soul. It is Satan that causes us to dwell in darkness. Our spirit is overwhelmed by our soul, when we allow Satan to persecute our soul, without calling on God for help. When Satan persecutes our soul, we must:

remember the days of old - His way with Israel;

meditate on God's works - remember His miracles;

muse on the works of His hands - His creation;

lift our hands unto Him (verses 5-7).

Verse 8 tells us to listen for His loving kindness, in the morning. We must ask God to:

cause us to hear Him;

deliver us from Satan;

teach us to do His Will;

lead us in the way of uprightness;

revive us and bring us out of trouble, because we are His servants (verses 9-12).

Father God, I know you as an ever present help in time of trouble. I need to be very careful to know you in all seasons, with the same intensity of desire. As a child, I selfishly called on you mostly for help. Now I need your ever present friendship and companionship. Thank you!

**I am so happy and privileged to be
a friend and companion of God,
the ruler of the universe.**

*"And Mordecai walked every day before the
court of the women's house, to know how
Esther did, and what should become of her."*
Esther 2:11

THE SPIRIT OF ADOPTION

We find a valuable example in Queen Esther. She
was adopted into Mordecai's family. As she followed his
wise instructions, she was successful in all her ways.
She was frightened and anxious as she waited to see if
the king would hold out the scepter. But she trusted
the guidance of Mordecai. He had accepted her as his
own and he would not give her counsel to harm her, for
he loved her, as himself. As soon as she acted out of
obedience and did just what he told her to do, God moved
on the king to bring him in line. As Mordecai was given
authority to act, he grew stronger and stronger and the
enemies were defeated.

We have been adopted into God's family, by the power
of the Holy Spirit. As we listen to the counsel of our
Mordecai, the Holy Spirit, and do our part, it brings
into action all of God's divine plan, and all the pieces fit
together in every life that is involved. It is a progressive
thing. As the Holy Spirit is given control and heard and
obeyed, He makes all the enemies flee before us.

*Father, how full your Word is of examples and
situations that we can apply to our own lives, and learn
how to flow in your ways. Thank you again for our
Mordecai, the Blessed Holy Spirit of God.*

**I may shake a little in situations, but I'm
going through!**

"Likewise, ye wives, be in subjection to your own husbands; that, if any obey not the Word, they also may without the Word be won by the conversation of the wives;"
I Peter 3:1

ORDER IN THE HOME

In verse 6 of I Peter 3, we read how Sarah obeyed Abraham. She followed his guidance and acknowledged his leadership over her by calling him lord, master, leader, authority. We are her true daughter if we do right and let nothing terrify us, nor give way to hysterical fears or let anxiety unnerve us. Ephesians 5:22-24 speaks of being submissive and adapting ourselves to our husbands, as a service unto the Lord. Colossians 3:18 tells us it is fitting, right and our proper duty to be subject to our husbands.

Looking at three of these terms, we can draw a Word picture of a godly wife. Subject is to see our husband as ruler, authority, or head in the relationship. Subordinate is to place oneself under leadership, ready to follow orders and sensitive to desires and wishes. To adapt is taking something that naturally does not fit and fixing it, so that it does. It is changing your ways and habits so that they "fit in" with the ways and plans of your husband.

Lord, this isn't a really popular subject in a lot of circles, but I have seen, by example, and by the teaching of your Word, that it only works this way. It needs to work. We are a broken and disjointed society, with our pieces and parts scattered all about. We need to return to the proper method of functioning, so we may be healed.

I am learning to see my marriage as God sees it.

*Humble yourselves therefore under the
mighty hand of God, that he may exalt you in
due time." – I Peter 5:6*

HUMBLE YOURSELF TO RECEIVE

II Chronicles 7:14 speaks of a condition to receiving a promise from God. "If my people humble themselves, pray, seek my face and turn from their wicked ways," then the promise, "I will forgive their sin and heal their land." James 4:10 puts forth the condition to, "humble yourself in the Lord's sight." Then the promise follows, "and he will lift you up."

Job 22:29 tells us God shall save the humble person.

In I Peter 5:5,6, the younger are told to submit to the older as a condition to receive grace from God. If we will humble ourselves under the mighty hand of God, we are promised that He will exalt us, in due time. Verse 7 reminds us that it is only the humble who will cast their care over on the Lord, for the proud feel as though they have to carry it themselves. Our wonderful promise, again, in verse 10, is that God, after we have suffered in humility for a while, will lift us to a new level and make us stable.

Father God, I willingly humble myself, I will pray and I will seek your face. I will turn from my wicked ways. I ask you, oh God, to hear my prayer, to forgive my sins and please, to heal my land.

**I submit myself to God, so that the enemy
will flee from me.**

"If my people, which are called by my name, shall humble themselves, and pray, and seek my face, and turn from their wicked ways; then will I hear from heaven, and will forgive their sin, and will heal their land."
II Chronicles 7:14

WHAT IT WILL TAKE TO GO ON

Isaiah 51:16-23 is descriptive of our nation - no one to lead, young men refusing to fight the enemies, who have their feet on our necks. We have fear of our enemies in our hearts, but God will lead us. He will put fear, by His fury, into our enemy's hearts.

Psalm 140 finds God's man humbling himself, praying and seeking God. We can pray the petition in verse 11 for ourselves and all people. Proverbs 1:23 reveals Jesus' longing to pour out His Spirit upon us and make known His words to us, but we must <u>turn</u> [repent] at His reproof. Verse 33 gives us wonderful hope and encouragement, as it shows us those who listen and take heed shall dwell safely, and not fear in the time of calamity.

Father, as we read and meditate on these verses which hold solemn and sobering instructions, we can also take great courage, if we will only heed the warnings. We thank you so much that you love us enough to have warned us thousands of years ago of dangers in life, and how to come safely through without fear. Fear will paralyze us and keep us locked away from enjoying life as you made it possible for us to live. Thank you for setting us free from fear. We love you, and praise you, Almighty God.

I will do something today, that fear has caused

me to back down from, to prove I am free!
"Because I will publish the name of the Lord:
ascribe ye greatness unto our God."
Deuteronomy 32:3

OH TO BE LIKE MOSES

In Deuteronomy 32:1-4, we read Moses' song as he sang his delight in the Lord, His God. In verse 2, he said, "my teaching shall drop as rain, my speech shall flow as the dew. It will be gentle to the unknowing, and like showers on the mature. It shall flow with the greatness of the name of the Lord. He is the rock, He is perfect, just and right, without iniquity."

In Luke 14:8-11, we have Jesus' instructions on humility. With all the ability God is providing to teach the Word, we are instructed when we go in to a place to always take the lowest seat. If then, we are promoted, it will be to God's Glory. Never attempt to take the high place. Anyone who attempts to exalt himself, God will bring down. He, that will humble himself, will be exalted.

Moses sang the song above in the presence of Israel after he had appointed Joshua, the new leader. He sang it, we are told, in its entirety. Moses was spoken of by God, as the humblest man alive. He left with Joshua and Israel the keys of greatness. Always attribute success to God, and stay humble in success.

Father, we are so prone to strut about in the headiness of victory. In that time, we are subject to the enemy of our souls, to be brought down and defeated. Thank you for carefully placing within your Word, warnings and instructions that, if heeded, will safeguard our service to you, and keep us effective for long years.

I want to sit quietly in my place, that I might mount up with wings, as my Lord calls me forth.

"And said, Verily I say unto you, Except ye be converted, and become as little children, ye shall not enter into the kingdom of heaven."
Matthew 18:3

TO KNOW MEANS TO DO

In II Samuel 6:1-7, the people that went with David to bring the ark to Jerusalem were chosen. They knew God's instructions concerning touching the ark. The oxen shook the ark, and Uzziah reached forth his hand impulsively to steady the ark. In verse 7, we read the anger of the Lord was kindled, as the result. God does not need, or want, any help from us concerning His part. He has given us laws and commands, and has even written them in our hearts, that we might not sin against Him. We must be so steeped in His Word, we are disciplined to it. No impulsive moves of our soul realm will be tolerated, or excused.

Matthew 18:1-5 is a teaching by Jesus to His disciples on the importance of child-likeness. Impulsive behavior is a result of not trusting the instruction and guidance of the adult authority. To partake of kingdom living, it is necessary according to the Word of God, to live and conduct ourselves as children in the household. We must see God as a functioning adult.

Father, we have been so undisciplined or over disciplined, by earthly parents, that we have difficulty trusting you where our lives are concerned. Oh God, please forgive us for seeing you incorrectly, because of conditioning. Help us yield to your Spirit, as He leads, directs, comforts and teaches us how to respond to you. We must begin to say quickly and easily, yes, Lord.

Without hesitation, today I chose to obey the Voice of God as He directs me through His Word.

"But put ye on the Lord Jesus Christ, and make not provision for the flesh, to fulfil the lusts thereof." – Romans 13: 14

MARINATING IN THE WORD

As we saturate our souls in the written Word, it becomes more and more difficult to act contrary to the Will of God.

In Ephesians 6:16, we see the shield of faith is raised against the enemy. There is no substitution for faith. The real thing is generated by the hearing of the written Word of God.

II Timothy 3 outlines how it will be to live in the last times. Verse 12 tells us that all who live Godly lives will suffer persecution. In verse 13, we see how Satan has opportunity to deceive us when we refuse to live Godly, with consequences following. Going on to verses 14 and 15, the apostle Paul admonishes us to continue on in the things we have learned and been assured of from the scriptures.

One of the saddest examples in the Word of God is found in Luke 6:39-49, showing that hearing the Word, without obeying the Word, is useless. How sad to think we can sit and read and get knowledge, and yet go away without having gained anything.

Father God, how sobering is this thought to us. We do not want to be hearers only, but doers of the Word. We thank you for your Holy Spirit interpreting the Word to us, and activating power in us, to go and do what we read.

I will spend time in the Word in order to saturate my soul.

"Now concerning spiritual gifts, brethren,
I would not have you ignorant."
I Corinthians 12:1

CONCERNING SPIRITUAL GIFTS

Different gifts-same Spirit.

Different kinds of service-same Lord.

Different operations-same God (I Corinthians 12:4-6).

God works all these gifts in all Christians. We do not need to seek to duplicate an action or a service. Even the same gift operates differently according to the Will of God. It is He that wills and He that does His good pleasure. The gifts are given for service. God uses the gifts in ways He deems necessary for us to perform as Jesus did, while on the earth. I Corinthians 12:11-13 reminds us the Spirit gives several gifts, as He chooses, and that God places them in the body as it pleases Him.

Mark 16:20 tells us as we go forth in obedience, and open our mouth in faith, God will fill it, and miracles will follow to confirm that Word.

Matthew 12:36 and 37 is a warning against having a bantering spirit, it will rob others of blessings. It warns against frivolity. The more we talk, the more likely we are to sin.

Father, we realize to be gifted by you for service in your kingdom carries with it a responsibility for stewarding that gift. We are prone to take the gifts and calling of God too lightly, thus your warning against frivolity. We must not rob others of the opportunity to receive from you, because we are insensitive to your Spirit.

Only to be faithful, oh Lord, please. I want
to be faithful in my service to you today.

**"Draw me, we will run after thee: the king
hath brought me into his chambers; we will be
glad and rejoice in thee; we will remember thy
love more than wine: the upright love thee."**
Song of Solomon 1:4

THE SONG OF SOLOMON

1:7 Does my spirit crave for the Divine Shepherd, even in the presence of the best the world has to offer me?

2:6 Do I have a constant sense of my shepherd's presence, regardless of my surroundings?

2:13 Do I take time to meet my good Shepherd every day, letting Him tell me of His love and cheering His heart, with my interest in Him?

2:14 Do I realize that my voice in praise and song is sweet to Him, or do I withhold it?

2:15 What is my greatest concern, the thing I most of all want help with? When He asks to hear my voice, what do I tell him?

4:8 Do I heed when He bids me come away from the lion's den of temptation and dwell with Him?

4:16 Am I willing for the north wind of adversity to blow upon me, if it will better fit me for Christ's presence?

5:3 In my weariness from earthly cares, do I hesitate to answer when the Divine Shepherd knocks at my door and turn him away from me?

5:16 Is my Savior Shepherd unquestionably the one altogether lovely, the one above all others, most precious to me?

My Lord and my God, what an intimate portrait of relationship with a personal Lord. It makes me long to experience, all the time, this wonderful intimacy. As I answer these questions, I can see the need for adjustments, to make this a possibility, is all on my side.

**With God helping me, I can have this
Divine intimacy.**

"And walk in love, as Christ also hath loved us, and hath given himself for us an offering and a sacrifice to God for a sweet smelling savour." – **Ephesians 5:2**

THE LOVE WALK

Until you are rooted and grounded in the love of God, you cannot comprehend the love of God. God is love. Everything He does is governed by love. His Word is a revelation of the love of God to man. What do people doubt most about God? It would seem to be they doubt He really loves them. We need to perfect our faith in His love, to believe He will use His mighty power for us, in our behalf.

God loves us. His Spirit came to reveal that love to us. We begin to move toward our loved ones in that same way, with no demands, just allowing love to flow toward them. In this way, we create an atmosphere of love around us.

The Bible declares we already have the love of God. John 3:16 says it is ours as soon as we take possession of it. When you were born again, you became an expression of the love of God. When you learn who you are in God, and begin to confess it, it becomes a part of you. Confession of sin must turn into confession of righteousness. The first thing you have to do to practice the love walk, is to confess it.

Father, feelings are not at issue here. We often times do not feel loved, but if we can begin to agree with what you say about your love for us, feelings will develop. Thank you for loving us, and sending Jesus to redeem us.

I am the love of God!

"Wilt thou yet say before him that slayeth thee, I am God? but thou shalt be a man, and no God, in the hand of him that slayeth thee."
Ezekiel 28:9

THE PRIDEFUL WILL FALL

The king of Tyre was condemned because of pride. In the Ezekiel chapter 28 account, we see the three steps of pride. It began in the heart [beauty, intelligence, money, position]. From there, it moved to his head, and his wisdom became corrupt. We see that the end was disaster [conceit, corruption and condemnation]. Nothing is as difficult to do gracefully, as getting down off your high horse! The warning here is clearly to humble yourself before God.

In Luke 8:43 and 44, we have the story of a woman sick for years, touching the hem of Jesus' garment as he passed by. As soon as she turned to Jesus, she was healed. We must seek Jesus for our healing, humbly throwing ourselves on His mercy. In verse 53, we read how they laughed him to scorn when he spoke of the dead living. We, too, will be laughed to scorn when we live as Jesus lived. We are not greater than our master.

Father God, we can see how important it is for us to be like those coming to Jesus for healing, rather than pridefully thinking we have all we need as the king of Tyre. It is a worthy goal to attain, this, laying aside all our abilities and possessions, and becoming like Jesus to the world. Help us, oh God, to freely follow Jesus and learn His ways.

Today I know I can't do it by myself. I must have the Holy Spirit to help me.

July 9

"And Jesus came and spake unto them, saying, All power is given unto me in heaven and in earth." – Matthew 28:18

THE COST OF REVIVAL

We always repeat Matthew 28:19 and 20 when referring to our commission as Christian workers, but without verse 18, 19 and 20 are a waste of time. Somehow, we, as the people of God, seem to have wasted a lot of time. And yet, God is sovereign - our Holy teacher. He has poured out His Spirit upon all flesh to prepare the way for the return of His son, Jesus.

There is no time, as there was before. It seems God is doing a new thing now. It is the same, only greatly accelerated. There is no time as there was before, and the old programs and procedures won't work now. They take too long. <u>Now</u> is the time. If you hear His voice it is the time for salvation. God is confirming His Word with signs and wonders (Mark 16:20).

Luke 24:52, 53 is a picture of the church in revival. They are worshipping Jesus, returning with great joy, and praising and blessing God continually, across the world where revival has already come.

Our Lord and our God, we are aware that in the places where revival has come, the people have paid a great price in repentance and prayer. We know it will require the same thing from us, but we are crying out to you to draw us to yourself. We are all hungry to be together, you and your people.

I will lay on my face and cry out for refreshing.

191

"Praising God, and having favour with all the people. And the Lord added to the church daily such as should be saved."
Acts 2:47

STAYING POWER

Jesus <u>grew</u> in stature and favor with God and man. The early Christians found favor with all men. God wants to use us as magnets to draw people to Him. A magnet is simply being in close proximity to the object needing to be drawn. God will move the magnet where He chooses to draw. The rest is accomplished by the Holy Spirit in us. Jesus empowers, and sends forth His disciples. As we allow Him to use us, all things are possible.

As we walk in love, we can accomplish all that is required. As we walk in love, we will be willing to do whatever is necessary, to minister the love of God. When God wanted to tell us how much He loved us, it took flesh – flesh, in the form of a living person, with a voice and a mind. When He wants to tell others He loves them, it still takes flesh, our flesh. You and I are God's love letter to the world.

A trail blazer is one who takes their position in the front lines, never flinching or fleeing. This will require the love of God, having been established in that heart, to stick it out.

Father God, it is evident to me, I'm not made of the right stuff in my own self. I have need of all you will impart to me to make me that front line soldier. I am willing. Help me become that.

I choose to love with God's love long after my love quits.

"There is no peace, saith my God, to the wicked." – Isaiah 57:21

TURN TO THE LIGHT

When we come up to the Word of the Lord in a personal way, it can seem very harsh, blunt even. This usually occurs when it's an area in our lives that needs correction. Take, for example, the passage in John 3:17-21. Verse 20 tells me that when I do evil, there is hate in my heart for the light, which is Jesus. In the shadow of every great love is always a perversion. Jesus said, "I am the light of the world." In His light, we see love as it really is.

Storms are generated from pressure fronts. Storms in our souls are generated from the pressure of our disobedience. God does not send these storms. Jesus was not with the disciples when the storm came, fear was. Jesus had said, "<u>fear not</u>," then the wind blew. They feared it and it became a full blown storm. Jesus came to them in the storm. We again recall these reassuring words, 'Fear not, peace be with you, I am with you. I'll never leave you nor forsake you.' Whatever storm pressure is causing in our lives, we do not need to look into the darkness of fear, but to turn and face the light.

Father God, I read these promises and I am encouraged, but when the wind blows, if I do not have your help, I will go into fear and loose my way in the dark. Please let me know you are here. I need you every hour.

I will seek diligently to find the light when I am faced with darkness and storms.

*"Be still, and know that I am God: I will be
exalted among the heathen, I will be exalted
in the earth." – Psalm 46:10*

CHILDLIKE ADULTS

There are two conditions to seeing the Glory of God. One is to stand still, and the other is to believe. You must believe in order to stand still. You cannot be content to do nothing, unless you trust in that thing before which you are still. To stand still is to be confident that the one you stand still before is capable and willing to do what you would do, only better. God wants to do for us. He wants His glory to be seen.

Stillness, confidence, and trust are words we use for little children in good relationship to their parents. Little children are preoccupied with their parents, much as we need to be preoccupied with Jesus. This preoccupation brings, as a by-product, all my needs fulfilled. I have then placed all the responsibility for myself upon God and choose to be a child.

Father God, we live in a time when the goal seems to be making adults out of children, and even begin teaching them in the crib to use computers! Then we read of Jesus telling the people He taught to become like little children in order to inherit the kingdom of God. It is all so confusing. May we, with your help, retain all the needed childlike qualities, while maturing into functioning adults in our world. This, indeed, is the fully formed creature you intended at creation.

**I will to be simple and uncomplicated
while making worthwhile contributions to
my world today.**

"No man hath seen God at any time. If we love one another, God dwelleth in us, and his love is perfected in us." – I John 4:12

LOVE PERFECTED

It is by loving one another that the love of God is perfected in us. We cannot sit at home and wait to be perfected before we go out and love. It is in the going that we are perfected. The evidence that God loves us is that we love one another. The Spirit in us is God's assurance that He dwells in us (I John 4:13).

The reason our love is perfected is so that we may have boldness in the day of judgement. As God is, so are we in the world. We are God's hands and feet, His channel. If we are God's extension here, we will be accountable on judgement day. The love of God dwelling in us will allow us to accomplish that which will give us boldness on that day. Isaiah 59:21 reminds us that all that God is, is inside of us. He expresses all of Himself through us, as we will allow Him to. It is love that allows God to make my life a life of service to God and man.

My Father, oh Lord, our God, what a call, what a plea from your heart, to use us as a vessel for your love, to pour through, to touch the loveless world. Oh Spirit of Grace, flow into our hearts, please, and shed the love of God abroad, so that we burn with desire to let it flow out of us.

I need a love transfusion today.

"So we see that they could not enter in because of unbelief." - **Hebrews 3:19**

THE KILLING SIN OF UNBELIEF

Everything we have comes to us as a blessing from Jesus, and in our response toward Him, in faith (Colossians 2:6, 7). The opposite of faith is unbelief. Many Christians believe Jesus for salvation, but do not have the faith to trust Him for daily bread. In Nazareth, among His own people, Jesus could do very little because of unbelief. Much of the reason for unanswered prayer is the killing sin of unbelief.

Let us look at some promises God has given us. In John 14:27 and Isaiah 26:3, we are assured of peace. In Luke 6:38, God promises material, physical and spiritual blessings. But fear of giving, a sin of unbelief, will bring a curse, instead of a blessing.

In John 15:11, we have a wonderful promise of joy as we read the words spoken by Jesus. We must be aware, however, that impression without expression will lead to depression. Again, if we wallow in unbelief, and do not activate our faith, the enemy has won a great battle.

Father God, as we look in your Word, we are reminded of the host of beloved children of God that stopped short of entering into all your provision, because of unbelief. Oh God, we believe, but help thou our unbelief. Do a mighty work of grace in our hearts. Circumcise the flesh that would hinder our entering in.

I do not want to miss God's Will because of unbelief. I choose to believe today.

"And Samuel said, Hath the Lord as great delight in burnt offerings and sacrifices, as in obeying the voice of the Lord? Behold, to obey is better than sacrifice, and to hearken than the fat of rams. " – I Samuel 15:22

SAY YES, LORD!

Obedience <u>is</u> better than sacrifice. We feel so good, often times, when we sacrifice before the Lord. In I Kings 8:5, we find King Saul standing before the altar in the temple he built for the Lord, sacrificing untold numbers of sheep and oxen. Out on the hillside, he was building palaces for heathen women with gardens where they could offer sacrifices to their gods.

God would have preferred obedience in not marrying foreign wives, rather than sacrifices made for the sin of doing so. If we would obey first, sacrifice is not necessary. Obedience brings us into God's presence, empty-handed. Sacrifice is an attempt to empty hands filled with foreign things.

Obedience is putting God first. Sacrifice is the attempt to bring God to the front, by putting to death those things which have been first. How it pleases the Father to be first, first!

My Lord God, this thought causes us to blush in the spirit and to say we have been found out. We run headlong after things of the world instead of placing you first. Then as we are convicted, we begin to "unload" them, so to speak, so that we can raise our hands and our hearts to you. Forgive us and cleanse us.

I want to make God first today, through obedience.

July 16

> *"Jesus said unto him, Thou shalt love the Lord thy God with all thy heart, and with all thy soul, and with all thy mind."*
> **Matthew 22:37**

THE GREATEST TRUTH OF ALL

It is not the situations or circumstances in our lives that count. It is our reaction to them. How do we feel about them? How do we handle them? The land was given to Israel by God. Joshua led them in. They conquered and possessed, but they didn't maintain the land. Maintenance is needed in our spiritual lives, to have unbroken fellowship. Sin must be confessed and restoration sought. Again, we see that to obey is better than sacrifices offered.

Half of our maintenance is within and half is without. Victories always come from God. He provides the way and the means to maintain by our obedience. We just need to get on God's side. What is true in the natural is also true in the spiritual.

Romans 12:1 says to present ourselves to God, a living sacrifice. In John 15:12, 13, Jesus said He laid down His life for His friends. Jesus and God are our friends. We will serve them through laying down our life. It doesn't matter about me, Lord.

Father, I see I have not maintained my land in the best possible way. That way is instant, unquestioning obedience, which shows you how much I truly love you. I ask your forgiveness, and I pray you fill me new and afresh with your love and grace.

I have been willing to die for my friends, now I am ready to live for my friends.

"And be not conformed to this world: but be ye transfromed by the renewing of your mind, that ye may prove what is that good, and acceptable, and perfect, will of God."
Romans 12:2

THE ART OF CONSTANCY IN LOVING GOD

The emotions are moved, the mind reasons it out and the will chooses. "I see it, I want it, should I or shouldn't I?" The will decides, yes or no. The emotion, the intellect, and the will make up the soul of man. "I choose today, now, this instant, in this situation to love God. The seat of my emotions is fixed on loving God. I will ask the Spirit of God to make this real to me."

The mind is like an old fashioned "jukebox." When the button is pushed, it plays that tune. The mind receives and stores up whatever is given to it. It does not choose. The world, the flesh and the devil push the buttons. By an act of our will, we can decide whether or not to play the tune recorded in the old life, or to play the new melody emanating form the life of Christ in us. If the seat of our emotions is fixed on loving God, we will choose to please Him and play the tune He wants to hear.

Father, I can look at these illustrations and see clearly I should do this way. Help me, my Lord, to permeate my being in your presence and to give your Spirit free reign to change me to be yielded to you and directed by your Word, so that I may grow and mature and become a stable, productive member of my earthly and spiritual family.

I do choose now, this instant, to love God with all my heart, soul and body. It is a choice!

"And be not conformed to this world: but be ye transfromed by the renewing of your mind, that ye may prove what is that good, and acceptable, and perfect, will of God."
Romans 12:2

THE ART OF CONSTANCY IN LOVING GOD

The emotions are moved, the mind reasons it out and the will chooses. "I see it, I want it, should I or shouldn't I?" The will decides, yes or no. The emotion, the intellect, and the will make up the soul of man. "I choose today, now, this instant, in this situation to love God. The seat of my emotions is fixed on loving God. I will ask the Spirit of God to make this real to me."

The mind is like an old fashioned "jukebox." When the button is pushed, it plays that tune. The mind receives and stores up whatever is given to it. It does not choose. The world, the flesh and the devil push the buttons. By an act of our will, we can decide whether or not to play the tune recorded in the old life, or to play the new melody emanating form the life of Christ in us. If the seat of our emotions is fixed on loving God, we will choose to please Him and play the tune He wants to hear.

Father, I can look at these illustrations and see clearly I should do this way. Help me, my Lord, to permeate my being in your presence and to give your Spirit free reign to change me to be yielded to you and directed by your Word, so that I may grow and mature and become a stable, productive member of my earthly and spiritual family.

I do choose now, this instant, to love God with all my heart, soul and body. It is a choice!

"I cried unto God with my voice, even unto God with my voice; and he gave ear unto me." – Psalm 77:1

COMFORTING COMES FROM GOD

Webster's dictionary gives the definition of comfort as to "soothe or console, consolation or solace. A state of ease and satisfaction of bodily wants." Do you sometimes just feel as though you need a hug? Psalm 77 gives us good instruction concerning looking for comfort. In verse 3, we read that complaining causes our spirit to be overcome. Complaining is in the area of the soul, 'I feel, I think;' therefore the soul is taking pre-eminence. Verse 5 reminds us to think back on good times with God. In verse 6, remember the song He gave you in the night. This is communing with God in the spirit, and the spirit begins to search out God.

We will to remember what God has done in the past (verses 10, 11), this builds faith. Take a moment now to read verses 12-15 to recall the goodness of God and to praise Him for it. God inhabits the praises of His people. Tell God your complaints, not someone else thus destroying your witness and weakening their faith.

Father God, in my need of comfort, I choose to be as the Psalmist of old. I want to recall your goodness and the times of joy I have had with you. I want to stop feeling lonely and discouraged. I desire to be at peace and to be at rest in you. Thank you for reminding me of your goodness in your Word.

I will read the Word, and pray, and sing hymns to myself, until I am happy again.

"Wherefore let them that suffer according to the will of God commit the keeping of their souls to him in well doing, as unto a faithful Creator." – I Peter 4:19

THE PLACE OF PRAYER

Is there one like the lowly Jesus? No, not one! In the cleansing process, we see ourselves talking to Father God concerning our sins, and asking that those sins be placed on Jesus. We can see Jesus standing between God and ourselves, perfectly still, willing although innocent, to have that sin placed upon His shoulders. Oh what a Savior, meek and lowly.

In Romans 8:1-5, we learn that because Jesus was capable and God willing, that He, Jesus, who knew no sin, became sin for us. Sin was condemned in the flesh, where the law was broken, so that we could fulfill the law if we walk in the spirit. Only through suffering can we be made whole. Jesus suffered, if we are to be like Him, we walk after His pattern. The suffering comes from the annihilation of my own personal will and choices. Death is painful. The body wants to live.

Gethsemane is a picture of the struggle of the soul to accept God's Will. Alone, each man goes through the death to our own abilities. Our only help is in prayer.

My Lord and my God, we see Gethsemane was the place of prayer, why do we think we will be the one to escape? It is such folly! We come now, humbly desiring to lay aside our own plans and to embrace yours. We will learn of the life on the other side of the cross, only through death.

I can see my sin on the shoulders of my dear Savior. Thank you, Jesus.

"Again I say unto you, That if two of you shall agree on earth as touching any thing that they shall ask, it shall be done for them of my Father which is in heaven." – **Matthew 18:19**

THE POWER OF AGREEMENT

How can two agree? In the Spirit. If one is speaking from the soul (as it feels) and the other from the spirit (as it is), they are not saying the same thing. It will be impossible to arrive at a common conclusion (the same thing). One will arrive at a false assumption, assuming I know what you're thinking instead of being open-minded to hear what you are saying, and not judging within my frame of reference but hearing you impartially. I mean hearing the other person out, not writing the script!

We see the outward, how it appears, and base our judgements on that. It is time we get God's viewpoint. How does He see it? Let this mind be in you which was in Christ Jesus (Philippians 2:5). Jesus was led by the Spirit. In Philippians 1:9, Paul's prayer for the Philippians was that they abound more and more in knowledge and judgements. Let us judge all things by the Word of God. Then let us agree. Let us ask of God together, that we might have what we ask of Him.

Father, I believe the prayer of Agreement is very strong and sure. It brings unity and makes harmony as a beautiful symphony, rising to your throne of grace. I believe it brings great joy to your heart, and that you delight in answering such prayers. Help us agree!

I will find agreement in the Spirit with someone and pray the Will of God.

"And the sight of the glory of the Lord was like devouring fire on the top of the mount in the eyes of the children of Israel." – **Exodus 24:17**

GOD IS A CONSUMING FIRE

The Glory of the Lord is the manifest presence of God, as in the burning bush and the tongues of cloven fire on Pentecost. The sacrifices burned up on the altars during Elijah's battle with Baal's prophets. Again I say, God's presence is a consuming fire. All that is not of Himself is consumed in His presence.

Adam was made in God's image. God could come into Adam's presence because he was like God and had the God-like nature. Adam sinned, and the love of God removed Adam from His presence, so he would not be destroyed. In Exodus 19:18, the Lord descended on Mt. Sinai in fire. All that is not of God when He is present is consumed.

Jesus is God. His presence is the same as God's. All that is in us that is of Jesus will stand. All that is not of Jesus will be burned up. He said, "I in them, and thou in me, that they may be made perfect in one; and that the world may know that thou has sent me, and hast loved them, as thou hast loved me" (John 17:23).

Father we are not really acquainted with you and all your ways. You desire to come once again and tabernacle with your people. You are who you are, and you cannot change, and if indeed you are a consuming fire, then we are the ones who must change. We must allow Jesus to arise and be more in us.

I quickly and happily say more, Lord, more!

**"If thy whole body therefore be full of light,
having no part dark, the whole shall be full
of light, as when the bright shining of a
candle doth give thee light." – Luke 11:36**

IT'S NO LAUGHING MATTER

Dear Father, that my whole body may be full of light and have no part darkness.

Love is patient and love is kind, even, no especially, when the object of that love has tried you past your ability to bear it. At that precise point, the love of God kicks in like overdrive and you go right on being patient and kind. This is the God kind of love in action.

Television shows us our sinful nature in an acceptable manner. We can take out that which we see in ourselves and judge it as unacceptable, and look at it played by a comedian and laugh and "get relief" from it. In days of old, the king had "fools" who portrayed the king's mistakes in character. This can do serious damage to us, by relieving the tension sin puts on our conscience, without confessing it as sin and cleansing our hearts. When we act unloving, unforgiving and hurtful towards another, it isn't funny. It is sin!

O God, let me see my old human nature as dead, poured into Jesus on Calvary, crucified with Jesus and in the tomb, not risen to do as it pleases regardless of the cost. Jesus arose and I arose with him to a brand new life. Thank you Father, that Jesus' life is now in me. Father, I know sin isn't a laughing matter and it has to be judged, either on me or on Jesus. Thank you for Jesus' death on Calvary, for my sin.

**Christ was formed in me, and He grows
until He can be seen in me.**

"In whom also we have obtained an inheritance, being predestinated according to the purpose of him who worketh all things after the counsel of his own will:" – Ephesians 1:11

MADE JUST RIGHT

Because Christ loved us, He died to present us spotless before Father God. We have become gifts God delights in. A son chooses a bride, brings her home as his and presents her to his father. Because the father loves and trusts the son's judgements (he is a son and he was taught by the father), he accepts the bride which his son brought home. She is accepted, in the beloved son, as a member of the family. He tells his father to look at what he has brought to him, the gift of a daughter.

God provided for Adam's need by forming Eve, out of Adam, so that the material of the two would be compatible. No foreign object to rub Adam the wrong way, but a complimentary person. To be bone of his bone and flesh of his flesh, so that he would not reject her. She was made out of Adam. This is a beautiful picture of a marriage, both natural and spiritual. We are made out of our husbands as women to be part of him, our earthly mates and our heavenly bridegroom, Jesus.

Father, how sad it is to see the striving between men and women when you made a place for all of us. It is not by scratching and clawing our way to the top that we find that place. It is rather a matter of accepting ourselves for who we were made to be and relaxing into the full possession of that inheritance. Oh Father, we want to relax and lay down our weapons of war and competition. We want to say, "Come, Holy Spirit, and fill us with the knowledge of the Glory of God."

I know I am fearfully and wonderfully made.

*"Not that I speak in respect of want: for I
have learned, in whatsoever state I am,
therewith to be content." – Philippians 4:11*

CONTENTMENT

If I have entrusted the totality of myself and my possessions to the Lord, I must now reckon upon God as my total resource, refusing every horizontal source as a final means of supply. I will now choose to begin to give from my new supply. I ask God, here and now, to give me positive direction. I expect God to work on my behalf, in my circumstances, in an obvious fashion. The following confession can be helpful:

"I _____ do here and now affirm that from this moment on, the government of my affairs will be upon His shoulders. I choose that Jesus Christ, and He alone, will be Lord of my life. I choose your plan, Lord, for my life. I am no longer my own, but yours. Put me to what you will, rank me with who you will, and put me to doing, or put me to suffering. Let me be employed by you or laid aside for you, exalted or brought low for you. Let me be full or let me be empty. Let me have all things or nothing. I freely and heartily yield all things to thy pleasure and disposal. This is my commitment to you, my Lord."

Father, coming to a place of commitment is a serious thing. But Lord, we believe we must express back to you how far we are willing to go with you. We believe it gives you a chance to work gloriously in our behalf and to set into motion some things that can and will change our lives.

**We quickly say to you today, help
yourself, Lord.**

"Whatsoever thy hand findeth to do, do it with thy might; for there is no work, nor device, nor knowledge, nor wisdom, in the grave, whither thou goest." – Ecclesiastes 9:10

THE WORD OF THE LORD

The following writing is offered as a series of instruction from the Lord:

"Know ye that I am the Lord. Know ye not that what I have spoken, that will I perform? Wait ye, I say upon the Lord, I will perform it."

"Cast your bread upon the water, for after many days it shall return unto you. What is your bread? It is that which I shall give unto you. Be thou not afraid, for I am with you. Whatever I give you, that is what you are to cast. Do it quickly, for the hour is late. The time is short."

I do nothing but what I tell my prophets first (Amos 3:7). Give no thought to what you will say. It is the Spirit of my Father which speaks in me (Matthew 10:20). Listen to my voice. Trust me to speak through you. Do not be afraid. It can be no other, for you are mine and I am yours. Everything you have is from me. Open your mouth to the Glory of God the Father. From him who will believe, rivers of living water will gush forth. Many will come to the fountain to drink.

Father, we receive these words of instruction from your heart, to our very own. We confirm these words in your written Word, and our spirits bear witness. Now, Lord, we pray for a spirit of boldness to come upon us, as we agree to move out and to speak your Word as you give opportunity. Yes, Lord!

I will open my mouth and show forth the praises of my God.

"And when he was come into the house, the
blind men came to him: and Jesus saith unto
them, Believe ye that I am able to do this? They
said unto him, Yea, Lord."
Matthew 9:28

YES LORD, WE BELIEVE

When God sets you in a place, you fit! And the place fits you! When God sets you in your high place, no one can uproot you! You are as secure as God is. When God sets you in your high place, it is a secure place. Neither time, nor things of this world can move, overcome, or devastate you.

Danger: Satan attempts to break your rhythm, to separate you within yourself - the physical (body) against the spiritual, the spiritual against the physical, the mental (soul) against the spiritual and the physical; body, soul, and spirit divided, not whole.

It takes whole people to make unwhole people whole. When the blind lead the blind, they both fall in the ditch (Matthew 15:14).

Matthew 9:28 is the condition of Christ's abiding presence. God cannot force His blessings on us. He seeks in every way to stir our desire, and to help us realize that He is able and willing to make His promises true. His all inclusive evidence is Christ resurrected from the dead.

Father, how it reassures our quivering heart to hear that nothing can separate us from you. We are careful to give you honor and thanksgiving, for having such high and lofty plans and purposes for us, your children. Help us to stay in trust and to move with you in accomplishing your highest.

I am being set in my place and nothing can move me away.

"Take my yoke upon you, and learn of me; for I am meek and lowly in heart: and ye shall find rest unto your souls." – Matthew 11:29

PMHR, MORE LORD

To learn of Christ is the same as to give up to P̲atience, M̲eekness, H̲umility and R̲esignation to God, or the same as to have faith in Him. I can only give up to p-m-h-r when I can trust Him. Trust means to allow Him to do for me what I cannot do for myself. I "faith it" when I trust Him with myself. It truly means giving up all that I am, and stepping over into faith, where I totally rely on someone. I call it free falling in the spirit.

When you shut yourself up to p-m-h-r, you are leaving all you have in exchange for Him. You are in the arms of Jesus, your whole heart is His dwelling place. He lives and works in you. Patience expects from God, standing still, and seeing Him move.

When your own self in pride or impatience attacks you, stand, turned to this humble resignation. Leave yourself to be helped by God. Wait, wait on the Lord. The Sabbath of the soul is freedom from the labor of self and resting in p-m-h-r.

Father God, our natural busy-minded self shudders at words like patience, meekness, humility and resignation. At the same time, our tired soul leaps with joy to hear words it knows will bring peace. Father, we truly long within our hearts to be at peace with you. We've spent all we have in time and energy to arrive at the place you have ordained in your sovereign mercy for us to dwell in. The problem is, it only comes through giving up, through p-m-h-r!

Today, I resign chairman of the board of me and give Christ first place.

**"For how great is his goodness, and how great
is his beauty! corn shall make the young men
cheerful, and new wine the maids."
Zechariah 9:17**

GOD'S GOODNESS

God is infinitely more desirous to give than we are to receive. We need to know He is and that He is the rewarder of them that diligently seek Him (Hebrews 11:6). He has promised us that we would find Him when we search for Him with all our heart (Jeremiah 29:13). There is no shadow of turning in God (James 1:17).

God created man to receive good. He can will nothing else to man, because God is good and He has to be true to Himself. God is always good toward creation. He does nothing but from love. He pours forth nothing but rich gifts to creation, to the extent it can receive them. In other words, we need to pray for Him to increase our capacity (more, Lord). We need to learn to be receivers. We can be prepared for receiving from God, by receiving from one another.

To rightly believe in God is to believe in His love toward us. The Glory of God is the manifestation of His goodness and His mercy. We must wait on God, wait before Him to shine His light into our hearts, so that His glory may arise upon us.

Father God, we, like Moses, would ask you to show us your glory, only to learn that your goodness is your glory. How easy it is for us to see, once we consider it, your goodness is all we could ever desire or require. We love you, we praise you and we thank you.

When I think on your goodness, I will see your Glory!

"Keep back thy servant also from presumptuous sins;" – Psalm 19:13

JESUS TEMPTED

Matthew 4:1-11 is a narration of Jesus' time in the wilderness given so that we might learn. Everyone who receives the Holy Spirit has to be tried. The Holy Spirit does not try or test. He leads into the place where Satan can try or test, either to a person, place, or circumstance, that a testing can be performed. Satan does not lead a child of God, the Holy Spirit does. Therefore, God has granted permission in His loving care for us.

Jesus' first temptation was to use Divine Power for personal satisfaction (verse 3). In verse 2, we see where Jesus was hungry and weak after fasting 40 days. Satan tempted Him where His weakness was, in His hunger. Satan always offers us a way, in our need, that would keep us from dependence on God as our source. We can learn much from Jesus' response to the temptation, in verse 4.

The second temptation was of presumption. It was an attempt to get Him to disregard God's law, because He was a child of God, expecting Him to intervene in His behalf (verse 6).

Father, we can see ourselves in both of these situations, and remember countless times we have succumbed to these temptations, and prayed for you to intervene in the resulting circumstances. Forgive us, we pray, for sins of presumption and acts of foolishness. Thank you for your mercy and your loving kindness, extended to us over and over again. Forgive us our trespasses, and lead us not into temptation.

I want to come through times of testing as Jesus did, by the Word of God.

*"Be careful for nothing: but in every thing by
prayer and supplication with thanksgiving
let your requests be made known unto God."*
Philippians 4:6

HOLY READJUSTMENTS

Only the fear and the weight of a burden are burned at the altar. This leaves the heart of it exposed to God. Then it is washed and purged in a Holy readjustment. Unseen but mighty forces take this heart of the problem and work it out on the basis of His truth and perfect harmony. Readjustment in the outer life must and will follow. Everything must be brought to God for readjustment to His laws.

In times of restlessness and aloneness, you must learn to be still. Burdens (cares and worries) are to be brought to the altar and left. Problems you bring in the same way, but something more is required of you. You are to talk them over freely with God, so you may learn to choose to use good judgement for growth. They need to be untangled, thought out, and worked through. Do not waste time in idle speculation. Come within, to the mind of Christ. Make Him not only master of your soul, but master of all outward conditions. As you lay the problem before Him, clear, all compelling, definite answers will come. All circumstances shall so evolve that there will be found only one course which you could consider taking.

Father, the readjusting of all things according to your will and your way brings great joy and peace to our heart. We must quickly run to you, and freely discuss our problems that we might find solutions. Thank you for caring.

I will seek answers and not be part of the problem.

*"And grieve not the holy Spirit of God,
whereby ye are sealed unto the day of
redemption." - Ephesians 4:30 "Quench not
the Spirit." – I Thessalonians 5:19*

THE SPIRIT OF GRACE AND TRUTH

Rebellion grieves the Holy Spirit of God.
Disobedience quenches the Holy Spirit.
Rebellion says, "I <u>will</u>." Disobedience says, "I won't!"
Fellowship, communion with God, the Father, through
Christ, in us, frees the Holy Spirit to teach, guide,
instruct, and lead us into all truth (John 14:26).

Sin breaks fellowship. It unplugs our life support
system. Our new life, like a baby that is growing inside
of us, cannot yet be seen. The Holy Spirit, our life support
system, is like an umbilical cord, feeding and nourishing
that baby life. Bringing it to birthing, that what is inside
can now be seen by the world around us – a life now
manifesting the Christ within us. Our growth is the
responsibility of the Holy Spirit. We must submit to our
teacher in order to grow and come forth.

The perogative of the Spirit of God is to teach true
and satisfactory knowledge of the scriptures. It is this
knowledge that leads us into all truth about the Father.

*Father God, thank you for your Holy Spirit, and for
His teaching and guiding us. Teach us how to be teachable
and obedient to all He shares with us, so we are not cast
away from your presence. Thank you for making a plain
way for us back to yourself.*

**I will obey what I know the Spirit of God is
telling me – and be quick to do so.**

"Let not your heart be troubled: ye believe in God, believe also in me." – John 14:1

BELIEVE ME!

All that Jesus did and said, while on earth, was so that man would see and hear and <u>believe</u>. God's wonderful plan of redemption was useless unless man believes - believes in God, believes in Jesus, believes in God's power and believes in Jesus' sacrifice. Man is no better off because of what Jesus has done, unless he believes it. All that God did in Jesus, all He is doing now, and will do in the future, is so that man will <u>believe</u>.

My life must be lived so that man will believe. Jesus went to the Father. And if I believe, greater works than Jesus did, I will do so that God will be glorified in Jesus. I am to live as Jesus lived, so that what I ask, in His name, will glorify God. What I ask for must be the same as what Jesus would ask if He were here, in my place.

In John 14:15 and verses following, Jesus admonished believers to live and walk in love by keeping His commands. Then, He and the Father can manifest themselves to us, in us and through us . It all hinges on that little four letter word again, love. Love for the Father and Jesus and our fellowman releases the power of God.

Father, John, chapter 14 was spoken by Jesus and written by the apostle for our edification, comfort and instruction. The love that Jesus portrayed to his disciple, before He went to the cross, is what we are all looking for. Thank you for publishing the Bible, as a testimony to us, of your intent toward us. We receive your love gladly and gratefully. Flow through us, Spirit of God.

Love will keep me following the laws of God from a willing and obedient heart.

"And he removed from thence unto a mountain on the east of Bethel and pitched his tent, having Bethel on the west, and Hai on the east: and there he builded an altar unto the Lord, and called upon the name of the Lord." – Genesis 12:8

WORSHIP

Worship is giving God the best He has given you. Whenever you receive a blessing from God, give it back to Him, as a love gift. Take time to meditate before God and offer the blessing back to Him, as a deliberate act of worship. Then God can multiply it, to bless others, as He did the loaves and fishes.

Bethel translates as a place of communion with God, and Hai, as the world and our public activity. We must keep a balance between our place of communion with God and our public activity. Our worth in the world is dependent on our private communion with God.

Jesus was unhastening and unresting. His worship, waiting and work all flowed together. The measure of our work is that our tents are pitched where we always have a quiet time, no matter how noisy our time with the world is.

Look again at our verse for today. Abraham pitched his tent. He settled down and lived a balanced life, communing with God, amid the chaos of life.

Father, we do often feel unbalanced, sort of dizzy and shaky. We understand the need to focus in on you and your presence with us all the time, in every circumstance. You have the words of life, because you are the source of life. We want to focus on learning how to commune with you. Holy Spirit, come and teach us.

Jesus told me to learn of Him. I gladly apply my heart today to learn of Him in His Word.

"Now therefore let me alone, that my wrath
may wax hot against them, and that I may
consume them; and I will make of thee a
great nation." – Exodus 32:10

A BETTER WAY

God used the circumstances at hand to allow Moses to empty his heart of any greed that may have been there. He offered him the chance to replace Abraham as the father of God's people. In turning down God's offer and choosing, rather, to intercede for Israel, it rid Moses' heart of any and all traces of greed. This enabled him to pray Exodus 32:31 and 32 honestly. How God's heart must have been pleased with Moses' response.

To empty the heart of greed is to disengage the life forces from the destructive bondage of selfishness. This, in turn, frees the soul into the liberty of the Spirit.

What wisdom can be gleaned from this encounter of Moses' with Jehovah God! We can see that every doorway of opportunity opened to us is not necessarily to be walked through. We need to see what the Lord is after and decide if we need to go through or to "give the opportunity away." Something much better could be waiting for our humble refusal.

Father, teach us, like Moses, to look for the higher good in every opportunity. It brought more glory to you to be able, by his prayer, to salvage the children of Israel. What an unselfish thing Moses did! That is what intercession is all about. We need to be praying for your leaders and your children, not trying to replace them.

I will look for opportunity to help my
brother by praying for him, today.

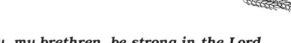

"Finally, my brethren, be strong in the Lord,
and in the power of his might."
Ephesians 6:10

SIMPLE SIMPLICITY

How can we be simple with the simplicity of Jesus? We must receive His Holy Spirit, and recognize who He is and rely on Him. This Holy Spirit is to be obeyed as He reveals the Word of God to us.

Here are some names of this Holy Spirit and also some of His functions on our behalf. He is the Spirit of truth, who will glorify Christ in us; the Spirit of love, who will shed the love of God abroad in our hearts. He is the Spirit of prayer, through whom our life may be one of continual prayer to the Father. We also see Him as the Spirit of wisdom, whereby He causes us to experience the power of God within us. There are other names He is known by, in the Word of God. My challenge to you is to discover all of them. In this way, you will become very familiar with Him.

Self-denial will enable us to accept the way of the cross. This is the way of obedience to the Word, as the Spirit of God teaches us. This is a life long process. We need to embrace the truths of God, take root, and grow right where we are.

Father, we so want to thank you that you answered the prayer of Jesus, and allowed your Holy Spirit to come and abide with us. He will lead us into all truth, and make our journey here good and acceptable to us.

I will call upon the Holy Spirit to reveal the truth of Gods's Word to my heart.

August 5

"Speak unto the children of Israel, and say unto them, When ye are passed over Jordan, into the land of Canaan;" — Numbers 33:51

INSTRUCTION FOR TAKING THE LAND

When we go on into the promised land, <u>then</u> we are to clear out the soul realm. Clear it of all the pictures, images and prideful ways as described in Numbers 33:51-53 and again in II Corinthians 10:3-6. (It will be helpful to stop and read these passages.) Let us see these <u>pictures</u> as emotions - I feel it, the <u>images</u> as intellect - I think it, the <u>high places</u> as the will (pride) - I'll do it.

The three areas Satan seeks to snare us in must be brought under subjection to the Lordship of Jesus Christ. All of the old habits and thought patterns must be driven out. They are driven out and replaced by submitting, in every situation, to the Lordship of Christ. Every action calls for a reaction; a situation must be yielded each time - not me Lord, but you.

We cannot do this by might, but by recognizing we cannot. This will bring the life of Jesus, in us, to the front. Verse 55 of Numbers 33 tells us that every area we allow the old habits and thoughts to live and rule in will become a vexation to us.

Father, it is obvious to us that this is to be a way of life. For it to work for me, I must yield to it and humbly ask you to work it into my experience. I realize that only as I submit to your Spirit will I have success.

I will submit my emotions, mind and will to the Spirit of God for retraining.

"For many are called, but few are chosen."
Matthew 22:14

WHICH WAY ARE YOU WALKING?

You have been chosen! "Many are called but few are chosen." God calls all men. The response of the heart to God's call is the key that opens the chosen. God calls. Man either keeps walking, or hears and turns around. Turning around allows us to see God pointing at us and saying, "you and you and you, come, follow me." We make the choosing possible, by having a listening heart. Those who don't listen keep walking farther away.

God keeps calling through circumstances, events, people. As they trod farther away, it gets darker. The farther they get from the light, the darker it is. The circumstances get harder. It gets colder and lonelier. Pride keeps them walking, thinking, "It'll get better. I can do it. I can make it better." They keep walking away, until they run out of will power - "I can't do it, I can't go on!"

God reaches down and says, "I have chosen you, come on home!" Pride has brought us so much pain and difficulty. The quicker we turn toward home, the better it will be.

Father, like the prodigal son, we have held on to areas of our life that we thought we could make better than you could. Forgive us of this awful sin of pride, and thank you for making the way back.

**I'm going home today. I've held out too
long for my own way.**

"Jesus answered and said unto them, This is the work of God, that ye believe on him whom he hath sent." – John 6:29

I OBEY WHAT I BELIEVE

The great need, in my life, is not to <u>do</u> things, but rather to <u>believe</u> things. I am what I believe. I only take action on what I believe. Redemption is what God has done through Jesus Christ. Atonement is what Jesus Christ has done through the power of the Holy Spirit, to bring me into right relationship with God. It is not an experience, it is a fact. I have to build my faith on that fact.

If I build on my experiences, it will create an atmosphere of spiritual bigotry. The reality of it is that I have experienced what God has done in Jesus Christ. It is not because of what I have experienced that God can use me. It is because of what I believe about what I have experienced. My believing brings me in line with absolute Deity. My believing is being obedient, and obedience is saying, "Yes, I do believe."

When two agree, as touching anything, it shall be done. God is already in line. My obedience brings me where God is. Then we are in agreement. Obedience is acting on my faith. The Grace of God, plus my obedience, means victory.

Lord my God, it is all about faith, trust, and belief. I need a revelation of you to cause belief and faith to rise up in my heart, then I will trust you. Spirit of God, thank you for revealing to me the truth of God's Word. From this revelation, I can believe.

I must read the Word of God for faith to come forth in my heart. The faith is in the Word I read.

"And Cain talked with Abel his brother: and it came to pass, when they were in the field, that Cain rose up against Abel his brother, and slew him." – Genesis 4:8

SIN

All sin can be traced to an omission, a failure to do, make, or use what we know. Every sin is the result of a chain reaction. Refresh your memory of the story about Cain and Abel by reading Genesis, chapter four. We see here, that Cain slew Abel, as the result of anger. Now let's follow the progression of a chain reaction. The anger was the result of jealousy. Jealousy was the result of an unacceptable sacrifice.

Why was Cain's sacrifice unacceptable to God? It was offered as the result of not heeding His instructions. The absence of obedience was because of an inattentive ear, or a heart that had grown cold toward God. The germ of one sin is the seed of another. We can always trace it back to some form of neglect as its beginning.

Looking at this scenario, we shiver to think of all the times we are deaf or inattentive to His instruction - the instruction that always comes to put us over, not to put us down.

Father, we can gratefully look to your Word for examples of living. We can see how it works for our good or how failure on our part brings chastisement. Help us be more attentive and submissive.

God is for me. I must listen to His instruction.

August 9

"But we have this treasure in earthen vessels, that the excellency of the power may be of God, and not of us." – II Corinthians 4:7

NEVER GIVE UP!

Treasure in earthen vessels, what unbelievable grace that is! It is the power of God at work, in spite of human frailties and failures. There are five crises listed in II Corinthians 4:7-12, where these earthen vessels would break down, except for the power from on high.

We see external pressures, in the form of situations, listed in verse 8, along with inner perplexities, brought about from our own self. Verse 9 lists inter-personal conflicts, day to day dealings with people around us. Also mentioned here are acute dangers, with the promise that God is still at work, even in defeat and mortal danger.

Verse 10 reminds us that all of life is a confrontation with death, bringing opportunity for triumph, as Christ exerts transcendent power in the mortal (earthen) vessel.

Looking at the verses in this passage of scripture is cause for rejoicing. Again, we are reminded that it isn't what we experience in life that is so important. It is how we relate to these experiences that make the differences.

Father, we need to pray that our light may so shine before men, that they will see and glorify you in heaven. All of life's situations can end in victory for your children, if we will not give up; if we will keep looking to you, as I Corinthians 10:13 encourages us to do. Thank you for never giving up on us.

Today, I will view my experiences as opportunities to praise God.

"Wherefore I also, after I heard of your faith in the Lord Jesus, and love unto all the saints, Cease not to give thanks for you, ... in my prayers:" – Ephesians 1:15,16

GOOD NEWS FOR SAINTS

In verses 18 & 19 of Ephesians 1, we see three things Paul prays that we know: 1) the hope of His calling; 2) the riches of the glory of His inheritance in the saints and 3) the exceeding greatness of His power, to us who believe.

The calling of hope is the absolute certainty that needs no visible foundation on which to rest. This calling is our life, our vocation. This hope means you are going to be who God called you to be. You are going to make it! I can begin to act like who God said that I am.

The Glory of God's inheritance is me, the saints – me and you! We are God's treasures. Paul prayed that we would know this.

Then, we need to look at the greatness of His power; we win! If we win, then we won. That means we are winners. We see here the calling, the riches, and the power of God. This includes it all. All we need for life and Godliness is provided by God. This prayer was for us to recognize who God is and to recognize who we are, then, for us to live in proper relationship to this fact.

Father God, I want to thank you again for arresting Paul on the Damascus Road, and for working with him to bring him through to be the apostle he was. What a legacy he has left us, the revelation of the mystery of Godliness. We can know you in fullness because of his sacrificial life. We know we are called on to make the same sacrifices he did. We are to pass on the Good News to those in darkness. We pray for an anointing of boldness to speak out.

I know I am a winner. God's Word told me I won!

"And he said, Thy name shall be called no more Jacob, but Israel: for as a prince hast thou power with God and with men, and hast prevailed." – **Genesis 32:28**

TWO ROADS, MY CHOICE

Not long ago, I was in a pressurized situation, knowing I had two avenues of action. The Spirit of God had the opportunity to reveal a truth to me, in this situation. I pray I can pass it along to you.

We stand in the same space, same situation or circumstance, either Spirit-controlled or flesh controlled. The difference in the outcome is measured by who is in control!

We see Jacob and Esau as examples here (Genesis 32 and 33). If flesh had stayed in control, Esau would have warred with Jacob. Jacob sought God and refused to let go, until God blessed him. Jacob was determined to go on with God, because of it he was willing to be Spirit-controlled. Esau went his way without harming Jacob.

When a child of God walks in the flesh, he lowers his protection. When he walks in the Spirit, situations change on his behalf. Our spiritual battles affect the other areas of our lives - physical, natural and financial.

Father, this is so important in the day we live in. There is so much anger and violence waiting to erupt all around us. It is our choice to react to the pressure, or step back and get in relation to you, and yield to the Spirit, before we respond. Teach us, oh Spirit of God, these life preserving principles.

I choose to be Spirit led and Spirit controlled today.

"So God created man in his own image, in the image of God created he him; male and female created he them." – Genesis 1:27

REVIVAL

Salvation is restoration of that state that man was intended to be in when he was created. When revival comes, the Spirit of God takes control of the inside of us and we become an adequate representative of what God is like; in other words, an image of the glory of God.

Man was made, or created, to reveal the character of God. Man was made to be what God is like. Sin is a lie about God. (He doesn't look like that.) The good news is that God has a plan! That plan is that I can live every day as the reflection of God. We are worth no more than what we exhibit of what we were made to be! We are, and will always be, valuable to God, because He loves us. But oh, the sadness that a thing so valuable to God can have so little value!

Jesus was the truth about God on display. The glory of a man is what he allows to be done in him. The intention of God in creation is brought to fruition, in a human being, by salvation.

Father, our heart's cry, now, is for revival, a revival where your Spirit gets inside of us and rearranges, changes, and cleans and clears the way for your image to come forth in us. We must have revival. Without it, we will perish. We cry and we plead. We beg for revival, please come.

I will ask God to send revival in me today.

"I am the good shepherd: the good shepherd giveth his life for the sheep." – John 10:11

WORRIED?

Worry is thinking turned toxic. It is imagination used to picture the worst. It will choke or strangle the worrier. It is a low grade form of agnosticism - boy, that's strong. No wonder the Bible tells us it is a sin! It is a lurking form of doubt, because it questions the adequacy of God to care for you. It is a terrible place of loneliness. Feelings of helplessness begin the cycle of worry. The mental anguish causes emotional distress and physical discomfort. It is a distortion of our capacity to care.

The good news is, Jesus is the answer to worry! Hebrews 13:5-6 is a wonderful promise we need to wave in the face of worry. Jesus, Himself, said He would never leave us or forsake us. He, as the good shepherd, stands between you and whatever would seek to harm you, misuse you, disturb or destroy you. The only <u>sure</u> <u>cure</u> for worry is the practice of the presence of Christ.

Father, we realize that anything toxic in our system is poison and that enough poison will shorten or end our life. We confess that worry about anything is a sin. We ask you to forgive us of this sin and to restore a right mind within us. We thank you for it.

The peace of God will gird my heart and my mind today, as I think on Him.

"Jesus said unto her, I am the resurrection, and the life: he that believeth in me, though he were dead, yet shall he live:" - **John 11:25**

HOPE IN DISCOURAGEMENT

We must have expectation when otherwise exasperated. When our computer is down and we don't have all the facts, it's easy to get desperate. Expectation, ie., hope, will keep us focused on the answer. In times of disappointment, we need to look for the Lord's appointment! Otherwise, disappointment will be a prelude to discouragement. We must be surrendered in order to thank God and expect a miracle.

When discouragement does come, we need to look for and to draw upon the resurrection power of God. The power that raised Jesus from the dead is ours.

We live in a new age of miracles. A miracle is the higher law of God's love. Discouragement presses us out onto the edge of a miracle! When we least expect it, God breaks through. Our only responsibility is to trust Him with whatever discourages us.

Look at the account of Thomas after Jesus' resurrection in John 20:24-29. Jesus assured Thomas it was more blessed to believe even when you cannot see.

Father, again we hear the clarion call, sounding in our heart, to stay focused on you, your purposes and your great love for us. We must stay in hope of your coming into all our circumstances with a miracle. We love you and we thank you.

I may get frustrated, exasperated, or even discouraged today, but it will not take away my hope!

August 15

*"These things have I spoken unto you, that
my joy might remain in you, and that your joy
might be full." – John 15:11*

DON'T MISS THE JOY!

Joy is a condition of the soul which is utterly unassailable by life's ups and downs. The joy spoken of in John 15:11 is conditional on verses 1-10. Please read these verses from the bottom up, beginning with ten and ending with one. The only thing that can give us life and joy is a love relationship with Jesus. He is the vine, we are the branches. Love is the life-giving sap and joy is the fruit.

Acts 13:52 tells us that joy and the Holy Spirit are closely related. We see in Romans 14:17 that the kingdom of God is joy, along with righteousness and peace. If this isn't enough, let's look at I Thessalonians 1:6, to see again, it's the joy of the Holy Spirit.

If we will abide in unbroken connection with a constant, active relationship to Jesus, we are guaranteed joy in our lives. Showing joy brings reproductivity. Experiencing joy reproduces our faith in others.

Father, I want the joy of Jesus to remain in me, and I want my joy to be full. This fullness of joy will draw others to a hunger and thirst for you. I want, more than anything, to be a fruit bearing branch. I give you full permission to prune my branches, to conserve my energy for fruit bearing.

I have the joy of Jesus down in my heart.

*"My brethren, count it all joy when ye fall
into divers temptation." – James 1:2*

SACRIFICING SUFFERING

In the listing of the fruit of the Spirit in Galatians 5:22 and 23, we see peace as the tandem companion of joy. To enjoy and be a participant of this fruit of peace, we are required to relinquish our suffering. We can see our hard places as judgement, condemnation, fate – or opportunities for learning. Joy is God's special gift to people, whose suffering has been submitted to Him. Nothing can happen to us that God cannot use for an experience of fresh grace and new growth.

James 1:2-4 helps us to see how "counting it all joy" will bring peace into our situations. The arrival of joy, in the midst of a trial, ushers in its companion peace. It opens the door, or paves the way, for peace to come and rule in our heart. Peace is necessary for patience to have it's perfect work. When we are unpeaceful, we tend to fly up and make serious blunders, thus delaying the healing processes.

II Chronicles 29:27 shows us that when the sacrifice begins, the song of joy springs forth.

Father, as we seriously contemplate the scriptures above, we have to see how holding on to hard places and bad experiences stunt our growth and hinder our possibilities. Help us learn to quickly relinquish our hard times to you and sacrifice them, so that joy will speedily come forth.

**I will see road blocks as opportunities to
learn and progress.**

"This is my commandment, That ye love one another, as I have loved you." – **John 15:12**

BROKEN THINGS

When we have experienced the Lord's love for broken things in us, we can become healers of the broken things in others (II Corinthians 1:4). We are to do and to say the loving thing, to touch that broken place carefully. To be attached to the vine (John 15:1) means to be actively engaged with the Lord in mending the broken things of this world.

Psalm 51:17 tells us the only cure for a broken heart is brokenness. We must move beyond cynicism, despair, rebellion, self pity and self-blame into sublime surrender. The miraculous, mysterious moment when we ask for God's perspective, we receive His peace and His power.

Here, we are on the hallowed ground of broken things, too broken to mend, the place of which it has been said, "I've never known a broken heart that was not healed when the person unreservedly surrendered the heart to God." From this sacred ground, we can most assuredly touch the broken heart of the world.

Father, the above being true, we can assume the only broken things not mended are those not brought to you. The woman at the well went everywhere proclaiming what Jesus had done for her and asking them to come see this man, Jesus. We need to bring others to meet Jesus.

**I plan to be sensitive to those around me.
Are they hurting?**

"Unto thee, O Lord, do I lift up my soul."
Psalm 25:1

A PRAYER FOR GUIDANCE

Unto God I will lift up my soul. I trust in God. These words open up Psalm 25, to reveal a prayer for guidance and protection. Read through the entire Psalm and then make the following prayer and confession yours, personally. When I wait upon God, I will not be ashamed. I ask God to show me His ways, to teach me His paths, and to lead me into truth.

Oh God, remember me in mercy for thy name's sake.

God will guide the meek in judgement by showing them the way to walk. He will teach the meek His way. God will teach the man that fears Him, in the way He chooses. That man shall dwell at ease and his seed shall inherit the earth. When I am looking to God, He will pluck my feet from the net. God delivers from desolation, affliction, trouble of heart, pain and sin.

Father God, we can look to your Word for comfort, for instruction and guidance – whatever need we have. The answer can be found in your Word, the Bible. We ask you, by your Holy Spirit, to lead and guide us into all truth. We can learn to trust you for protection and guidance, as we get to know you more intimately, through your Word.

**God will keep my soul and deliver me
because I trust Him to do so.**

"Yea, let none that wait on thee be ashamed:
let them be ashamed which transgress
without cause." – Psalm 25:3

WAITING

Psalm 25 tells me they that wait upon the Lord will not be ashamed. Waiting on God brings excellency of plans, programs and performances. Waiting will always be right, and will minister to the need and bring fruit. God's ways are not our ways. Waiting takes us past compulsion to reliance on God's way. We can have maximum results with minimum effort - economy of energy.

God gave Abram a vision, and immediately darkness resulted. The vision brought Abram into God's presence. Darkness resulted from an excess of light. In the darkness, <u>wait</u>. In the darkness, God is creating. In Genesis 17:5, we learn in the darkness God changed Abram to Abraham.

When the light resumes, it is to be moved out on, as a vehicle for travel. It will take you straight to the need. It will fix the need. Light heals, because light is God. Trust God enough to be faithful, to take that light where it needs to go!

Often times we see a great need and, without waiting for the light to come from God, we rush to the scene. In being ill-equipped, we create a mess, or, at best, a false hope. We need to be prepared with the truth and light of God to really be effective.

Father, dare we ask you to teach us to wait? How much better it will be if we voluntarily learn to wait, through trust. It is humbling to learn we aren't the answer to the world's problems. It's also the beginning of wisdom. By your grace, we'll get it straight. We're just the errand boy!

The truth of the matter is, God is never late,
He's always on time!

August 20

"Then spake Jesus again unto them, saying, I am the light of the world; he that followeth me shall not walk in darkness, but shall have the light of life." – John 8:12

THE TRUE LIGHT

When you have delivered the light, your job is finished. You are just the delivery boy. How the package is received and what is done with it, by the recipient, is not your responsibility. Do not be moved by the person with the need, but rather by God with the answer.

When approached with a need, any need, even one you think you can handle, go to God for guidance (light). Take the need and the needy one by the hand and lead them to the Father, through Jesus Christ. Do not become part of the problem. Rather, stay on the side of the answer. Then, when the light comes, deliver it, trusting the needy one to God.

Bring men to the light. Take the light to men. You have no answers. You know the Answer. Attempt not one thing on your own, no matter how simple it appears. Bring the Supernatural into the natural, to have everlasting results, in any situation.

Father, life is a serious matter. When we are putting our opinions into other people's lives, that, too, is very serious. May we be taken with the awesome responsibility that we have to minister the light and truth of life to those needy ones who come into our lives. It is only in knowing you and who you are that we can input into another's life.

I will pray and seek to hear God today, before I speak into another's life.

"Thy word is a lamp unto my feet, and a light unto my path." — **Psalm 119:105**

THE PATHWAY OF FAITH

When we are meek and humble before God in an attitude of submissiveness, He can guide us. It is like walking on a beam of light, from God's presence, to the deed He asked us and empowered us to perform. As we walk on that beam of light, Satan is along in the shadows whispering, causing fears and doubts, reasonings and imaginations, to creep in. We must walk on in the light from God to Jesus, the author and finisher of our faith, who is walking before us.

There are witnesses, in the stands, who have done it before us, as an encouragement that we can do it also (Hebrews 12:1). We are never alone on the pathway of faith. Jesus is in us. The Holy Spirit is in us and alongside, behind, and in front of us!

We come to God, in our quiet time, just fellowshipping with Him, enjoying and loving Him. He may speak a Word that will require action. This is when we start out on the faith walk, not looking to the right or left, but pressing on in unwavering faith.

Father God, we get excited when we look at the faith walk for what it really is - a journey through life with a very faithful and familiar friend, one we can trust!

Faith is a fact! Faith is also an act!

"Serve the Lord with gladness; come before his presence with singing." – Psalm 100:2

PRAISE

We search for God and it is right that we do so. His promise is that we will find Him when we search with all our heart (Jeremiah 29:13). Our times of obedience are accomplishing that. More of our heart joins in the search each time (Psalm 4:4). We must not grow weary in our search. Rather, we are to know that He is more anxious to reveal Himself, than we could ever be to find Him.

The reason He reveals Himself to us, when there is no conscious effort on our part, is so we will know it could not have been anything we did to bring it forth. You see, He is God, and we can never program Him. We can bring certain things about by operating certain laws, but He is God. His presence cannot be programmed.

It is His presence our heart must desire more than His works. We must come into His presence with thanksgiving and praise, and let our requests be made known to Him. Here are some of the advantages gained through praise. It:

Pleases the Lord
Raises our spirit
Arouses our productivity
Instills confidence and peace
Stimulates enthusiasm
Expands and extends our vision

Father, just thinking on these things makes our heart grow lighter. We do love you, and we want to move deeper into praise. We want to be always searching for and discovering more of you. This will take time in your presence, depending upon your Holy Spirit.

I believe God waits to reveal Himself to me. I need to go to His presence and wait before Him.

*"Ask, and it shall be given you; seek, and ye
shall find; knock, and it shall be opened
unto you:"* – Matthew 7:7

SEEKING GOD

Why don't we pray? We don't have anything to pray for! Most people want so little and are satisfied with almost nothing. Prayer is for the adventurous life. Nine out of ten people do not have a definite plan in life. Wanting nothing, they pray for nothing.

Matthew 7:7 tells us to ask. Asking is not a condition of God's giving, but rather a condition of our ability and willingness to receive. "Ye have not because ye ask not" (James 4:2). Deep desire will lead you to ask, to seek and to knock. God responds to desires, not needs. These three prayer words, in the Greek, are present tense and call for continuing action. Keep on!

Ask in admission of helplessness. I cannot earn it or provide it for myself. Children ask without shame. Seek is asking, plus effort. Many of God's gifts come as ore, to be dug out. Knock is asking with effort and persistence.

Father, if prayer is an adventure and I need to be adventuresome, in order to pray, I set my heart to ask and to seek and to knock. I will need to determine what I want you to do for me. If you answer desires, I must get in touch with what I want, in order to know what to pray for.

**This is going to be a good discovery. It will
put me in touch with myself, as well as
God.**

"But cleave unto the Lord your God, as ye have done unto this day." – Joshua 23:8

STAY CLOSE TO JESUS

Man shall live "by every word that proceeds out of the mouth of God." This is the last part of the verse Jesus quoted when tempted to rely on something else (Matthew 4:4). In John 5:17, we understand that the Father shows the Son all He does. To stay close to Jesus is a life-preserving edict.

Joshua, the mighty man of God, that led Israel into the promised land, lay dying and called the people around him. In Joshua 23, we read the final words of instruction from this precious saint of God. Verse 8 echoes the words we've already shared, when he tells them to "hold fast to the Lord." He goes on in verse 14, to assure them they can trust the Lord. Not one of His promises has failed.

May it be said of us, if Jesus tarries His return, that when we called our families around us for the final instruction, we uttered these same life-giving words to our loved ones. To say, "stay close to Jesus, not one thing He has ever promised will fail," would be a priceless legacy.

Father, we do love our families so much. We want to reassure them, at the end of our journey, that we wouldn't change a thing. Help us to adjust our lives, today, to so closely follow after Jesus that we may be able to say this.

I will listen and take instruction from the Spirit of God, to know where Jesus is, that I may be there.

*"And I will give them one heart, and one way,
that they may fear me for ever, for the good
of them, and of their children after them:"*
Jeremiah 32:39

GUIDANCE THROUGH DIRECTION

The following thoughts will be helpful to those seeking direction and guidance from the Lord. Our first directive is to <u>ask</u> the Holy Spirit to give the single eye. It is utmost in importance to focus in, when seeking direction from the Lord. Next, let God take, break and make us, after His Will. Subordination is will surrendered, not extinguished. So often, we don't know where to go, because we have such mixed emotions. We need to be surrendered to the right way.

Then, we need to feed our minds with facts. We need reliable information (truth). This comes from the Word of God and experiences of the past, both ours and others. This will require much prayer, behind closed doors. It will require some enterprises to cease, for a time of quietness and waiting. The big <u>W</u> Word, is our last point, waiting. Wait on the unfolding plan of God. This comes as impressions within, the Word without, and circumstances around.

Father, you so want to be involved in every aspect of our lives that you give several avenues by which we can determine the route we are to take. Your Holy Spirit, your Word, and our lives bear witness. Thank you.

**Have I checked the map and gotten my
correct readings for today's trip?**

*"Therefore now let it please thee to bless the
house of thy servant, that it may continue for
ever before thee: for thou, O Lord God, hast
spoken it: and with thy blessing let the house of
thy servant be blessed for ever."* – **II Samuel 7:29**

THE SECRET OF CONFESSION

In II Samuel 7, we have a record of God's promise to
David. We see, in verses 27-29, David praying to God in
acceptance and thanksgiving of this promise. David
acknowledged it, praised God, thanked Him and
confessed it was so. We understand that God's kingdom
operates by sowing and reaping. Our heart is the soil.
We sow the seed by speaking it out of our mouth. We
confess then, with David, that we will reap the harvest.

The secret of confession and of dominating faith
lies in getting a true understanding of what Jesus
actually did for you, what you are in Him, as a result of
it and what the Word promises that you can do, as a
result of His finished work in you. This understanding
comes from reading and meditating on the Word of God.
You may want to refer to Psalm 119:97-104, for further
insight into the importance of keeping the Word ever
before your eyes.

*Father God, how many times and how many ways
can you continue to encourage us to stay close to you
through the Word you have given us? Why do we so quickly
succumb to pressures around us, and abandon you and
the time we could spend with you? My Lord and my God,
I humbly beg your forgiveness for my neglect of you.*

**I will hurry to the place to be with my Lord,
not hurry away from it.**

"I therefore, the prisoner of the Lord, beseech
you that ye walk worthy of the vocation
wherewith ye are called, ..."
Ephesians 4:1

VOCATION: MY LIFE PURPOSE

Paul considered himself a prisoner of Christ, taken captive, with no choice, but to remain in bonds, serving a sentence - a sentence which qualified him to beseech, beg, and strongly urge, you and me, to walk worthy, to live up to, to give a good showing of, the vocation we are called to. The vocation is our life's purpose, the reason we were called.

Paul continuously urged his hearers to make the one who called them, which is God, proud to say, "this is mine!" Our vocation, then, is God's purpose for our lives; to walk humbly before our God, to be obedient to His wishes and commands. In other words, to grow up into the stature of Christ, who gave Himself, to be a servant to all. He said He could do nothing of Himself, but came to work the works of His Father. You can't get any better than this, children. It isn't about promotion, it's about reduction - less of me for more of Him. Paul was captivated by this very vocation.

Father, we know the apostle Paul was pleasing to you. He followed the pattern of Jesus, by laying aside his own aspirations and following after his vocation. It is in our heart to be as pleasing to you. We yield our plans and desires, and take up our cross to follow Jesus.

**I must stop today and seek to hear my
Savior's footsteps falling softly on the path
ahead, so that I don't miss the way.**

*"With all lowliness and meekness, with
longsuffering, forbearing one another
in love; "* **– Ephesians 4:2**

THE SERVANT HEART

"With all lowliness and meekness," these are not popular words in this age that we live in. This is the time to "rise up, sue for my rights, make my needs known and buddy you are going to pay for them!" This is so opposite of, "take my yoke upon you and learn of me, for I am meek and lowly." Yet, this is the way to walk worthy of our vocation, after the manner of Jesus, laying aside our kingly garments, to be identified with humanity.

Longsuffering is going the extra mile, the giving of our cloak and esteeming the other one higher than ourselves. It's forgiving 70 x 7. It's forbearing one another in love. It's saying, "it doesn't matter what you do to me, I'm going to stand right here and love you."

Living our vocation with all these attributes, no exceptions, no loopholes, not blaming others, no matter how bad it gets, is following Jesus. If I fail, I don't quit, but rather accept responsibility for failing, confess it, get up and go on. Our attitude must be, "what I want for myself, I want for you." This is truly being a servant.

Father, we have difficulty equating these words with our responses to situations, in our life experiences. Your Word shows us, without exception, these are requirements for living and ministering, as Jesus did. We do desire to be as He was on the earth. We yield to your Holy Spirit, to do a work in us.

**I will lay aside my rights today, to live and
walk as Jesus did.**

*"To whom he said, This is the rest wherewith
ye may cause the weary to rest; and this is
the refreshing: yet they would not hear."*
Isaiah 28:12

A TRIP TO THE SPA

Allow me to give a brief outline of Psalm 19:7 and 8. It will encourage our hearts. The <u>law</u> of the Lord restores the soul (verse 7). The <u>testimony</u> of the Lord makes the simple wise (verse 7). The <u>statutes</u> of the Lord rejoice the heart (verse 8). And the <u>commandments</u> of the Lord enlighten the eyes (verse 8). In these two verses we have a picture of restoration, through the Word of God, for our whole man; spirit, soul and body. One might say it's like going to a health clinic for a rest. We are always talking of taking mini-vacations, etc. Well, a trip into the Word of God is the best vacation of all!

All we need to be perfected is found in God's Word. By it we are warned, and we are rewarded for keeping it. All that we need for life and godliness are found within its pages. What use is it, to us, to have access to this knowledge, if we do not avail ourselves of it? Oh foolish men that we are, when we neglect so great a salvation.

Father, we earnestly desire your rest and your refreshing. We do not want to be foolish and look into your Word and go away, and forget what we heard. Help us to contain your truths and, by your Spirit, be changed from glory to glory.

**I want to get away with the Lord today and
have a refreshing.**

"And when Jesus had cried with a loud voice, he said, Father, into thy hands I commend my spirit: and having said thus, he gave up the ghost." – **Luke 23:46**

A GRAIN OF WHEAT, DYING

Up to this time, Jesus had surrendered His will to the Father, had chosen God's Will over His own. Here is something new. Here, He completely loses His own will, in death. The ultimate in trusting, He sank down into darkness, into death, where His will was dead, trusting in the Father to both keep Him in the darkness and to raise Him up.

We must have the same mind about the cross that Jesus had. We must see that there is nothing to save in our Adamic nature. We must agree with God, that it needs to die. The life of Christ, the resurrection life, needs to live in us. A grain of wheat must die to produce a stalk of wheat. We must totally cast ourself on God, not knowing how He will bring about the new life, leaving it completely up to Him.

Our Lord and our God, it's a new perspective to view our own life on the cross; to yield up the life force and allow you to bury us away in the darkness; to lie there until you bring forth that stalk of wheat, that new life. It could be frightening except we see Jesus. What a beautiful relationship He had with you. We hunger and thirst for that same relationship. We also know it only comes through death (trusting).

I want to go to the place with God, where I am not free to will or to choose, but where my will is lost in His, where we are so one that His will is mine and mine is His.

"Take, my brethren, the prophets, who have spoken in the name of the Lord, for an example of suffering affliction, and of patience."
James 5:10

OVERCOMERS ENDURE

God has given the accounts of the prophets' reactions to circumstances, similar to our every day life, for examples to us. Suffering is the struggle of the soul to react spiritually, rather than carnally, to afflictions that are put upon us by the carnal and the worldly. Patience can be said to be, "keeping on, keeping on" with the message God has given us, in spite of sufferings and afflictions.

Verse 11 of James 5 reveals real happiness that comes from enduring. Giving up and failing to "keep on" brings guilt, frustration and conviction. We see Job as an example. He never gave up. He endured to the end with God. Through it, we see God's tender mercy revealed. God repays endurance beyond anything we ever dreamed. Job endured, Jesus endured, Abraham endured, and Paul endured – just to name a few.

God endures. He never gives up. He is making us like Himself. So endurance must be developed in us, at all cost. We endure suffering and affliction with patience, in order to work endurance into our character.

Father, we do want to look like you. It's hard to accept suffering, until we realize it is just a mold. Before we are melted and poured into that mold, by the fire of affliction, we do not look like you. We are made into your image by the things we suffer. We say, "turn up the heat Lord, we will melt!" We cry for your mercy, Lord, not to be removed from the fire, but to endure it. Thank you for your mercy and your grace.

Joy is endurance!

244

September 1

*"Teach me thy way, O Lord, and lead me
in a plain path, because of mine enemies."*
Psalm 27:11

SPIRITUAL AEROBICS

Trials are necessary for faith to operate, and in order to go on into endurance. In every trial, we are tempted to sin. We have opportunity to choose life or death. God has provided all we need to withstand the temptation, and to be victorious in Jesus Christ, through our faith in Him.

According to James 1:12, temptation to deny the faith comes in the trial. God allows the trial, although the temptation does not come from Him (verse 13). The temptation is to give in to the flesh. When we give in to the flesh, we have become trapped (14-15). God has provided an escape through our faith. When we use that escape, our faith is developed (I Corinthians 10:13). It is like exercising - we get stronger and better able to withstand temptation.

Psalm 27:13 and 14 bring much hope for rejoicing. We must believe in the goodness of God. Wait on the Lord. Trust in Him and faith it!

Father God, the promise here is that if we wait upon you, you will strengthen our hearts. That's what is meant by developing endurance. Strength is needed to face life with its trials and temptations. We are thankful we have opportunity to develop our faith muscles!

**I will do my workout today. I will stretch a
little farther than I did yesterday.**

245

*"Neither shall they say, Lo here! or, lo there!
for, behold, the kingdom of God is within
you." – Luke 17:21*

KINGDOM LIVING

The Kingdom of God is within us. God has always wanted to dwell within His people. He cannot dwell in a perverse world. His holiness would burn it up. God seeks sanctuaries to dwell in, sanctuaries that are cleansed and holy. God dwells within His children.

Jesus and the Holy Spirit make this possible: Jesus, by sprinkling His blood continuously on our spirit, our holy of holies, and the Holy Spirit with His teaching, convicting, leading, guiding and keeping. In this manner, God can dwell in us. Kingdom living is simply having God living in us.

God cannot dwell in the earth in any other way than <u>IN</u> His children. He tabernacles with mankind through His children. It isn't what we do, it is who we are; cleansed, holy vessels, wherein God can abide. Then as we live and move and have our being in Him, His purpose is carried out on the earth, as it is in heaven.

Oh Father God, what a concept! What a thought! What a truth! If your interaction with mankind depends on your dwelling inside your people, which depends on Jesus' finished work in us, and the Holy Spirit's keeping power - we need to get serious about yielding to your cleansing power. We will never be holy any other way. We are to be holy <u>as you are</u> holy. That is you in me, being you. Help yourself, Lord.

**I will see myself today as a dwelling house
for God Almighty, and clean house!**

"...because the love of God is shed abroad in our hearts by the Holy Ghost which is given unto us." – **Romans 5:5**

THOUGHTS ON LOVE

Love is:
    patient
    kind
    happy with the truth
    eternal
    the greatest thing
    a gift from God
Love is not:
    jealous
    conceited
    ill-mannered
    selfish
    irritable
    happy with evil
Love never:
    gives up
    Hope, faith and patience fail, but love, never!

This stretches our mind to encompass attributes of God that He wants in our lives. For God is love, therefore, rightly relating to God requires a love attitude flowing in and through us. In looking at the lists above, we can easily see where self-love can be reversed in every list. This is why we are admonished to lay down our own lives, embrace the cross life of Christ and love as He loves.

Father, I cannot, of my own strength, love in this manner – I must yield to the workings in my life, of your Spirit.

I desire to love more perfectly today.

September 4

"Now the God of hope fill you with all joy and peace in believing, that ye may abound in hope, through the power of the Holy Ghost."
Romans 15:13

HOPE IS ETERNAL

We are to be filled with joy and peace in believing and to abound in hope, through the power of the Holy Spirit. God, Himself, is the source of hope. As we believe, we are filled with joy and peace. Jesus was filled with all joy, peace and hope. He believed God. God gives as we believe. As we believe, we receive. Believing unleashes the power of the Holy Spirit to work in us.

Biblical hope is not defined as the world uses the word. This definition of hope is a firm expectation based on certain fundamental truths and actions. This hope leads one to think and to work. Belief in God is conformity to the image of Christ. To the degree that we believe, we are Christ-like.

A good definition of faith is to continue to believe in certain truths, no matter what happens. Take another look at our verse for today, and see how the prayer for our joy and peace in believing comes from our God of hope. It all works as one principle. Our hope is as sure as our God. Hallelujah!

Father God, Lord of our hope, I feel so charged in my spirit to stand in faith in certain situations, in my life, that would seem hopeless if I used the worldly definition of hope. But when I see hope and faith are one and the same, so far as believing in unalterable facts, I can hope against hope, and shift into trusting you with all things that concern me.

My hope is sure, because it is anchored on Jesus and His righteousness. It can never fail.

"Having predestinated us unto the adoption
of children by Jesus Christ to himself,
according to the good pleasure of his will, ..."
Ephesians 1:5

CHOSEN OUT OF LOVE

Look with me, if you will, at one of the most fulfilling texts in the Bible. Ephesians 1:4-8 tells of God's love and desire toward His children. I will paraphrase it in the first person for full effect.

Before the foundation of the world, God chose me, in Jesus, that I should be holy, without blame, before Him, in love. The love of God begot me. The love of God allows me to stand before Him, because He loves me. He chose my destiny for me, to be adopted into His family by Jesus Christ. It is all according to God's will. He picked me out of the world's orphanage to be His own child.

It was to be to the glory of His grace, His unmerited favor. God, being God, was free to choose whomever He pleased. God can do anything by His grace. Now the whole universal system can observe God being God, by His accepting me in the beloved.

God knew in His wisdom exactly what it would take to redeem man. Exactly what man would respond to, God dealt with us according to understanding.

Father, one of the most comforting thoughts of all, is that you understand me. The cry of the human heart is for someone to understand, which we interpret to mean love. Nowhere on the earth can anyone have the depth of love and understanding that the human heart requires to be fully satisfied. Nowhere else can we find this depth, than with you, our maker and our God. Thank you for all your dealings with us, and especially for not turning away from us in our sin, but coming to us in salvation.

I am comforted and fulfilled in knowing
God loves me so much.

"The sacrifices of God are a broken spirit: a broken and a contrite heart, O God, thou wilt not despise." – Psalm 51:17

PLEASING SACRIFICES

A doubt-plagued believer may feel guilty about bad conduct or ungodly attitudes. They want to get rid of that guilt feeling, but aren't ready to confess and forsake their sin. So they begin doubting the Christian faith or their salvation, often shifting the blame for their guilt feelings from the real cause to an issue that won't make as many demands on them.

If you want peace of mind, you must be honest with yourself. You cannot be joyous and assured as a Christian, without daily confession and renunciation of evil practices. If you are practicing sin, harboring wicked thoughts and attitudes, you must confess it as sin and reject it. When you do, your doubts will disappear. God wants an honest and contrite heart.

Consecration means the <u>continual</u> separating (committing) of myself to one particular thing. You cannot consecrate, once and for all. Am I continuously separating myself to consider God, every day of my life?

Father, this is what is meant by coming away and receiving from you, the fresh anointing for each day - the consecrating, or giving myself to you, ever new and fresh. I pray to stay in this path of separating.

Today, I choose to come away early and receive impartation for today. Thank you, Lord.
"Charity never faileth: but whether there be

prophecies, they shall fail; whether there be
tongues, they shall cease; whether there be
knowledge, it shall vanish away."
I Corinthians 13:8

LOVE NEVER FAILS

Sometime ago, I put together some scripture based thoughts on the love walk. I'd like to share some of them with you here. The love of God must be perfected in me to walk the love walk [I John 4:7-21]. Love comes from God because God is love. Christ living in me is the love of God personified in me.

Love is God loving us and sending His Son to be the forgiveness of our sins. Love is made perfect in us, as we love one another. This one is good to pause and think on: we are practicing the perfecting of love through opportunities presented by others!

Love is made perfect in us in order that we may have courage on Judgement Day. When on Judgement Day we see what would have happened to us apart from the love of God, we would perish without the courage given to us, through the perfecting love of God, in us. Only in the judgement of God is the righteousness of God revealed. I John 4:17 tells us how much we rely on the love of God, in this world now, and the world to come.

Father, we thank you that you first loved us. Even when we were in sin, you reached down your loving hand and lifted us unto yourself.

I am comforted to know that
I am loved by God.

September 8

"And the sons of Aaron the priest shall put fire upon the altar, and lay the wood in order upon the fire:" – **Leviticus 1:7**

FIRE ON THE ALTAR

Fire always shall burn upon the altar which the priest shall nourish, putting wood underneath in the morning every day that the fire may not go out (Leviticus 6:12). We can see here a picture of the fire of love lighted in the soul of a devout saint, which is the altar of God. The priest shall <u>every morning</u>, 'lay to it' holy Psalms (songs), clean thoughts, and fervent desire to nourish the fire of love, that it may not go out.

The equipment needed for a time of prayer is a quiet place, a quiet hour, and a quiet heart. As we faithfully make our way to this place of prayer, we will find the thoughts above helpful in quieting our hearts. Once our devotion has been rekindled and fired, white-hot, by the Word of the Lord (Jeremiah 23:29), may we then see Jesus coming to us as a flaming fire, and enter into a period of passionate praying, as the Spirit leads.

Father, if our prayers are devoid of passion, then we are truly missing the reason for praying. Heat our hearts, Lord, with the fire of your presence. As we faithfully lay our wood in order, come with yourself, and set us ablaze.

The fire of love for the Lord burns strong after I have tended the altar.

"He that hath my commandments, and keepeth them, he it is that loveth me: and he that loveth me shall be loved of my Father, and I will love him, and will manifest myself to him." – John 14:21

OBEDIENCE: AN ACT OF LOVE

The Holy Spirit came to reveal Jesus' presence as ever with us. Christ, through the Holy Spirit, would manifest Himself to us. Through the Spirit's revelation, we would know Him, Jesus, in a new, divine, spiritual way (John 14:15-21).

Love is the condition to the above revelation. It is the love with which Christ loved us, revealed to us by the Holy Spirit. The proof that God's love has been shed abroad in our heart is that we will respond in the love of a full and absolute obedience. Obedience is a demonstration of love.

Father, we accept your teaching about the need for obedience from us toward things you have told us. Here we begin to understand what obedience is. It is showing you and all the universe, worlds without end, our love for you. We love you in response to your first having loved us. We realize that you are love and that love is demonstratable. Obedience is a positive response to the love you have held out to us. Thank you so much!

I <u>want</u> to obey Jesus' words. It's something I can do to show Him I love Him. Yes, Lord!

 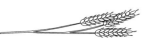

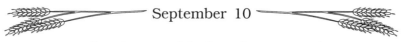

September 10

"Thou hast ravished my heart, my sister, my spouse: thou hast ravished my heart with one of thine eyes, with one chain of thy neck." – **Song of Solomon 4:9**

LOVE'S RESPONSE

The love of God needs our love, in which to reveal itself. His love moved toward us and the heart that responds is the one which is saved. God, seeing my love responding to Jesus' love (deep calling to deep). Divine love and human love united, wed, married. True marriage is God entering the soul of a man and consuming it. While the soul dwells in the holy of holies with the Spirit of God, held there before God, it is consumed. This is love beyond our ability to conceive with our natural mind.

God sees this heart of mine responding, accepting and receiving the love He offers. He is pleased. He shows His pleasure by resting His love on this soul. It is a special love drawn out of God, by the love of that heart. This kind of love causes the Lord to manifest Himself. It brings the Shekinah glory down. The Song of Solomon is a beautiful picture of the developing of this love relationship.

Father God, our Father, and the Father of our Lord Jesus Christ, we cry with the Shulamite woman in Song of Solomon 1:4, draw us, we will run after thee. We want to present ourself to you as that responding heart, that one full with desire for this love relationship you are offering. May we stay before you until you consume us with your love.

I am actively involved in responding to the overtures of love expressed to me, by my Lord.

"Herein is love, not that we loved God, but that he loved us, and sent his Son to be the propitiation for our sins." – I John 4:10

UNBELIEF CANNOT LIVE HERE

God sees our response to the love of Jesus, His Son, as the measure of our love for Him. How much <u>do</u> I love Him? My actions will show my obedience to His Word. I will show you my love (faith) by my works (James 2:18). What I do (action) is a visible measure of the depth of my love. Love and faith are inseparable. I cannot have faith that is not expressed in love. I cannot love that which I can place no faith in. See I John 4:7-21 for further revelation on this matter.

I cannot, and I will not, surrender myself to anything or anyone I cannot have total faith in. Any unbelief will hinder total surrender. We need to cry out with His followers, "Lord I believe; help thou my unbelief" (Mark 9:24).

God can come and tabernacle in a heart that is totally surrendered to Him in this beautiful love relationship, This is when we enter into the rest of God.

Father, our heart, like the saints of old, cries out to enter into this absolute oneness, this marriage of two hearts; wedded to you in a love beyond words to express. This is a work of your Holy Spirit, as we present ourselves to you. Come, oh Spirit of God, and consume us.

I place myself and all I am on the altar today, to be burned with the fire of God.

"For we are made partakers of Christ, if we hold the beginning of our confidence steadfast unto the end;" – **Hebrews 3:14**
"Whom have I in heaven but thee? and there is none upon earth that I desire beside thee."
Psalm 73:25

THE OBJECT OF OUR AFFECTION

Believing, simply, only, truly, fully, in what Jesus Christ is, and can be to us every moment, must become the main focus of our existence. He is the Son of the Living God, the resurrection that gives us power to be victorious over sin and Satan. He is our life, our true self. Blessed are those who have not seen and yet believe (John 20:29).

This is the faith that overcomes the world. Jesus must be the object of our desire and our confidence. Wanting Him and trusting Him results in loving Him. The fruit of that love will be peace and joy. When He is the object of our desire and confidence, He will manifest Himself to us in divine power. To such love, even struggling with unbelief as Thomas was, Jesus will still manifest Himself. Faith in His Word, in His divine power and in His holy abiding presence is to be the one thing that masters our whole being.

Father, we hear you calling to us and instructing us to focus in on Jesus as the object of our desire. We also hear you warning us to put our confidence in Him and no where else. Even on the mount of transfiguration you instructed the disciples to hear your Son. Lord God, we want to hear your Son, to follow after Him as He leads us home. Spirit of God, make Jesus bigger in us today.

I place my trust in Jesus and make Him my all today.

"Nevertheless I tell you the truth; It is expedient for you that I go away: for if I go not away, the Comforter will not come unto you; but if I depart, I will send him unto you." – John 16:7

THE WORK OF THE HOLY SPIRIT

The devotion we have to God is worked in us by the Holy Spirit. It is the office of the Holy Spirit to reveal God <u>to</u> us, by salvation; God <u>in</u> us, through sanctification; and God <u>through</u> us, in glorification. The revelation of God to us is our belief in Jesus Christ's work, on our behalf, to save us from sin. The revelation in us is of God's goodness. This involves all we need to rise above sin and inadequacy. The work of the Holy Spirit, through us, will deliver others.

As we look in John 16:7-11, we see these various offices and works of the Holy Spirit, promised by Jesus, before He was crucified. Verse 13 tells us the Holy Spirit will guide us into all truth. John 8:32 assures us we shall know the truth and the truth shall set us free. It is the office of the Holy Spirit to reveal the truth about God to us. He is referred to, in the Word of God, as the Spirit of truth.

Father God, we are so very thankful and grateful to you for answering Jesus' prayer to send us the Holy Spirit. Jesus had been with us personally, and He knew how limited we are in grasping the truth. He knew the temptations and the pull of the evil one against the things of God. He, therefore, requested of you to send us the Spirit of truth. Thank you for your down payment, so to speak, on eternity - your earnest money of the Holy Spirit. We yield ourselves to receive truth from Him.

I realize the Holy Spirit is a person, and He has feelings, just like I do. I don't want to grieve Him.

*"And he said unto me, Son of man, go, get
thee unto the house of Israel, and speak with
my words unto them." – Ezekiel 3:4*

WHAT TO DO WITH
THE WORD OF THE LORD

The instruction of the Lord in Ezekiel 3 is to be His
mouthpiece. He told him to let His words sink deep into
his heart. First, to listen to them carefully, himself, then
go afterwards to the people. He told him to go shut himself
up in his house whenever He gave him a message. Then
He would loosen his tongue and let him speak.

As Christians, we so often receive a new truth, and
then we deliver it before it has become life to us. Then,
because it is only head knowledge, we have to either give
it up or defend it, when others refuse to receive it. When
that happens, brothers are divided.

Wait until the revelation proves its reality. Wait until
it burns in your heart as a living thing that must be
shared in humble confidence. It lives because it is truth.
The truth of God's Word needs no defense. It needs only
to be shared.

*Father, where we have gotten ahead of you and hurt
our brothers, we ask your forgiveness. Help us to ponder
your revelatory truths until all self is washed away and
your living Word is left burning in our soul. We want to be
so much in your presence that we hear your heart. We also
know how much flesh has to die out of us.*

**I don't want to be premature, like Joseph,
and offend my brothers.**

September 15

"But Jonah rose up to flee unto Tarshish from the presence of the Lord ..." – Jonah 1:3

THE SIN OF DISOBEDIENCE

Jonah was a man guilty of the sin of disobedience. In Chapter 1, we see a man running from the commandment of God. If it had not been for the whale, he would have drowned. What we call hardship, very often is God's hand of provision. In Chapter 2, verse 9, we hear Jonah reluctantly coming along to God's way of thinking.

In Chapter 3, we can know God speaks to us more than once. He speaks as many times as is necessary. Jonah was a difficult man and viewed Ninevah as his enemy. Nevertheless, the people heard God and not Jonah. Their response was to repent. Verse 10 says when God saw their heart, He changed His mind.

Jonah preached, they bowed, and Jonah got mad! It has been said that 99% of those who commit suicide are mad at God because they can't have their own way. We are disobedient to God because He is trying to get us to deal with our enemies! In Chapter 4, verses 4 and 9, God asked Jonah the same question twice. In His loving kindness, He continues to deal with us according to our sin, so that we might be reconciled to God.

Father, may we earnestly take a look at our own hearts and see if there be any of Jonah's sins lurking inside of us. Are we hiding, or running, from facing our enemies so that we shut them up in judgement rather than mercy? Oh God, how we deal with our enemies will be how we are dealt with. Lord God, I want mercy, So, I choose to give mercy.

I'll go wherever God sends me, and speak salvation to whoever He wants to hear. As much as is within my power, I will be at peace with my enemies.

259

"Awake to righteousness, and sin not; for some have not the knowledge of God: I speak this to your shame." – I Corinthians 15:34

APPROVED FOR SERVICE

"Be still and know that I am God; I will be exalted among the nations; I will be exalted in the earth" (Psalm 46:10). Thoughts enter the mind from two sources: the devil from the outside, and our human spirit from the inside. As you stay (be still) in close fellowship with God through prayer, meditation, and study of God's Word, you learn to determine where the thought came from.

We renew our mind by studying God's Word – <u>confession</u> is affirming something we believe. To have the mind of Christ is to study His Word – <u>testimony</u> is something I know. When we believe His Word in our heart and act upon it, we are <u>witnessing</u> for a truth we have embraced. Here we have confession, testimony, and witnessing. Three levels, so to speak, of sharing the Word of God. It is dependent on the time we spend in the Word, how we share it.

Father, your Word said some of us lack the knowledge of God. Is it any wonder we are unable to bring a witness of you to those we live and work with? If we are empty clouds holding no rain, we have nothing to give. Your Word also tells us to "study to show thyself approved, a workman that needeth not be ashamed" (II Timothy 2:15). To be of any value to others, we need the goods. We confess we have not spent enough time in your Word.

I will apply myself to the knowledge of God's Word.

September 17

"And hath raised us up together, and made us sit together in heavenly places in Christ Jesus:" — **Ephesians 2:6**

WORSHIP COMES FIRST

Ephesians 2:5, 6 reveals to us that we are seated with Christ, at the right hand of God. The right hand is the place of authority. If we are Christ's body (the church), the body has to be where the head is. God carries out His plans and programs, through His right hand. This takes the form of intercession, inter-go in for another and cession - do it for them. God and Jesus are praying all the time. They are praying for the plans and programs of God to be accomplished on the earth.

Intercession comes out of worship. In worship we submit ourselves to God. We seek the mind of Christ for those He assigns us to, and we resist Satan for them. Intercession is necessary when they cannot seek the mind of Christ for themselves. We always return to the place of worship. It is the bowing down of the whole being and recognizing the God of all creation, His Son, Jesus, and the Holy Spirit, as rulers and Lords over our very lives. In this place of recognition, it is easy to submit ourselves to the highest service we can perform, that of intercession.

Father, we do want to pause just now and worship at your footstool. We recognize your sovereignty and lordship. We pay you tribute and bring you honor. Pray through us, for your world around us.

I will wait and listen for my call to intercede for others.

September 18

*"Redeeming the time, because the
days are evil."* – **Ephesians 5:16**
*"Walk in wisdom toward them that are
without, redeeming the time."* – **Colossians 4:5**

TIME MANAGEMENT MADE EASY

To redeem the time means to buy up for oneself. A time in which something is seasonable, this moment will never pass this way again. Tomorrow, even this afternoon, will be too late for now. Grab this time, seize upon, squeeze all that is in it out like toothpaste from a tube. Don't miss being one with God, in this opportunity.

I must live in 'moment-prepared compartments.' All the talent, gifting, preparation, supplies and energies are furnished by God for that specific moment. "And thine ear shall hear a Word behind thee, saying, this is the way, walk ye in it, when ye turn to the right hand and when ye turn to the left" (Isaiah 30:21). Anything else will be a direct drain on the battery, so to speak. The energizing power of the Holy Spirit is for union with God in the experiences of life. Everything else will be wasted.

Father God, life can be an exciting, challenging opportunity, or it can be just wasted time. What a delight to expect to hear your voice behind us, leading us in the direction of adventure and fulfillment. This, indeed, is Spirit-filled, Spirit-led living. Thank you for choosing to let us in on what you are doing.

**Today, I will be listening for the voice of
God to lead me.**

"Wherefore, my beloved, as ye have always obeyed, not as in my presence only, but now much more in my absence, work out your own salvation with fear and trembling."
Philippians 2:12

GOING ON TO MATURITY

Look with me at the verses in Philippians 1:7-11. Paul prayed for their love to abound more and more in real knowledge and discernment, so that they could approve the things that were excellent, in order to be sincere and blameless, until the day of Christ. Chapter 2:8 tells how Jesus humbled himself by becoming obedient, and verse 12 speaks of how they always obeyed. Because of this, Paul encouraged them to work out their salvation (by obedience). God works it in by the hearing of the Word. The only way for it to become real in us is through obedience. Hearing from God is the working in, doing whatever He says is the working it out.

If we are truly God's, He makes His Will known to us by circumstances, people, situations, His Word, and the inner witness. We do not want to take action, so we deceive ourselves into thinking we cannot act, because we do not know God's Will. We blame God, people, things or circumstances for our failure to heed God's prompting. Nothing, absolutely nothing, can keep us out of the Will of God, but our own will!

Father, I ask you to give me boldness to speak the truth, as you reveal it to me; boldness to walk into the gates of hell and snatch the dying out for you; boldness to do all things, to work out my salvation. I know it is you at work in me, giving me tailor-made opportunities to work out what you are working into me.

I will do the Will of God without murmuring or complaining. I want to be a blameless child of God (Philippians 2:14, 15).

September 20

*"Then answered the Lord unto Job out of the whirlwind,
and said, Gird up thy loins now like a man:
I will demand of thee, and declare thou unto me."*
Job 40:6, 7

PREPARE TO ACT LIKE
A NEW PERSON

Job repented. He was sorry for trying to hide from the truth. He stopped feeling sorry for himself. This is the point where healing begins. It begins when we are ready to stop making excuses for the way we have been acting; when we quit trying to prove we are right, stop all the talking, quit making alibis and start admitting our attitudes are all wrong. Being teachable is the first sign of honesty - becoming helpless and allowing others to show us the way.

In Job 42:10, we see Job taking the final step to healing. We have to do more than forgive the hurt. We have to get concerned about the needs of the ones who have hurt us and must pray for them. Let's view three important steps to healing. First, make a list of all who have hurt you, then, forgive them from your heart. The last step is to begin to pray for them and ask God to bless them. Pray that God will allow you to help them in some way. Be mad at no one, get rid of every grudge.

Father, it is frightening to even consider how many hurts and offenses have come into our lives over our lifetime. Then to realize keeping these in our hearts may very well be making us ill is beyond our comprehension. By faith, we believe this is true, and we faithfully set about, with your help, to clean our slate and to heal our minds, souls and bodies, through forgiveness. We ask the help of your Holy Spirit to recall all the hidden hurts.

**I want to walk out into a life totally devoid
of hurts and offenses!**

"But godliness with contentment is great gain."
I Timothy 6:6
"And when Moses heard that, he was content."
Leviticus 10:20

THE SATISFIED LIFE

The dictionary definition of contentment is, "modestly satisfied." When our motives are right, our hearts pure, and we move on the command of the Lord, we can say we are living modestly contented lives. This way of life will require us to receive a renewed mind. Proverbs 2:8 tells us that "God keepeth the paths of judgement and preserveth the ways of His saints." We are also told that He (God) lays a stone in Zion and those who know that are never in haste (I Peter 2:6).

Haste is the flesh not wanting to suffer, but hurry and "get it over with." Notice how much quicker you take a cold shower or hurry into a warm place out of the cold? Satan will use the impatience of our flesh to wear us out! Hastening can drive us quickly beyond God's Will, or cause us to move prematurely and miss opportunities to succeed. There is a temptation in haste to do more than we should. We are exhorted in Luke 21:19, "in your patience, possess ye your souls."

Father, we can honestly say that at times we feel like we are driven by forces to hurry, to speed along at break neck speeds and then not be able to rest when we arrive. This is not living life as you put it forth to us. It is being worn out and misused and made to feel of no use. Help us move into this area of modest contentment where our soul is satisfied. Thank you for promising never to leave or forsake us (Hebrews 13:5). This knowledge brings great comfort to our hearts.

**I am satisfied with Jesus, and my life must
reflect that to others.**

"...the lust of the flesh, and the lust of the eyes, and the pride of life, is not of the Father, but is of the world." – I John 2:16

LOVE NOT THE WORLD

God wants us to see, know, recognize, admit and then quickly repent of the fact that there is no good thing in us. Those God can use mightily are quick to repent. They are quick to recognize the need of repentance, because of the lack of any good of their own. They are quick to take action on this revelation, and to keep 'short accounts' with God. We must judge every thought, Word and deed by Jesus Christ and His righteousness. We must choose to be done with sin.

Repentance is saying, "I am done with and want no part or portion in sin. I am agreeing with God against my sin and I am moving over to His side of the line." Repentance lines me back up with God's verdict against sin. Repentance is choosing God's way over mine.

The "pride of life" is choosing my way over God's. The pride of life always resists the true work of the Holy Spirit (Acts 7:51). Pride of life, in operation, strikes fear in the heart - fear, guilt, doubt, works of the flesh, and then depression (Romans 3:20). What a tool of the enemy, to bring us into the place of utter uselessness. Repentance is trusting God, depending on God.

Father, how quickly we get caught in the web of self-fulfillment, and what a ride to destruction it brings. In humbly coming into your presence, confessing that we "blew it" and turning from the path of destruction in obedience, we find our peace and joy restored. Thank you for I John 1:9 and the way of restoration, through Jesus Christ.

I will be quick to admit my failures and sins.

September 23

"Submit yourselves therefore to God. Resist the devil, and he will flee from you." – James 4:7

ISN'T THERE AN EASIER WAY?

God has made provision for us in every area: for sin– the blood of Jesus Christ, for the flesh – the cross of Calvary, and for Satan– the name of Jesus. The blood will not work on the old man (flesh), nor will it work for the devil and his demons. You cannot wash demons in the blood.

We are to confess the sin and crucify the flesh, cutting the ground out from under Satan. He needs live flesh to work his will through. Last of all, we cast them out and break their power, by the name of Jesus. As we confess sin, and enter into God's presence, then submit to Him by crucifying the flesh, we come under authority, and the name of Jesus is rightfully ours to use against Satan, and he has to flee!

More times than a few, we find ourselves calling someone to pray with or for us, because we are "under-attack." All the while, the flesh is the culprit. Let us study the above maxims and seek to discover the truth.

Father, we confess we always want the easy out when left on our own. It is only by the convicting power of your Spirit that we are brought face to face with things as they really are. Until we throw ourselves wholly over on your side we will not have victory. We've used enough band-aids, we need open-heart surgery. Thank you for making all provisions for us.

I choose to submit my flesh to the work of the cross so that I might be under God's authority.

"And after six days Jesus taketh Peter,
James, and John his brother, and bringeth
them up into an high mountain apart, ..."
Matthew 17:1

ALONE IN HIS PRESENCE

Follow the disciples up the mountain with Jesus as it is recorded for us in Matthew 17:1-8. Jesus took Peter, James and John up to a high mountain and as they beheld Him, His countenance changed. They began to behold Him in His Glory, not as a surface view reveals. They began to have spiritual truths revealed to them as they were alone in His presence.

In verse 4, Peter wanted to make the things pointing to Jesus equal with Jesus. Isn't this just like us? Not knowing how to act in the Lord's presence, we try to do something religious! Verse 5 shows God Himself instructing Peter in the truth of Jesus' position, above all else. He was saying, 'I have given Him my stamp of Divine Approval. You better listen to Him!'

If we are to learn the supreme truth of this passage we need to understand verse 8. As they lifted up their eyes, they saw no man but Jesus. Times alone with the Lord draw us into His presence where we get in touch with Him as He really is.

Father, we see here the truth that we will not know Jesus as He is until we draw apart into a place with Him alone. In this place, you will reveal the truth about Jesus to our hearts by your Holy Spirit.

I will run to the quiet place
to learn about Jesus.

"See then that ye walk circumspectly, not as fools, but as wise," – Ephesians 5:15

A FOOL VERSUS THE WISE MAN

The dictionary definition of a fool is: without reason, reckless and inconsiderate habit of mind. It is lack of common sense perception of the reality of things, natural and spiritual. It is a moral reproach as contrasted with sobriety in Ephesians 1:17 and I Peter 2:15. We see a fool referred to as being without discernment or understanding in Romans 1:21. He is also described as unintelligent. Therefore, his heart is darkened.

Again, in Ecclesiastes 2:19, the fool is contrasted with the wise man. Ephesians 5:15 exhorts us not to walk as fools, while Job 5:2 tells us wrath killed the foolish man. Proverbs 20:3 infers that fools walk into areas that the wise would stay away from, such as strife.

For the ultimate comparison of the fool and the wise man, we need to read the story of the ten virgins in Matthew 25:1 13. As the closing hours of this age as we know it draw near, we are hereby warned not to be foolish. Rather, we need to spend our days applying ourselves to wisdom, so that when the Bridegroom appears, we will be ready!

Lord God, we are sure of the definition of a fool, through your Word. We now want to declare unto you, we would not be foolish. Teach us, by your Spirit of wisdom, how to be wise. Then we can fill our vessels with oil and be prepared.

I will apply my heart to wisdom and my hands to obedience.

September 26

*"But ye, beloved, building up yourselves
on your most holy faith, praying in the
Holy Ghost, ..." – Jude 20*

PRAYING IN THE SPIRIT

Praying in the Spirit builds up the Christian to live the ordinary life every day. It helps us to grow in faith. We are admonished to fight the good fight of faith (I Timothy 6:12). It is always a matter of faith, for the just shall live by faith (Romans 1:17). If we are told to live by faith, then we need a bunch of it. It stands to reason that our faith needs to grow, so we will always have enough for all occasions.

The Word tells us it is impossible to please God without faith (Hebrews 11:6). We don't always understand, and lack of understanding makes us depressed. Praying in the Spirit builds faith when our understanding is darkened. It is a bridge between what we know and the faith we need to believe what we don't know. I Corinthians 14:2 says the Spirit speaks mysteries to God. Mysteries are things I am ignorant of because my understanding is darkened. As I pray in the Spirit, I get understanding.

Father God, what a precious thing you have done for us, in allowing your Holy Spirit to be available to us, and providing the opportunity for us to receive the faith we need to meet all of life's challenges. We yield ourselves to your Spirit, to pray through us, things we don't even know we need.

**I believe the Words of God written in
Romans 8:26-27 and trust the Holy Spirit
to pray for me.**

"Rest in the Lord, and wait patiently for him ..."
Psalm 37:7a

ACTIVE IN REST

The Word for today is "faith." There is an action that is necessary in a waiting time. Submission of will and desire is required and then a posture of obedience. It is not a passive rest, but rather a posturing of readiness for quick obedience. The Word of God continuously exhorts us to action, to be strong in faith, give Glory to God and to be fully persuaded. We are also encouraged not to let our heart be troubled, neither let it be afraid. We are not even to permit fearfulness.

We are to keep our heart, to gird up our minds, to follow peace and to offer praise. Actions of faith are required, even in the rest periods. Acts of obedience show forth good faith. Things are never as they seem. It is Satan's strategy to interpret things to you, through your mind, by getting control of your thinking process. You must keep control of your mind. You have a choice of what you think about. Let the Word of God, by faith, interpret the reality of things to you. Get the Word on it, accept it by faith, and your senses will come along.

Father, we can see, by the instructions above, we are not to wait by sitting idly with folded hands. Rather, we are to be actively exercising our senses in faith. We are to rely on your faithfulness and act when the time is right.

**A time of rest is a good time to acquaint
myself with the Lord.**

"And when ye stand praying, forgive, if ye have ought against any; that your Father also which is in heaven may forgive you your trespasses." – Mark 11:25

FORGIVENESS

I do not have to excuse sin in order to forgive. I only forgive the person the hurt their sin inflicted on me. We live in an imperfect world, among imperfect people. Forgiving is releasing the other from expectations I had for them to perform, in a manner prescribed by me! God has a right to expect certain behavior. I do not! When a person falls short, or misses the mark of God's prescribed behavior, it is sin, accountable only to God.

A person related to me, by whatever means, can and does affect me when they sin. This is why we are to forgive them, as God has forgiven us. I cannot forgive the sin, that's God place. What I am to forgive is the sinner and what his sin did to me.

You bind the person you cannot forgive to you. It is a soul tie. You are in the thing with them. Forgiveness looses the person to God for action, either forgiveness or judgement.

Father, all of us have painful memories of wrongs and hurts suffered because of another's harshness or rudeness. We have carried many of these hurts a lifetime, only to have them surface at inappropriate times, and damage our lives. May we lay each one of them at your feet – and forgive. It's not worth carrying these loads to our own destruction.

I choose to forgive every person I can consciously recall hurting me in any way.

For the kingdom of God is not in word, but in power." – I Corinthians 4:20

RETURN TO OUR FIRST LOVE

The kingdom of God consists of power, moral power and excellency of the soul. We live in a moral universe. III John 2 says, "I would that you prosper," or have a good journey. In John 10:10, Jesus said He came that we would have life and enjoy it. Life does not consist of things we have. It is the quality that counts not the quantity.

III John 2 goes on to say we will have a good journey, even as our soul prospers. Excellency of soul is a requirement for a good life. We must go back to where we got off, if we are to go on with God. We, as the people of God, have lost our first love (Revelation 2:4 and 5). There must be repentance for having strayed from God before restoration can come. That will bring revival.

It is not enough to say we are sorry. We have to prove it by our works, by returning, retracing our steps to where we got off. One day the church will judge the world. Now, in preparation for that time, God is judging us.

Lord God, no stronger or more serious charge can ever be laid to your people than that of forgetting or forsaking our first love. It is in this love relationship that we will be perfected now, as well as that quality we will need in judgement.

I am serious about turning from my sin of cold love and going back to the place of burning love for my Lord.

"...for the joy of the Lord is your strength."
Nehemiah 8:10b

THE PRESENCE OF GOD

What emotion is evoked when you stand in the presence of the Lord? Peace, joy, love, anger, fear, pain? In Genesis 3:8, I believe Adam and Eve felt fear when God approached. In Exodus 33:14, God promised Moses rest. I believe that brought forth peace in Moses. Over in Jonah 4:6, it seems like anger was present in Jonah's encounter. A look at Acts 6:9-15 shows an incredible story of love coming forth from God's presence. Peter, in Matthew 26:69-75, experienced a deep and burning pain when he denied knowing Jesus.

There are many other examples throughout the Bible, but let's look at one more. Hebrews 12:2 mentions that it was joy our Lord experienced in the embracing of the cross life. We can look at many scriptures that indicate joy is a very accessible reaction to the presence of the Lord. It is even recommended often, by Jesus Himself, as the secret of enduring many hard places in life.

Lord God, we want to look again at the emotions displayed by various individuals, as they had encounters with you. Which of these will be our experience? Oh God, cleanse our hearts, so we will be free to experience love, peace and joy only in your presence.

**I will draw joy from the wells of
salvation today!**

"But he said unto me, Behold, thou shalt conceive, and bear a son; and now drink no wine nor strong drink, neither eat any unclean thing: for the child shall be a Nazarite to God from the womb to the day of his death." – Judges 13:7

EYE TROUBLE

Today, let's consider Samson's life. In Judges 14-16. Samson had eye (I) trouble! It was his eyes (I's) that opened the door for the oppressors to put his eyes out (16:24). We see in Chapter 14, verse 8, that he had killed the lion, but it's carcass wasn't buried. We renounce some besetting sins, but leave their "carcasses" lying around and, in weak moments, we return to them for nourishment to our flesh.

His was a life called of God before he was born. Judges 13 records his conception and birth. Yet, as we watch his life progress, he was always going after the things he <u>saw</u> and wanted, forbidden things. What a challenge he must have been for his parents, knowing the call of God on his life (13:7). In Chapter 14:1, he <u>saw</u> a woman and married her. Yet, it wasn't a good thing. Read the entire fourteenth chapter for the whole story. We all know his problems with Delilah, his eventual imprisonment, and the loss of his eyes.

We don't have to leave Samson here. We see, in Judges 16:28, when Samson prayed to God, he was used mightily to bring down the enemy's house.

Father, you place a high calling on the lives of those you would use. We also know the calling is so inadequately followed, because of our willfulness. What a comfort it is, for those of us who have messed up a lot, to read of Samson's end. How much better it would be, though, to come into obedience at an early age.

I'll forget my failures, as I have repented, and go on to fulfill the call on my life, <u>now</u>.

"But the Lord said unto Samuel, Look not on his countenance, or on the height of his stature; because I have refused him: for the Lord seeth not as man seeth; for man looketh on the outward appearance, but the Lord looketh on the heart."
I Samuel 16:7

LETTING GOD CHOOSE

In I Samuel 16:7-9, we have a powerful example of God giving His people what they want, so they could learn what He tried to tell them. We have two ways to learn, experience or obedience. Unfortunately, we seldom learn any way but through experience. In Chapter 7:3, Samuel carefully laid out for Israel the steps for deliverance and success. For a season, they did as God commanded. As long as Samuel led them, they prospered. In Chapter 8:4 and 5, their elders saw Samuel fading and his sons coming to leadership. They asked for a king, instead, like all the other nations around them.

It was a sad day for Israel, Samuel, and the Lord. Nevertheless, God told Samuel to do as they asked (8:7-8). They were so delighted to have their own way, they didn't hear what a king would require of them (verses 11-18). The saddest words of all are found in verse 20, "We want to be like everyone else!"

In their selection of a king, they looked after the outward man (Chapter 9:2). God has warned us to always look after the heart. He used Saul to drive these truths home to the Israelites.

Father, we still look at the outward man when selecting our leaders. After we set them up in places of leadership and their true nature surfaces, it is a bitter pill we swallow. You had chosen David, a shepherd boy, ruddy of complexion and seemingly too simple. What a battle ensued before the right leader was raised up. We repent of looking at the Madison Avenue slick covers and choose to seek your leaders.

I will be careful about who I follow. I want to be sure it is God's ordained leader.

"I therefore, the prisoner of the Lord beseech you that ye walk worthy of the vocation wherewith ye are called." – Ephesians 4:1

WHO DO I LOOK LIKE?

In I Peter 2:3-5, we have a description of a holy priesthood, a call to the private ministry unto the Lord, so beautiful to Him. Going on to verses 9 and 10, we learn about the elect, the public ministry of the children of God. Ephesians 4:1 is a call to walk worthy once the Holy Spirit has come upon us to possess us for the purposes of God. Also, the admonition is to see that everything in our inner life corresponds to that purpose.

In John 1:12,13, we have the Greek word, "Tek'non," used for the sons of God, describing the birth, rather than the dignity and character of the relationship between child and parent. Over in Romans 8:19, the word, "huios," describes the relationship of a child to its parent, manifesting the character or nature of the parent. In simple language, we can say that we are born babies, still children of God, but encouraged to grow into the full stature of adult children; children who can then go on into a productive relationship, as partnered with the parent.

Father, you invest all of yourself and your kingdom in "rearing" your children. We see how you sacrificed Jesus, your only son, to birth us, and then gave your Spirit to nurture us, to bring us to adulthood. We want to thank you and tell you how humbled we are to have experienced all of this individual care and tutoring. We want to take our place now as mature, functioning children and sons in your household. Lead us where you would have us go.

I will be recognizable as a child of God by my God-like character.

"And if any man shall take away from the words of the book of this prophecy, God shall take away his part out of the book of life, and out of the holy city, and from the things which are written in this book." – **Revelation 22:19**

LIVING WITHIN BOUNDS

Boundaries are for our good and for our well being. God gives us boundaries for this reason. Moving or altering these boundaries will get us in trouble. Within these boundaries are joy, peace and righteousness. Salvation is the boundary for the people of God. History is a story of mankind altering and moving boundaries prescribed by God, for preservation and safety. It's man's laws versus God's laws. As man lowers his law more and more; we are called more clearly to follow the higher law of God. For a time, it appeared, there was a grey area, but as the end time approaches, it's clear to see it is only black or white.

As the bride is preparing herself to meet her king, there is more pressure being applied to be responsible for the keeping of God's law. In practical application, we can see that moving boundaries consists of putting in my own willful intentions, and refusing to let the Word of God have its way in my life. It's a form of idolatry and rebellion. In these days, it's a dangerous place to be in, this place of uncertain landmarks.

Father, we take your words of warning to heart, and we quickly move to restore and to cleanse our boundaries, by confessing where we have willfully disobeyed your teachings and commandments to us. It is the only safe place we have, this land you have given to us and designated as our inheritance.

I will be bold to lift the banner of God's truth higher today.

**"The Lord doth build up Jerusalem: he
gathereth together the outcasts of Israel."
Psalm 147:2**

BLACK AND WHITE

In Genesis 30:32-43, we have the account of Jacob's
cattle. He had worked as a hireling for his uncle Laban
and earned his wives and all that he had. Now he is
starting his own herd and it's all spotted and mingled.
Laban's herds were perfect and he was willing to give up
the less perfect ones to keep Jacob working for him.

We can look at Jacob's flocks and herds and see a
picture of the new thing God has said He would do on the
earth (Isaiah 43:19). He has promised to build up
Jerusalem and He is starting with the outcasts. There are
several references, in the Word of God, to the saints being
the off-scouring of the earth and not many wise among
them. We are looking at a soon coming move of God, that
will sweep many, who now feel like outcasts, into the
kingdom of God.

To be presented to God, we must be perfect. That lets
all the "spotted and mingled" out, doesn't it? No. No way,
for Jesus is perfect! We are all gathered into His bosom
and become perfect, in Him. It is Jesus, our shepherd and
high priest, who presents us perfect to the Father.

*Father, we know how spotted and mingled we were
when you "cut us out of the world's herd" and presented us
perfect in Jesus. Now, from this place, we must see every
person we meet, as perfect in Jesus. The outcasts of the
world are the beginnings of great herds and flocks for you.*

**I will remember where I came from when
tempted to look down on another.**

"And fear not them which kill the body, but are not able to kill the soul: but rather fear him which is able to destroy both soul and body in hell." – Matthew 10:28

FEAR

Vine's dictionary defines fear as "phobias." It first had the meaning of flight caused by being scared. It denotes cowardice and timidity. I Timothy 1:7 tells us this "spirit of fear" is not given to us by God. In Revelation 21:8, the fearful are first in the list of transgressors.

Anxiety can be referred to as a disturbed state of mind, produced by real or imaginary fears, a condition resulting from fear of failure. This fear is an emotion that overpowers the reasoning ability of the mind. It yells "Danger!" – danger that says risk or peril is at hand, and throws you into fright or flight. Anxiety brought about by fear temporarily bypasses reasoning and goes into imagination. Look with me at II Corinthians 10:3-5 where we find a very important exhortation to pull down imaginations and not let them become strongholds in our minds.

Fear can be a paralyzing emotion and, if entertained, can bring us into a state of anxiety that causes all kinds of problems. The right kind of fear is a reverent state of heart and mind toward God and it brings great peace.

Father, we recognize fear and anxiety as crippling enemies that Satan uses to isolate and hurt us. It can put us into such a place of separation, that we have no life. Your Word tells us you came to give us abundant life (John 10:10). We will not be denied. We cast imaginations down, and we return to normal patterns of thought, by keeping our minds fixed on you.

**I will not fear what man may do to me.
I will walk freely and serve my Lord.**

*"For we have not an high priest which
cannot be touched with the feeling of our
infirmities; but was in all points tempted like
as we are, yet without sin."* – **Hebrews 4:15**

I MUST TELL JESUS

We are telling everyone we know, instead of telling Jesus. They can listen and commiserate with us, or offer alternative problem-causing solutions. But Jesus can give us the answer. We often times cry out <u>at</u> Him, railing against Him, against the thing He has moved into our path, to bring about some changes in us.

Reading His Word is like watching a video of the scenario facing us, and seeing how Jesus responded in similar circumstances. When we do this, we can see how we are to be changed by responding in our circumstances as Jesus did, in like circumstances, in His life.

The Epistles expound on the Gospels, teaching us, by revelation, how we can act like Jesus. They are letters of instruction to actual churches. Just read the Word of God and pray for the power to do likewise. We have the power residing in us. We have to pray to release it. We must give the Spirit of Grace permission to make Jesus real in our experience, every day.

Father, we can see Jesus in the Word and He becomes so much more real to us. When we see Him responding to things we are facing, we know He's been there and that He can understand. This, in turn, makes me want to talk things over with Him.

**I will tell Jesus all about my problems and
let Him give me the right answers.**

*"Nevertheless God, that comforteth those
that are cast down, comforted us by the
coming of Titus;"* – II Corinthians 7:6

RECEIVE THE COMFORT OF GOD

One of the ways God comforts us, is by sending those we love to us, in a time of need. Paul was dejected by the strain of things. He had trouble at every turn, wrangling all around him, even fears in his own mind. God never removed the strain, He comforted him in that strain.

Paul's letter had caused the Corinthians pain and they were upset with him. Nevertheless, they allowed the pain to be guided by God, and it worked Godly repentance. This caused them to be sorry for being upset at Paul. He was human, and when he caused pain, even directed by God, he suffered. This pain did not cause Paul to stop being obedient to God, but he suffered because of it.

In this time of loneliness and hurting, God sent Titus to him. He was just what Paul needed. Look with me at II Corinthians 7:7, "And not by his coming only, but by the consolation wherewith he was comforted in you, when he told us your earnest desire, your mourning, your fervent mind toward me; so that I rejoiced the more."

Father, we see here a picture of the minister taking the Word of the Lord to a people. This Word can sometimes be one of correction and not always received well. At the same time, we see a group of believers who took the Word of the Lord, at all costs, and let it find its mark. What a wonderful picture of true believers, living Godly lives. We also get a glimpse of your heart, in going the rest of the way and sending comfort, in the form of Titus, to your beloved Paul. We want to be believers like these, ministers and saints.

**I will both give and receive the Word of the
Lord, without counting the cost to myself.**

"The Lord shall increase you more and more, you and your children." – **Psalm 115:14**

SEEDS OF RIGHTEOUSNESS

Over the years of teaching many young women, a recurring concern has been, "What about the damage my sins have caused my children?" They are well aware of the forgiveness of the sins, but they also know the repercussions they caused. Today, I have wonderful words of promise to all our hearts that are deeply concerned about our families. Look with me in Psalm 115:12-14 and read of the promise that our families will get purer and purer!

Some families begin on the wrong foot, but later improve. Judah was one family like that, and so may yours be. Do not despair if your family began on the wrong track. Whatever has happened in the past, you can now claim the righteousness of God for your family (II Corinthians 5:21).

I encourage you to continue planting your fields with seeds of righteousness. For a season the tares will continue to grow with the wheat, but as you persevere in righteousness, those tares will be choked out by the good crops, and you will yield the harvest in the lives of your children and your grandchildren.

Father, these promises are like fresh rain falling down from heaven on our hearts. We get our eyes off of you at times and get caught up in our failures. Thank you for restoring our hope and our faith to keep on keeping on. We realize we will reap if we faint not. The joyous reward is seeing our Godly offspring.

I will sow seeds of righteousness into my children and grandchildren today.

**"He giveth power to the faint: and to them
that have no might he increaseth strength."
Isaiah 40:29**

JUST A GLANCE

In verse 28, we read that God faints not, neither is He weary. This is part of His six-fold omnipotence. We go on, in verse 29, to be reminded that He gives this ability to those who do not have it. Therefore, when we are reminded often, in scripture, to wait upon the Lord, it sounds like a great idea! Wait, here is a Hebrew word, "qaval,"—to expect, to bind together by twisting. Wow! When He and I are bound together in this manner, how can I not be strong?

Psalm 25:3 tells us none of them that wait on God will be ashamed. Psalm 37:9 says they that wait upon Him inherit the earth. A fuller description of wait, as used here, is to look for, to wait patiently, to trust, to be confident and to look for patiently. This is a posture of waiting for a good thing to happen!

Psalm 123:2 is a favorite of mine: waiting for just a glance. That's all it takes for one who has assumed a posture of waiting; to know it's time to move out. Isaiah 40:31 then tells us of the glorious results of waiting in the above described manner. It is a time of renewed strength and going forth, without fainting or being weary. Can we want anything less?

Father, we are encouraged so many times, in your Word, to WAIT on you. We are like little children, always running ahead, getting into all kinds of mischief, when matching our stride to yours can be all glorious. Help us to get in step, Holy Spirit.

**I want to match my steps to God's
and not run ahead.**

*"And the thing was known to Mordecai, who
told it unto Esther the queen; and Esther
certified the king thereof in Mordecai's name."*
Esther 2:22

RELEASING THE HAND OF GOD

Prayer gives God the moral right to act. It releases the righteous nature of God to act on our behalf, and still be righteous and fair to the enemy. What we often fail to understand is the moral nature of God and the way the universe operates. Our day is a time of gross immorality, and it is a temptation to try to get God to "cut corners," so to speak, and shave off knotty problems. No, God will always be true to His nature. Prayer can and will bring us into line, in asking and releasing God's hand to move in righteousness.

As Jesus realized personally, in His humanity, that He could do nothing, He entered into His closet. It was a quiet place where His spirit and the Spirit of God became one, so that when He returned, He returned with the solution. Personally, then as a man, Jesus did the works of His Father, to the Glory of God.

We can see Queen Esther as a human vessel, made aware of a need by Mordecai (the Holy Spirit). Her response was as Jesus' was and as ours is to be. She quickly went to the king with the matter. Verse 23 tells us of the success of her endeavor.

Father, when we realize you move, in your universe, in response to the prayers of your people, we will become serious about praying. In Philippians 4:6, you told us to pray about everything. Holy Spirit of God, move on us with a spirit of prayer, that we might desire to be about our Father's business.

**Today, I receive the call to pray about
things that concern God.**

 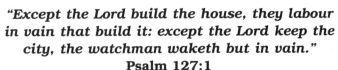

"Except the Lord build the house, they labour
in vain that build it: except the Lord keep the
city, the watchman waketh but in vain."
Psalm 127:1

BOW OR BREAK?

Nebuchadnezzar was a ruler in Daniel's day. We see, in Daniel 4:30, he was surveying his kingdom, all he had accomplished. In verse 31, we see that God decreed he would be taken away from it all, for a period, until he recognized it was all of God and none of his own doing, until he confessed God supreme in every affair of man, the raising up and the putting down as God's sovereign choice.

There are no self-made, lone rangers in the body of Christ. Unless the Lord builds the house, they that build it labor in vain. II Chronicles 20 records, for us, the story of a king with a problem. He was instructed by God to position himself and watch the Lord deliver him (verse 17). In verse 20, the king told Judah to listen to him and put their trust in the Lord their God and they would be established. Read the entire twentieth chapter to see the reverse of the fate of Nebuchadnezzar. We stand in the way of these kings who were mere men. The choice is ours.

Father God, who would want to be Nebuchadnezzar when they could be like Jehoshaphat? The results always come out the same. Those that bow and humbly recognize the Lord come out winners, and those who will not bow always break, eventually. We do want to pause, just now, and give you thanksgiving and all the praise and honor you so richly deserve.

I will be quick to lay all the crowns of life at
the feet of my Savior, Jesus Christ.

*"O Lord, how manifold are thy works! in
wisdom hast thou made them all: the earth
is full of thy riches."* – Psalm 104:24

ORDER IN CREATION

The works of darkness are done in the night (the place of darkness). Man was given the day to work and the night to rest. By greed and selfishness, mankind has "entered into" the realm of the wild things. Man was to have dominion over them, instead, he has "gone over" into the realm of darkness and has partaken of the tree of knowledge.

We are living in the day of technology ruling. There are not enough hours in the day to <u>acquire</u> all that can be acquired by the mind of man. Those of you who are wondering where this came from, please go with me to Psalm 104:19-23. This Psalm is labeled, God is the Creator. It describes His divine order in creation.

Verse 23 tells that it is safe for men to come in the day. Man has been so overcome by the beasts of darkness, that he now seeks for the darkness in the day, in bars and dens of iniquity. We are told to walk as children of light and to have nothing to do with the unfruitful works of darkness.

Oh Lord, we would cry out with Jeremiah of old, and beseech you to come, in the brilliance of yourself, and destroy the unfruitful works of darkness. Strike your sons and your daughters with a spirit of repentance, that they would be restored. We pray to reclaim them from the filth and greed of this world. Oh God, have mercy on our souls.

**I will curse every deed of darkness as I
encounter it on my way.**

"...for the Lord God had not caused it to rain upon the earth, and there was not a man to till the ground." – Genesis 2:5b

COMMIT TO HOE AND IT WILL RAIN

God will not cause it to rain on the earth until a man is available to till it. We have enough moisture for survival, but not enough for revival. God has spoken and asked, "If I send revival now, who will till the garden?" There are many hard places just now - hard from lack of tilling so that the water can penetrate when it comes.

Will you go and till this hard ground? Will you break up the clods, the hard spots, that don't want to be penetratcd with the love and goodness of God? Habakkuk 2:14 gives us a sure word, that the earth shall be filled with the knowledge of the Glory of the Lord. The Glory of the Lord is His goodness and His mercy. The call is going out for men and women to go to the ends of the earth with the message of the Glory of God. The knowledge of His goodness is not known everywhere now. This is what is known as digging up that <u>hard</u> ground, that has, heretofore, refused that knowledge!

Father, we want to be volunteers to go with this message. The catch is that it has to be worked into our lives first. We must become personally acquainted with your mercy and your goodness; so filled up with the experiential knowledge of that goodness, that it spills out, over, and onto everyone we meet!

First of all, I will be filled up with the knowledge of the Lord, and then I will go.

October 15

"My sheep hear my voice, and I know them, and they follow me." – **John 10:27**

FOLLOW JESUS

My sheep <u>hear</u> (obey, understand) with the ears of the mind. My sheep <u>follow</u> (to move quickly and straight, to be attendant) on to obey. It means cleaving to Jesus with believing trust and obedience, following His leading, and acting according to His example. In the western world of today, it's rare to see a shepherd with his sheep, but when we do, it is an amazing sight. The shepherd truly has given his life to the care and keeping of his sheep. When they hear his voice, which they recognize readily as their particular shepherd, and follow him, he leads them into green pastures and places of safety. Refresh yourself by reading Psalm 23, written by the shepherd king of Israel.

We could fill volumes with admonitions to follow Jesus, but we can only refer to a few here. John 12:26 follows with a promise of honor from God. I Samuel 12:14 calls for wholehearted devotion. And I Kings 14:8 speaks of David following with all of his heart. Psalm 63:8 is an expression of a soul who will not be denied. And Hosea 6:3 so beautifully sums it all up with, we shall know the Lord, if we follow on.

Our Lord and our God, the beauty of the promise is that we will come to the place where we will become intimately acquainted with you, if we will only follow on. It is a journey, this trip we are on, from a foreign land, to the very heart of God. The place we came from is the fall and separation of sin. Now we know the cry of our heart has always been for you.

My heart will not be satisfied until it finds it's rest in thee!

October 16

"Yet hear the word of the Lord, O ye women, and let your ear receive the word of his mouth, and teach your daughters wailing, and every one her neighbor lamentation. "
Jeremiah 9:20

WEEPING OR WAILING?

When we petition the Lord for a desire of our heart with strong wailing and weeping, we will be in a place to do business with Him. Desire creates an image of the thing desired. As we have stated another time, God responds to desires, not needs. Psalm 37:4 instructs us to delight ourself in the Lord and He will give us the desires of our hearts. We find desire here to be a craving, a petition. When we delight ourself in the Lord, He can fill our "craving" without bringing harm to us. The thing we desire will then be Godly.

Esther 4:3 speaks of the people being in a hard place. It caused them to weep and to wail in their distress. To wail is to take up a lament (Jeremiah 9:20). It is an act of the spirit doing business with God about a matter that is not right. Our desire should be to change the matter from wrong to right, not just get relief.

We go on to understand that weeping is a soulish emotion, brought about by personal discomfort over a matter. It looks at how I am affected in the thing that is troubling me. We can see our need to get beyond weeping (our need) to wailing (wanting to bring change), when we approach God with our desires. It's getting over on God's side in the matter and not just pleading our case.

Father, we will choose to delight ourself in you, to learn what your desire is, that we may have the same desire. Teach us to pray with strong wailing, so that our very soul enters into the petition. We will call this praying with passion.

May the passion and the zeal of the Lord set my prayers afire upon the altar of my heart.

"I delight to do thy will, O my God; yea, thy law is within my heart." – Psalm 40:8

A SERVANT

Psalm 40:6-8 is a good description of a servant heart, a body prepared by God, through which His good pleasure is accomplished. The nature of the service of a servant is to do the Will of God. Matthew 11:29, 30 speaks of yokeship; being in a yoke with Jesus.

Let's look at the character of a servant. There is a discipline of kingly character being built in them. In this training, they are being disciplined. Old habits are shed. New habits are being formed. There will be fundamental adjustments taking place, in the life, to bring it into harmony with the work they will be asked to perform.

Mark 10:45 states that even the Son of Man, Jesus, came not to be ministered unto but to minister, or serve. The character of a servant is made up of diligence, compassion, selflessness, gentleness and confidence in God. We can easily see why a child of God is of great value in the kingdom of God, once he has reached servanthood. We need to press on, so that being valuable to God isn't the end. We can also be of value to the kingdom through servanthood.

Our Father, we see by this list we have a long way to go. But we know, at the same time, that by yielding our lives completely to the work of your Holy Spirit, you can bring us along rapidly. You can do a quick work. Help yourself to us Lord. Mold us and make us after thy will.

I want to be of value, even while I am still on earth. I want to serve.

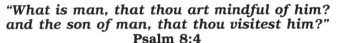

"What is man, that thou art mindful of him?
and the son of man, that thou visitest him?"
Psalm 8:4

BE A PERSON

A common definition of a person is personality, the sum total of character. The sum total of character is personality, years of character buildup. The individuality stays the same. The personality changes. Each temperament is different, so don't copy anyone else. Be yourself.

When we were born again, we had the character of Adam. This must be changed to the character of Jesus. Let's look at some aspects of His character. He had a transparent life. He was honest, true and real. He had a dependent life. (His whole life was totally dependent on God.) He never acted independently or on His own initiative. Luke chronicled His life as one of prayer. Then, we see His life as a big life. He had a big heart and it was always open, experiencing everything that came His way. We couldn't end without seeing Jesus' life as a simple one. He took life seriously and didn't waste Himself on unimportant issues. Again, we look at Matthew 11:29, 30, where Jesus encouraged us to take His yoke upon ourselves and learn to live as He did. He promised us it would be easy because His burden is light.

Father God, we don't take life too seriously, we take ourselves too seriously! Life is a gift from you, given with opportunity to grow, develop, enlarge and become something beautiful. We grasp it as a burden, and hide it in a hole in the ground, and dare it to grow or expand. We spend our entire lives putting walls, fences and no trespassing signs up. Oh God, forgive us for our stupidity! We throw away all our barriers and open our hearts and lives to you, and say, "Come, Lord Jesus!"

**I'm taking down dams and barriers. I want
the river of life to flow through me.**

"In him was life; and the life was the light of men." – John 1:4

JESUS - GOD AND MAN

In Luke, we see Jesus as the Son of Man. He was born, grew to adulthood, went into ministry and died. We are careful to remember His birth was an incarnation. The Holy Spirit of God overshadowed the virgin Mary and Jesus was the result. He stepped out when He was grown, and Luke records what He said and did in ministry.

John then shows Jesus as the Son of God. In Jesus, the Father God is fully revealed, fully manifested. Our Lord, Jesus Christ, is the mystery of God revealed. By His sacrificial death on the cross, He redeemed mankind back to the relationship with Father God that we had before Adam sinned.

Now, by Jesus, God is with us! This is grace. When love is translated into human practical expression, that is grace. God is light, light translated into human expression. That is truth. Words of truth bring light. Works of grace bring love. We now see more fully that Jesus became a man to redeem mankind. Jesus was God, at the same time, because only what is of God is perfect and acceptable to God. In this love of the Father, all the requirements were met. Hallelujah! What a Savior we have, Immanuel, God with us!

Thank you Father, Son, and Holy Spirit for grace. Thank you for love and redemption. While we were yet sinners, you made a way to bring us back to your heart. You are everything. I thank you again and again.

**Praises be to the Lord God Jehovah,
who was, and is, and is to come!
Hallelujah!**

"This beginning of miracles did Jesus in Cana of Galilee, and manifested forth his glory; and his disciples believed on him." – John 2:11

THE FIRST MIRACLE IS JOY

John 2:1-11 is the account of Jesus' very first miracle. He changed water into wine at a wedding. Can we look at this as a picture of our new life in Jesus? Our old life was running out of steam, or wine. It was insufficient. Jesus shows up and uses water to make wine – flat, tasteless water. He used what we had to get us started. Then He transformed it.

The servants were told to fill the pots back up with water. They had to start in simple obedience to the Word of the Lord. Then, Jesus put something new in that water. He put Himself in and it transformed that water to an abundance of really good wine! Flesh will always be flesh, but the Spirit of Christ Jesus coming into your clay pot displaces the old life in you, so that His life can be manifested in you.

Wine is a symbol of joy. Joy makes the heart glad and makes us forget our sorrows. The life of Jesus is full of taste (John 2:10), full of joy. Can we see the first miracle of Jesus was to produce joy? Do we have joy and have it full and running over? If not, why not?

Father, I believe that I see that joy is so important to you that you gave it first in Jesus' public ministry. That tells me I need it really bad, and I must not let anything steal my joy. I won't give it away and I won't let the lying devil steal it. The joy of my Lord is my strength.

Today, I will take joy as my portion. I may have to fill my jug with ordinary water, but Jesus will transform it!

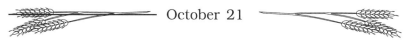

"I am crucified with Christ: nevertheless I live; yet not I, but Christ liveth in me; and the life which I now live in the flesh I live by the faith of the Son of God, who loved me, and gave himself for me." – **Galatians 2:20**

TRANSFORMATION

New life comes into our soul and displaces self or flesh. Christ begins to reign and self-reigning comes to an end. You are still there, but it is not you, it is Christ who lives in you. It is now a life of meaning and strength. The second miracle of Jesus was the healing of a fever; confusion was cleared up. Jesus gives us His life, with purpose, direction, and with goals. Then, He imparts the strength to go forward.

This life, with Jesus ruling and reigning, is a life of deliverance and Sabbath rest. Follow on, as Jesus walks His earthly ministry in John 5, when he finds a man who has given up hope and become paralyzed by self effort. Verse 8 shows him getting up and going on. Chapter 6 shows this is an abundant life, Jesus providing the daily nourishment. Chapter 9 reveals it as a life of light. All men are born blind, until Jesus gives them light. They live in imagination and supposition which leads to deception.

Chapter 11 tells of a life that overcomes death and Chapter 20 reveals the victorious life. The resurrection of Jesus robbed death of its power. Because of this, we have a life of love and sacrifice made possible (Chapter 21). Let us hasten now to the fields. The harvest is waiting!

Father God, thank you for giving us life and that more abundantly.

I have experienced transformation. Now I am free to progress into life with all of its fullness.

"Nevertheless I have somewhat against thee, because thou hast left thy first love." – **Revelation 2:4**

PRIORITIES

Revelation 2:1-7 is an address to the church in Ephesus. There are several interpretations of the relevance to you and I, but one thing is certain: the church <u>has</u> left it's first love. It is evident to all with eyes to see. We can take these words to heart and profit greatly by them. The judgement, of course, is that they had left their first love. They had fallen away backward. Service had replaced relationship.

The exhortation came in Jeremiah 4:3 and Hosea 10:12 to break up the fallow ground, in light of where you were, where you are now, and where you are going. Take a step backward and repent, get your balance, and then you will take many steps forward. With everything you've gotten in Revelation 2:1-7, get your face to face relationship right. I will be so bold as to say, in any area where work has replaced relationship, let it go. Get away somewhere, into the presence of God and get restored. If you feel to resume the activity, after that, fine, just as long as it is God-breathed and a result of your love for Him.

Father, this Word comes to us at a time when we are overloaded and seeking more hours in the day to carry out all we have added to our load of responsibilities. Thank you for the book of Revelation and for the Apostle John. He had been pulled aside from all activity and placed in seclusion. Here, you showed him your plan for the ages to come. We believe you will show us things to come, also, as we pull aside.

I will find my place of seclusion and get my priorities right. I am to love the Lord with all my heart, all my soul, and all my mind.

"And hast made us unto our God kings and priests; and we shall reign on the earth." – **Revelation 5:10**

KINGS AND PRIESTS

Let us look briefly at the two sides of our calling. This is to be both kings and priests unto our God.

As kings, we have the authority of one seated with Jesus on the throne, and to command deliverances and bring things into being, by achieving faith.

As priests, we are brought, by the Spirit, into the lamb life. We lay down our life vicariously, as an intercessor, taking the place of the one for whom we intercede. Here is where the "H" word comes to us again. Jesus described Himself as humble. Every leader of His people had to have this quality. Humility is the place of entire dependance on God, the sense of total nothingness, which comes, when we see how truly God is all, and in which we make way for God to be all.

We must consent, by our will, our mind and our affections, to be the form and the vessel in which the life and the glory can work and manifest. Humility is simply acknowledging the truth of my position as a human being, and yielding to God His place.

Father God, we often view ruling and reigning as a high and lofty position. We fail to look at it from your perspective, that of servanthood. When we look at the king seated on the throne of Heaven, we see a lamb. Oh my Lord, we must enter the lamb life to truly reign with you.

I never want to loose the picture of a lamb on the throne. What is a lamb really like? Like Jesus, of course!

"By which also ye are saved, if ye keep in memory what I preached unto you, unless ye have believed in vain." – I Corinthians 15:2

PROVE THE WILL OF GOD

In order to prove the Will of God, we need intuition, imagination, memory and will. These are four faculties of the mind. Memory is the ability to recall past experiences and interpret them correctly. We need to be in a posture of thankfulness for all God has done for you. This will keep our memory cleansed and available to prove the Will of God. We must discern the will of God, then prove it, by our response. In order to discern the Will of God, we have to have an intact memory.

There are four questions in every journey with God:
1. Who am I? This question cannot be answered in a vacuum. We find ourselves in relationships.
2. Where did I come form? I came from eternity past in the heart of God.
3. Why am I here? If we ask this with an attitude, we won't receive an answer
4. Where am I going? After it's all over, what will my life be like with God in eternity?

A good memory will be required to hold fast the questions of life. Memory is referred to in the Greek as bringing a ship toward the shore. We definitely do not want to be a derelict ship.

Father, your Word tells us to have the mind of Christ and to let the mind of Christ be in us. This renewing of the mind will be necessary to keep a good memory. We do not need to get trapped in the darkness of our minds. We plead the blood of Jesus over our minds and our memories, and we renew them, by the washing of the water of the Word.

I will let this mind, that was in Christ Jesus, be in me today.

"My brethren, count it all joy when ye fall into divers temptations;" — **James 1:2**

EMBRACING THE WILL OF GOD

To submit is to subject oneself to, to give in to imposed conditions. To embrace is to clasp, as in your arms, to press to your bosom, as an expression of love and affection. This is a pretty big order, isn't it? Let's look somewhere other than ourself for such an example of embracing the Will of God, in a very undesirable situation. We go again to Jacob. Poor Jacob; he has a most interesting life experience with the Father. Why don't you refresh your memory of his life by reading Genesis 27-35 and beyond. For today's purposes we are considering Chapter 32:22-32. He was preparing to meet a brother he had cheated, defrauded and hidden from for many years. What was going to transpire was uppermost in Jacob's mind. I'd like to paraphrase a prayer Jacob prayed as he spent the night before the meeting, alone with God. If you like, why don't you consider making the prayer yours?

Oh God, this situation is too much for me. I've manipulated and tried to make things happen, but I'm tired of doing things my way! I can't run any more, Lord, I want my life to be right with you. Esau may kill me and my family. He may take everything I have, but I'd rather be with you, in glory, than go another day living this way.

I choose to embrace the Will of God, by submitting to God, in my circumstances.

"What doth it profit, my brethren, though a man say he hath faith, and have not works? can faith save him?" – **James 2:14**

FAITH

Faith gives you access to God. It is not what you do, it is what you believe. Believing is receiving. Faith without works is dead (James 2:17). Faith is a noun. Believing is a verb. Faith brings you to believe in God. We go from a noun, faith, descriptive of know, to a verb, works, describing action. You faith it (know it) <u>and</u> you believe it (do it), to complete a transaction with God (Romans 9:9). Faith is the first step, believing is the corresponding action, step 2.

We are speaking here of faith in the inner man. This faith motivates us, reaches out to God and believes God. Abraham just lived in God's presence. His actions, go, stop, move, hear, do, were simply responses to hearing God. These responses were perfected, as he learned God's ways more perfectly.

Psalm 37:5 compels us to trust, also, in the Lord. <u>Faith</u> is the act of the will. <u>Belief</u> is the act of the mind or intellect. And <u>trust</u> is the language of the heart. Trust sees and feels and leans upon.

Father, we often refer to Abraham as the Father of our faith. Then, if he lived his life in this manner, we must live likewise, to be included in the household of faith. We have come to rely so much on our own abilities, we are missing it by a mile! Forgive us, and help us get back on the faith route. It is the only way it really works!

I choose to live by faith – by every Word that proceeds out of the mouth of God.

"Now faith is the substance of things hoped for, the evidence of things not seen." – Hebrews 11:1

FAITH IS

Faith is another world, a wheel in a wheel. Faith is another place, another dimension, another realm. It is a sphere of reality, outside of our sense realm. For a thing to be of faith, it has to be unseen. You have to go to the place where it is, outside the human function and bring it back.

Believing is the action of going to that faith realm, to bring back the answer. Naaman was required, by faith, in Elisha's word, to go dip in the Jordan (II Kings 5:10).

Prayer is an act of faith. It is going for the answer, bringing it back and then acting on it. To pray and obey means to fight the good fight of faith. In other words, fight your sense realm that is screaming unbelief.

Faith is perceiving as real what is not revealed to the senses. It is outside the sense realm. Faith is tried by a need, under pressure, to get the solution. Talking will keep you in the sense realm. Silence makes room for God to work

Father, faith is really putting our money where our mouth is. We either believe you, and act like it, by living in faith, or we are just making a joke. The knowledge that faith is a place to go to, to get what we need, that isn't seen, is really overwhelming! Help us learn to go to that faith place more often, because it is the realm where you are. It is heaven's address, the throne room of our God. It is a good place to be and to settle down and abide.

I want to live in the place of faith. I want to make faith my habitation.

*He that hath no rule over his own spirit is
like a city that is broken down, and without
walls." – Proverbs 25:28*

RETURN TO PARADISE

Rule, in the verse above, is meant as restraint. It isn't a very popular thing to talk about, but very needy, in light of the day we live in. II Timothy 3:1-5 gives a description of these days, and speaks of those without restraint. This is not a new condition, it is just increasing, as we near the time of the Lord's return.

Adam lost his first estate because he did not keep rule over his own spirit. He allowed himself to be influenced wrongly by Eve, who had herself been deceived by Satan. The last part of our verse for today likens an unruled spirit to a city that has been broken down. Remember how Adam lost his place, in the garde,n prepared for him, by God, and was cast out to work by the sweat of his brow. Satan took Adam's place as ruler on the earth, and has attempted to have authority over the souls of men ever since!

The good news is that Jesus came into the earth and took Adam's place. He returned the rule of man to his own spirit. Now are we free to choose, to rule our own spirit and to accept God's way of redemption, back to Himself – paradise restored!

Father, we know that judgement came into the earth in Jesus. His death on the cross judged sin once and for all. Now we have to decide what we are going to do with our sin. It has to be on Jesus, or it has to be on us. Thank you for redeeming us from the penalty of sin and death, and transferring us, by our faith, into the kingdom of your dear Son. When it is completed, Jesus will turn it all back over to you.

**I will have rule over my spirit, so my city is
not desolate, nor my walls broken down.**

"And the manna ceased on the morrow after they had eaten of the old corn of the land; neither had the children of Israel manna any more; but they did eat of the fruit of the land of Canaan that year." – Joshua 5:12

STEPS TO VICTORY

Wilderness food continued for the children of Israel until they were circumcised, took the passover, ate the old corn of the land and met the captain of the host. After this, they possessed the land. Read about it with me, in Chapter 5 of Joshua. The uncircumcised could not possess the land, even though they had passed over the Jordan. Manna sustained, but never satisfied. In order to be satisfied, we need to get prepared to possess the land. They were never meant to stay on manna. It was wilderness food.

We can see these four steps to victory for our own help:

1. Circumcision, the cutting away of the flesh so the spirit takes preeminence.

2. Passover, or the testimony of the blood of Jesus, His work of redemption.

3. Feeding on the corn, the Word of God, necessary for strength and instruction in Godliness.

4. Subject to Christ, as Lord, accepting Him as captain, permitting Him the plans and obeying Him fully.

Father God, these steps to victory were given to Joshua as an earthly picture of all that the spiritual life requires to succeed. We are no different from Israel, same weaknesses and sinful tendencies. It requires step-by-step instruction to bring us along your way. Thank you for the Holy Spirit, our guide and our interpreter of the heavenly way.

Unbelief and disobedience will not keep me out of the Promised Land. I say yes, Lord.

 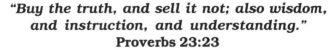

"Buy the truth, and sell it not; also wisdom, and instruction, and understanding."
Proverbs 23:23

WISDOM

If we know there is going to be a shortage or some much desired object is going to be scarce, we tend to get larger than usual amounts of it. Some even go so far as to horde some items. Can we look here at truth, wisdom, instruction and understanding in that light? We are instructed to buy it and not to sell it. We need to horde it up, so to speak, for the time it will be scarce or rare.

Wisdom relates to being wise, to acting wisely, to being intelligent. It also can be said to be prudent, cunning and clever. It is to have an intelligent attitude toward the experience of life. This above definition is according to the Greek. Before we pass on, we must consider Hebrew wisdom. A personal God, who is holy and just, expects us to live our lives according to His principles. The Hebrew did not speculate, like the Greek. They emphasized the human will of the heart not the head. They were very practical, becoming wise by praying and obeying. A wise man gave particular advice, based on divine revelation, in addition to his own experience and personal observation.

Father, we would cry out for wise men! In our days of very foolish things, we see a shortage of wise men. We pray both for wise men and that we may become wise.

My cry is for wisdom, instruction and understanding, that I may know truth.

"And Joseph dreamed a dream, and he told it his brethren: and they hated him yet the more."
Genesis 37:5

JOSEPH WAS DIFFERENT

In Genesis 37-50, we have the lengthy story of Joseph. It is well worth taking the time needed to review. In the meantime, I'll tell the shorter version. The purpose of God is to pour out His Spirit on the whole world, through men and women who walk faithfully with Him. Jacob's ambition was to be an anointed agent, by whom God would fulfill His Will. He was prepared and ready to move into his birthright and so was his son, Joseph. Jacob understood Joseph. They could fellowship around God's purposes. This set Joseph apart as evidenced in his coat of many colors. It was a mark of separation.

Joseph had an inner-consciousness of God. He was already fixed in God's calling, when he told his father that he would bow down to him. Faith is a conviction that God has said something, and we can say, "I know it." We could speak of the reaction Joseph's family had to this announcement, but that is not our goal. We are looking here at the certainty with which one can set the course of his life, when he knows he has heard the call of God!

Father God, it is exciting to read the account of Joseph's life. He was a man submitted to your Will for his life, and he endured the consequences it brought. No wonder he is said to be a type of Christ, portrayed in the Old Testament. He never aborted his mission by giving in to the hardships of a dedicated life. Thank you for giving us such role models. We can learn how to stand, with your help, when it gets rough going.

I won't give up, nor will I deny the direction of the call of God - ever onward and upward!

"Not that I speak in respect of want: for I have learned, in whatsoever state I am, herewith to be content." – Philippians 4:11

TRAINING FOR REIGNING

Joseph's years with Potiphar were training to rule in Egypt. In slavery, he did his best job, knowing God meant him to be there. This knowing he was in the Will of God brought poise to his spirit. This poise brings peace and freedom. All who observe this poise of peace are aware of the freedom. This is a testimony to the Will of God. All who live this way prosper.

Joseph was happy and free in his spirit, understanding himself to be God's man in this situation. It wasn't where Joseph was, it was who he was. In operating like this, all he did was blessed. He got comfortable in Potiphar's house. He even got comfortable in prison. This attitude freed Joseph to perform at maximum capacity. He prospered in all his hands found to do, because he was doing it as unto the Lord.

In several passages in the Word, we are admonished to have no stress, nor to be anxious, and to be content wherever we find ourself. Joseph is a good example of life lived in rythmn to the Will and Purposes of God.

Father, we can stand and look, with amazement, at the turns in Joseph's life, or we can understand it was you, and the way you dealt with him is the way you long to deal with all your children. We know we aren't all called to be ambassadors to Egypt, but we are called to rule and reign where we are! Help us, oh God, to find our rest in you, whatever the circumstances may be.

I choose to settle down and to be content where I am, knowing it's the will of God for me. Fixed consciousness will keep me fresh!

*"**Neither yield ye your members as instruments of unrighteousness unto sin: but yield yourselves unto God, as those that are alive from the dead, and your members as instruments of righteousness unto God.**" – **Romans 6:13***

RE-LIFING

Jesus alters our disposition by regeneration, re-lifing, starting a new generation. The old is passed away, dead. Now we have to bring our body, this old physical case, into harmony with that new disposition. This is a process spoken of as renewing the mind (Romans 12:2). This will take stern discipline, a great deal of cutting away and building of spiritual character. It's sort of like remodeling an old house. A lot has to go that was once useful.

Let's follow the progression of renewing the mind to bring about the transformation. First of all, it takes practice, continually doing that which no one sees or knows but me. I hate to say it, but practice does make perfect. The result of practice is a habit, the doing becomes second nature. Every habit is purely mechanical. When we form a habit, it makes a material difference in the brain. The material of the brain alters slowly, but it does alter. Repetition forms a groove in the brain, so that the practice becomes easier. It becomes unconscious.

When we are regenerated, we can reform, by the power and the presence of God, every habit that is not in accordance with His life in us.

Father God, we begin to see beyond salvation, beyond the cross, to the resurrection life, to the call to discipleship. We understand it is a walk. By your Spirit and with your help we make the decision to be one of those who go on to know you in fullness. We want our life to be transformed by your power through our obedience.

I will to practice walking in the Spirit until it becomes natural to me – until I can do it without conscious effort.

"And when the Lord thy God shall deliver them before thee; thou shalt smite them, and utterly destroy them; thou shalt make no covenant with them, nor shew mercy unto them." – Deuteronomy 7:2

DEALING WITH THE ITE'S

In Deuteronomy 7:1, God spoke to Israel concerning seven enemies they would encounter when seeking to possess their inheritance. We would do well to take a look at them, and thereby, take heed for ourselves.

1. Canaanites - the spirit of materialism, known for their business skills and material possessions.

2. Hittites - the spirit of fear produced by brutal, warring ones.

3. Hivittes - the spirit of humanism, the exaltation of man to the place of God.

4. Perrizites - the spirit of immorality, open, unwalled.

5. Girgashites - the spirit of compromise produces confusion and brings frustration.

6. Amorites - the spirit of pride shuts one out of the presence and provision of God.

7. Jebusites - discouragement and condemnation.

Verse 2 gives specific instruction from the Lord on how to deal with these enemies. We are told to utterly destroy them, and to make no covenant with them. It would be a good idea to read the entire seventh chapter to be built up in faith and knowledge of our relationship with God.

Father God, it is easy to see, from the above list, that there are many enemies we will encounter that seek to block the possession of our inheritance in you. We know, by your Spirit, and in direct obedience to your commands, we can overcome all our enemies and dwell in our Promised Land.

I want no part of anything that will hinder my spiritual growth or my relationship to God.

"And Jabez called on the God of Israel, saying, Oh that thou wouldest bless me indeed, and enlarge my coast, and that thine hand might be with me, and that thou wouldest keep me from evil, and it may not grieve me! And God granted him that which he requested."
I Chronicles 4:10

FOCUSING IN ON GOD

One would hardly look in the Old Testament for the Lord's prayer. Yet we find Jabez, a descendant of Judah, uttering this prayer in I Chronicles 4:10. Jesus brought those things concealed in the Old Testament to the light in the new.

Let us now look briefly at this prayer called the model for praying as found in Luke 11:1-4. Our Father - a personal relationship. Hallowed be thy name - my evaluation of Him. Thy kingdom come - my invitation to Him. Thy will be done on earth as it is in heaven - my yielding to Him. Give us this day our daily bread - my reliance on Him. And forgive us our debts as we forgive our debtors - humbly asking forgiveness. And lead us not into temptation but deliver us from evil - trusting Him for preservation. For thine is the kingdom and the power and the glory forever and ever, Amen - acknowledging He is able to keep what I commit to Him.

The following prayer can be prayed by us, as we use this prayer for guidance.

Father, because I acknowledge your authority and acknowledge your lordship, I don't need to be tempted. My relationship with you is right and pure. I ask you, therefore, to keep me from evil. My heart is following wholly after you, my Lord and my God. Lead me with your eye, not with the bit and bridle (Psalm 32:8,9). Thank you, Father, for your keeping power.

**I am safe in the keeping of my Father God.
No evil will come near me.**

*"And I will establish my covenant between me
and thee and thy seed after thee in their
generations for an everlasting covenant, to be
a God unto thee, and to they seed after thee."*
Genesis 17:7

ANCIENT MYSTERIES

Jerusalem was built as a statement of faith. It had no other purpose for being the chosen place. Mt. Moriah was the spot where Abraham, a man, was willing to sacrifice himself for God. Calvary was the spot where God, in matching faith, sacrificed Himself for man.

David chose this place for his capital city, a land that belongs to no one. It is God's land! God called it a place for His people, a place of their own where they would not be disturbed. David gave too much attention to the military and God brought judgement as a curse. David repented and asked God to stay the curse. He sent an angel. At the spot the plague stopped, David built an altar. Later on, this became the site for the temple.

Thirty seven years after the death and resurrection of Jesus, Jerusalem was destroyed, all but the western wall. Jerusalem is a testimony to the world of God's seriousness about His covenant with a man. Nothing can ever annul or change God's decree.

Father of Abraham, Jacob and Isaac, you are the Father of my Lord Jesus Christ. I know you have made a covenant of faith with me at Calvary. I know it is forever and throughout all eternity. Thank you for covenant.

**I see Jerusalem as a sign of
God's faithfulness.**

"For thus saith the Lord God, the Holy One of Israel; in returning and rest shall ye be saved; in quietness and in confidence shall be your strength: and ye would not."
Isaiah 30:15

WHERE IS OUR RELIANCE?

In verse 7 of this chapter, we read their strength was to <u>sit still</u> without interruption. In this stage of civilization the above statement sounds like a joke. Everyone is plugged in all the time. Computers, beepers, cell phones, you name it, no one even stands still in line. They go around in circles. Yet, God gave instruction concerning security. He warned in this 30th chapter of Isaiah against going to other places and paying large sums of money for help and support. Instead, he cautioned Israel to get quiet, to become motionless, cease from activity, settle down and plug in to Him!

Let's consider three words, quietness, stillness and confidence. Quietness means to settle down into the Lord. Stillness means be still, remain there and don't flit about. Confidence means to hope in the Lord, to do what needs to be done. Quietness ploughs the ground and waits and hopes (I Corinthians 9.10). It means to wait with confidence, desiring some good with expectation of attaining it. A foundation of hope is to trust someone. God is the one to build this foundation. You will never be disappointed!

Father God, hope deferred makes the heart sick. We are very sick of heart where we have misplaced our hope. The world and all that is in it is transitory and passing away. It is shifting sand. No wonder we are never still! As we take action to quiet our hearts and shake off these compulsions to start and run, we will become quiet in the center of our being. When we get quiet, you can speak to us.

I am sorry I have been dashing about here and there. I desire to get still.

*"Till we all come in the unity of the faith, and
of the knowledge of the Son of God, unto a
perfect man, unto the measure of the stature
of the fullness of Christ:"* – **Ephesians 4:13**

SEVEN TESTS OF CHRISTIAN CHARACTER

1.   If your enemy is hungry, feed him (Romans 12:20).

2.   When you make a dinner, don't call your rich neighbors, call the poor (Luke 14:12, 13).

3.   Go the second mile (Matthew 5:41).

4.   Esteem others better than yourself (Philippians 2:3).

5.   As you would have men do to you, do also to them (Matthew 7:12).

6.   Handle the other person as though he were Jesus Himself in disguise (Matthew 25:40).

7.   Take up your cross daily and follow Jesus (Luke 9:23).

When we buy a car, we take it in to the dealer for regular check-ups to be sure its functioning as the warranty promised. When we were born again and entered covenant with God, we got a warranty, so to speak. We need to keep our appointments for our check-ups, to see that we are functioning as the warranty promised.

Father, we know your Word is a light unto our path, to show us where we are walking. It is your Word that we can look into to see how we are measuring up. Thank you for the Bible that leads us into all truth. Thank you for the Holy Spirit who makes that truth known to our hearts.

**I will stay in the Word of God, to know how
my character is developing.**

"But if ye turn unto me, and keep my commandments, and do them: though there were of you cast out unto the uttermost part of the heaven, yet will I gather them from thence, and will bring them unto the place that I have chosen to set my name there." – Nehemiah 1:9

HEALERS OF THE BREACH

The desire and purpose of the heart of God is that the body of Christ may appear to the world as something worthy of God. He wants His body to become aware of this desire and that they be moved to cooperate with Him in bringing this worthy thing about. God is committed to the recovery and completion of His testimony. In Nehemiah, we have a picture of the house of God in disarray and the walls broken down.

The walls represented Jerusalem, the seat of worship unto God. They were broken down; anything could get in and out. Everything in Jerusalem was to focus on God, be for God. So much outside stuff had come in through the open places, it distracted from God and led to self-worship. Nehemiah picked up the burden of the Lord to repair the walls. If you are to be a Nehemiah, a restorer, a comforter, you must so love the child of God. You must take no thought for personal comfort, gain or welfare. You must be so identified with the desire of God's heart toward that broken down one, that you see nothing else but the assignment to redeem, rebuild and restore to the former state of beauty.

Father, broken things are not always lovable. You haven't called your church to the lovable, you've called them to the needy, the outcasts, the runaways, the rebellious and the hurting. We have been anointed with the same anointing of Jesus – and that is to go to the lost sheep, bind up their wounds, and carry them back home.

I will begin to rebuild the wall where I am. That's my part.

*"And it came to pass, when I heard these
words, that I sat down and wept, and mourned
certain days, and fasted, and prayed before
the God of heaven." –* **Nehemiah 1:4**

NEHEMIAHS NEEDED

The first information we receive about Nehemiah is his burden for Jerusalem and the people of God in captivity. The report he received concerning them, recorded in Nehemiah 1:2,3, was not good news. Verse 4 reveals how the report affected this man of God. There have always been forces at work determined to undermine, undercut, and work the destruction of God's testimony.

In these days, when the forces of evil are dead set against the testimony of God, God is developing warring elements and characteristics in His instruments. We need Nehemiahs in our time, people of great heart burdens. He took responsibility before the Lord and prayed vicarious prayers over the situation. He prayed hidden and alone before God (Nehemiah 1:4-11).

God wants vessels, travailers, to travail for His spiritual interests. God baptizes such souls into an anguish, and throws over them the mantle of God's own terrible disappointments, dissatisfaction and grief over things spiritually, among His people.

Father, we easily see that the spiritual condition of your people is not good. We need intercessors to raise up the cry and to travail before your altars, until the spirit of repentance comes and visits your church. Oh God, we need revival. We need to turn back to our first love.

**Oh Lord, raise up Nehemiahs
for your people.**

"For ye have need of patience, that, after ye have done the will of God, ye might receive the promise." - **Hebrews 10:36**

HOW PATIENT ARE YOU?

I would like to examine patience in three areas in order to explore our question: patience in our walk with God; patience in doing His work; and patience in His work in us. We will need to familiarize ourselves with Luke 8:11-15 to find our answer. There are four types of soil referred to here that the farmer sows seed in. The soil is the heart of man and the seed is the Word of God. The type of soil determines the crop. 1.) The wayside refers to a heart that is trodden down after years of hearing without heeding. We see these as the most impatient people of all, they hear and reject. 2.) The rootless, or hard ground, refers to the heart that hears and receives joyfully, but when temptation comes, they fall away, not waiting patiently for God to deliver them. 3.) The thorny place is the man that goes on with his life, allowing the cares of the world to choke out the seed, not willing to wait for the blessings of God, but rather runs after riches. 4.) We have the good ground, a good honest heart, a heart that is set on loving God, one that is convinced that Jesus will always deliver, just on time! The last line of verse 15 says this heart keeps the Word and brings forth fruit with patience. Where do we find ourselves in this patience check?

Father, we are again reminded that you, the Almighty God of the universe, are calling the sons of men to be patient with you! We can hardly fathom this plea of your heart. We can see, though, that impatience is a deadly enemy to our soul. Work a work of faith in our hearts that will make them good soil. The farmer often times needs a lot of fertilizer and additives to bring soil up to good quality.

I trust God to be my husbandman and to add what I need to make me good soil!

"Yea doubtless, and I count all things but loss for the excellency of the knowledge of Christ Jesus my Lord: for whom I have suffered the loss of all things, and do count them but dung, that I may win Christ."
Philippians 3:8

BITTER OR BETTER?

When we don't willingly, by free choice, lay down our lives for Christ's sake, we suffer loss by resenting the cause, the person or the assignment. Resentment causes anger, either outward as wrath or inward as rage. This resentment does harm to its victim, either yourself or others. Loss brings one to anxiety that cannot be settled until the loss is freely accepted and the grief allowed to surface.

Loss can come from having something taken without consent, something taken, as opposed to given up, something rendered from by force, rather than being laid down. The process will be loss, anxiety, anger, hurt, guilt or loss accepted, given up freely, and counted as gain. A root of bitterness develops from feelings of loss turned toward whoever you perceive to have caused the loss. Who are you mad a? What constrains you? What motivates you? The zeal of God needs to be our motivator, and we are to be constrained by the love of God.

Please Lord, do a remodeling job in me. Tear down old restraints and take out old wiring and plumbing. Put in new, larger pipes for a large flow of water, and bigger bulbs for more amperage, so there will be flood lights and free flowing water.

I want large pipes and bright lights!

"For the eyes of the Lord run to and fro throughout the whole earth, to shew himself strong in the behalf of them whose heart is perfect toward him. Herein thou hast done foolishly: therefore from henceforth thou shalt have wars." – II Chronicles 16:9

BOOT CAMP FOR HARVESTERS

There is coming a harvest, the like of which the world has never seen. It will be those sent by God who will gather in the wheat, those who know Him and those He can trust to do what He will require of them. No one knows the heart of man but God and those to whom He chooses to reveal it. There will be different procedures for tares and wheat (Matthew 13:30).

Jesus needs chosen vessels, prepared vessels, ready vessels, through which to work, to bring to climax all that has been prepared. He needs hands, feet, and voices to represent Him in the earth, to bring forth all that the Father planned.

The Holy Spirit is sent forth, in the earth, to inhabit these vessels. He is the Spirit of Christ, two bodies could not inhabit the same space, but spirit and body can. It is a spiritual time on the earth. The Spirit of God must have bodies through which to manifest the power of God.

The harvesters will be specifically called by Jesus to be His representatives. If we will stay in our place, we will be trained and ready to go when the call comes.

Father, we know it is a special time on the earth, and we have to be specifically trained to live rightly in this time. We volunteer to be vessels, the rest is up to you! Help yourself.

I'm a candidate for training!

"But in a great house there are not only vessels of gold and of silver, but also of wood and of earth; and some to honor, and some to dishonor." – II Timothy 2:20

RIGHT KIND OF VESSELS

If you are rightly related to God, you have come to the place where no one ever thinks of noticing you! This will take some thinking about. Here's the rest of the story; all that is noticed is that the power of God comes through you all the time. The real test of faithfulness is life, just like it is.

The most illuminating illustration found in the Bible to describe useful lives is that of the vessel. A vessel is strictly limited to one function only, it exists to be a container. When I see this humbling truth of my relation as human to God, I only exist to contain Him, I will be rightly related to Him.

Questions about the qualifications of the vessel could be like these. Is it ready for the master's hand? Is it handy for the master's use? Is it hallowed to the master's ends? If the answer is yes, then it is indeed a vessel of honor. Do we see the validity now of the opening statement? We then are ready to be borne about to do whatever the master has need of, and not be concerned with the impression we are making.

Father God, it is our desire to be so lost in bearing about within ourself, the very essence of the Godhead, to be oblivious to the attention it may bring, much as Mary must have learned to live while she was obviously pregnant with Jesus.

Oh, to completely forget about myself!

"Therefore say unto the house of Israel, Thus saith the Lord God; Repent, and turn yourselves from your idols; and turn away your faces from all your abominations." -
Ezekiel 14:6

SELL ALL

Anything that causes you hurt separates you from God who delivered you from all pain and death. That which can cause you hurt is an idol in your heart. Luke 9:57-62 is a recording of Jesus' conversation with a certain man seeking to be a follower. Please read it for understanding on today's sayings. He instructed him to "sell all (Matthew 19:21) and come and follow me."

The instruction not to look back was a warning of the pull of all you have not sold. It is a longing after what you left behind, but did not sell. Selling is a transfer of ownership. It legally removes it, by your free choice, from your possession. Looking back, (pining for, mooning over) hinders your progress. You can stumble, fall, hurt yourself, get lost or even perish if you don't look where you are going.

Matthew 6:33 could very well be the best piece of advice you ever receive, "Seek ye first the kingdom of God." Everything else will fall into place when you do this.

Early in our walk with you, Lord, you began to impart this wisdom to our heart. Every time we forget and grasp after something, to the exclusion of your kingdom, we are reminded, "seek ye, first." Thank you for always bringing us back to safety, away from dangerous traps.

I will be careful to put the kingdom of God first place in my life.

"And said, I cried by reason of mine affliction unto the Lord, and he heard me; out of the belly of hell cried I, and thou heardest my voice." – Jonah 2:2

CAUSE FOR THANKS-GIVING!

Jonah prayed unto the Lord out of the fish's belly. God had prepared a whale for Jonah to arrest his activity (Jonah 1:17). Three days Jonah was in the whale. He died to his own plans and purposes in those three days. Three nights, he was in total darkness and silence. Verse 2 tells us he cried by reason of his affliction. He was in hell and he cried out to God! He recognized that God had cast him into the deep, into the midst of the sea, and the floods encompassed him. All of God's billows and waves passed over him.

In all his pain of death, Jonah <u>looked toward</u> God. He remembered the Lord, and his prayer came up to God's holy temple. Look back at verse 2 where Jonah <u>recognized</u> that God heard his voice. What cause for the thanksgiving that Jonah then expresses in verse 9! He goes on to say that he will pay that which he vowed. Oh, beloved child of God, take these steps to heart and recognize your God, in your time of need. He waits ever so patiently to do for you what He did for Jonah in verse 10, 'the Lord spoke unto the fish.'

Father God, we suffer so much, needlessly. We sin, get rebellious, seek to run and hide from you and you prepare a fish for us. It is ever the record of your dealing with your child. We then get in such a fix that we cry out. It is beyond our understanding that you always answer that cry and speak into our need! Yes, indeed, this is a cause for great joy and thanksgiving.

I will not wait until I get in a fish's belly to seek my God. Early will I seek His face!

*"The Lord shall fight for you, and ye shall
hold your peace." – Exodus 14:14*

THE LORD MAKES A WAY

Exodus 14 is an exciting picture of the God of Israel versus Pharaoh, or the god of this world. We can be assured that God will be honored before the enemies of His people (verse 4). In verse 10, we see what fear of the world can do to us, " They looked up, saw the enemy and were afraid." They turn, in their fear and anger, and jump on Moses, the man appointed by God to lead them out of bondage. They became so overwhelmed by their circumstances, they decided they would rather live in bondage than to die in the unknown.

Moses, the man chosen of God, gave them the solution in verses 13 and 14. Fear sees the circumstances; faith sees the solution. We must keep looking away from the fear-causing circumstances unto Jesus, who is the answer. These attacks of the enemy are to stop us in our walk with the Lord. They cause us to hide from God, as Adam did, and make us become unfruitful in righteousness.

Father God, we take the words of Moses, in verse 13, and say, "we will not be afraid." With you being our helper, we will stand still and know you will bring things to the right conclusion. Too long we have allowed our fears to dictate our actions, and we refuse to do that anymore. We know, by faith, that you will make a way for us – where there is no way.

Trust is being willing to wait for God to act.

"For unto us a child is born, unto us a son is given: and the government shall be upon his shoulder: and his name shall be called Wonderful, Counsellor, The mighty God, The everlasting Father, The Prince of Peace."
Isaiah 9:6

THE PEOPLE OF GOD

Adam and Eve rebelled against God at the beginning of recorded history. The results, down through the ages, have been corrupt political and religious systems. Those not under God's government will always worship idols. Only faith in Jesus will bring us under God's rule. Jesus came to establish God's rule. He was always under the authority of God. He was perfected through obedience.

Any government not headed by and subject to Almighty God is, and will be, corrupt. Jesus was 100% under the rule of God. Ungodly religious and political systems empower one another. Greed for money is the power of sin.

Jesus has redeemed, unto Himself, a people - a people to be like Christ now, involved in the redemption of mankind, out of the corrupt systems of the world.

Father, I renounce all the habits, ways, customs, traditions and thought patterns of the past. I choose, by my will, to live in the now with you, in the presence of the Son of God, as revealed to me by the Spirit of God, so that I might live in unbroken fellowship with God the Father. In this glorious relationship, I can be a worker with Jesus, to bring in the kingdom of God in its fullness.

At the end of the millennial reign - Christ will hand a totally submissive creation back to the Father.

*"Therefore with joy shall ye draw water out
of the wells of salvation." – Isaiah 12:3*

FAITH AND HOPE: TWINS

Hebrews 11:1 reminds us that faith is the substance of things hoped for. Hope is the rope that lets the bucket down. Let the bucket go down, and draw up water from the wells of salvation. Upon receiving Christ as your personal Savior, you gave Him permission to begin to dig wells within your inner life. Now we can, in assurance of hope, draw up out of those very wells, by the bucket of expectation, what we need for life and godliness. Faith draws the bucket up, believing it to be full.

Hope drops it down, faith draws it up. My bucket is my place of need. It's empty, but it's my vehicle to get to my source of supply. Hope anticipates an answer to my need to the desire of my heart. Hope sends the bucket down to the place of supply, the well of my salvation. It is now easy to see why we draw up with joy. Faith is joyful because it knows the bucket isn't coming up empty.

Father God, it's easy to see, by this example, we've all had needs and empty buckets. How wonderful! You tell us to let the buckets down into our own wells, and then to draw the bucket up, full. What joy! Realizing the truth of this promise of provision, faith leaps into our wildly beating bosom. What calm and peace it brings.

**I will let down my bucket today and draw
out water for my need.**

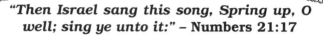

"Then Israel sang this song, Spring up, O well; sing ye unto it:" – **Numbers 21:17**

FAITH TO GROW BY

What great instruction we can receive as we are faithful to search the scriptures with a bent towards applying what we receive to our own lives. The above scripture instructs us to sing to the well, to sing it into fullness. If you dig a well in the natural, you must use a shovel. Well singing scoops out the hole for the water to come in! Psalm 84:6 may well be another description of the man in verse 5, who knows where his strength is and makes a well as he passes through a dry place. Again, in Proverbs 10:11, we see reference to the mouth of the righteous being a well of life, also in Song of Solomon 4:15.

John 4:10 and 14, with John 7:37 and 38, is a wonderful teaching from Jesus, Himself, of the living water that shall flow from the belly of the believer like a river. To catch the vision of growing, by faith in the Word of promise that God would send the water, look at Isaiah 44:3, 4. The willow tree is a graceful thing of beauty, as it blows and bends in the wind. It grows by the water and it stays supple and pliable, not breaking in the storms.

Father, your promise of wells that are full to overflowing brings great joy and peace to our hearts. Father, we desire to be green and pliable and growing by the river, all the days of our lives. Thank you for the waters of life, that come from Jesus, the wells of salvation that will never run dry or suffer a shortage.

My mouth is the mouth of the righteous and living water to give life must flow from my lips.

"And said unto him, Go, wash in the pool
of Siloam, (which by interpretation, Sent.)
He went his way therefore, and washed
and came seeing." – John 9:7

THE WATER OF LIFE

In Isaiah 8:6, is reference to the waters of Shiloah that go softly, like a gentle river, refreshing everywhere it goes. The Word of the Lord has this gentle, refreshing quality. Philippians 2:11 states that "every tongue shall confess that Jesus Christ is Lord, to the Glory of the Father." As this gentle, refreshing Word begins to break forth, from the fountains of life, in each believer's heart. It will become a mighty river of life, covering the earth.

The mercy of God is like a river. It washes our dry, barren ground, renews it, and brings life everywhere it touches. Joel 3:18 is a beautiful description of that day, when the river of God flows in its fullness. Nehemiah 3:15 tells of the pool of Shiloah being by the king's garden. The gate of the fountain was repaired when Nehemiah was rebuilding Jerusalem. This was a work necessary in that day and in ours. The walls and the gates have fallen in disrepair in the king's garden. It is revival that will repair the walls! We need revival!

Our Lord and our God, our tongues will confess, everywhere, every day, to every man, that Jesus is Lord. We must clean the debris out of the pool. The fresh, clear water is ready to flow and must not be polluted by the junk in the pool!

Oh God, send your Spirit of repentance to clean up the pool.

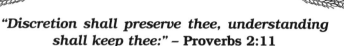
"Discretion shall preserve thee, understanding shall keep thee:" – **Proverbs 2:11**

TWO RIVERS

There are two rivers flowing today. Both are flooding their banks. One of these rivers is life and one is destruction. Look again, with me, at Isaiah 8:6. The pool of Shiloah was a wonder, fed from deep underground, and was always sweet and refreshing. The Euphrates river ran strong and turbulent. In verses 6 and 7, God said to the prophet that because the people had refused the river of life, or the quiet, gentle pool supplied for them, that He would raise the mighty river up to flow over them.

I was awakened early one morning with Proverbs 2:11, as instruction. Discretion means meditation, thought, prudence, plan, device or purpose. The thought came that as we, the children of God, follow His plans and purposes, we will be preserved. This is the plan of safety, following hard after the Lord and staying in the river of life provided by Him, and the waters of destruction will not overtake us. Proverbs 6:20-23 is good for further understanding.

Father, by your Holy Spirit, continue to bring light to our hungry hearts and to lead us by the still waters. We see that there are definitely two ways to go, but only one leads to you. Thank you for the river of life, that flowed from Jesus' side on Calvary.

I will stay, by the Grace of God, in the River of God.

"Howbeit for this cause I obtained mercy, that in me first Jesus Christ might shew forth all longsuffering, for a pattern to them which should hereafter believe on him to life everlasting." – I Timothy 1:16

A MODEL OF LONGSUFFERING

The apostle Paul stated, 'for <u>this</u> cause I obtained mercy!' Why have we obtained such mercy from God Almighty? That in me (each of us, as in Paul), first Christ might show forth all longsuffering. Longsuffering is restraint of mind, before it gives room to action or passion. The person who has the ability to revenge himself, yet refrains. This is referred to as giving space for repentance. During this time, we, in Christ's stead, forgive the iniquity and transgressions occurring in the life, who has the grace of this space. This, by no means, clears the guilty. It just frees God to work a little longer, desiring that they come to repentance. During this time, we may pray for pardon because of His mercy.

Paul said Christ could use him as a pattern to those who should come to believe in Christ, for life everlasting. A pattern is used as an example, a sketch, a form, or mold, into which the very life of Christ was to be modeled. We are very visual, and it takes visuals for us to see.

Father, what a high honor you have called us to! That we would model your life on the runway of this world, so that all who would see it are called to this life, by repentance. We must have our "fittings," so that the garment of your life fits us!

Father, try your garments on me and then whittle me to the right size.

327

**"But of him are ye in Christ Jesus who of God
is made unto us wisdom, and righteousness,
and sanctification, and redemption:"**
I Corinthians 1:30

SANCTIFICATION

Oh Lord, show me what sanctification is for me.

It is holiness, separation unto God. It is the ability to be holy, even as God is holy. We can know, by the verse above, it is not a process, but the result of being in Christ. It is the holiness of Jesus becoming manifested in me, God making sanctification as real in me, as it is in His Word. We must experience it as impartation of the qualities of Jesus, all manifested in and through our soul. Qualities of godliness, faith, holiness, purity, patience, love, etc. - all the perfections of Jesus at my disposal, as I <u>draw</u> on Him.

Slowly and surely, I begin to live a life of order, sanity, and holiness, kept by the power of God. The people of God have gone off, over their history, into a lot of ditches trying to achieve sanctification as something they do rather than someone they receive.

Jesus has been made unto us sanctification. Father, we read this in your Word, and for some reason quickly forget it and try to put on some form of godliness we think you will accept. How you must despair of us, if it were not for your holiness! The very thing we need is what keeps you from annihilating us. Thank you for being God.

**Holiness is a person who lives in me and
wants to come out and be seen.**

*"And I will settle you after your old estates,
and will do better unto you than at your
beginnings; and ye shall know that I am
the Lord." – Ezekiel 36:11b*

FORMER ESTATES RECLAIMED

I want to bless you today with revelation from the Word of God concerning you. The Word tells us the knowledge of the Glory of God will cover the earth before Jesus returns. You must know the Glory of God is His goodness and His mercy. Lock this information into your heart and never lose it. God has come into your life to do you good, real good! It is His intention to restore you to His purpose for you, before the fall.

Ezekiel 16:55 speaks of a returning to former estates. This is referring to a former pristine state, before the fall, the way the Lord had ordained for you. It has not entered the mind of man, the beauty and perfection God created man to be. We have only lived in the fallen state, restored, to a measure, through salvation and our obedience to the work of the Holy Spirit. But still, we have had the grave clothes of the fall holding us in unperfected areas of our lives. Now we begin to glimpse at the purpose, the plan God had when He made man. The promise comes ringing down through eternity, that our boundaries are going to be established from the original deed!

Father, we believe in our hearts that an interloper has taken much land that belonged to us, by inheritance. Now, armed with this revelation, we want to set ourselves in faith to reclaim that land and all that belongs to us. We want to be all that you planned for us to be in eternity past. We want to stand as testimonies to the Glory of the God of Israel, and our God. We know it can only be done to us according to our faith in you.

**I believe God is working in my life and I
believe it is all for good.**

"But Jesus answered them, My Father worketh hitherto, and I work." – John 5:17

TAKE NO THOUGHT

<u>See</u> what the Father is doing. He is showing you what and how He wants a thing done. His instruction to us is that we are to take no thought, in the matter. Jesus said He worked because He <u>saw</u> the Father working. We don't need to think up something to do for God. We see what He is doing, and that is Him showing us how to do the thing He wants done. We could say He uses visual aids.

The obstacle before us appears as concrete, immovable, a mountain, so to speak. We begin to think about this mountain, and we come up with various plans and schemes to move it about or to get around it. The Word of the Lord would say to us to stop it. Stop all action of the mind. Stop taking thought and reasoning, and <u>see</u> what God has in mind. What is He doing? Integrity is the key, having done all, stand and <u>see</u>. Don't help, or assist, let light <u>be</u>. It comes as a foreign sound to our ears, when God tells us we don't need to fight, just stand and see God. What a challenge He has delivered to us today.

Father, as we mentally review your Word, we remember that many of your leaders gave the Word to their charges in times of great stress, "Stand still and see the salvation (the work) of God." The battle is not ours, but the Lord's. Jesus is the captain of the host of God's army. What an exciting challenge! Lord we understand the key Word here to be, "see." See must mean to behold, to recognize what's being done. I also believe it is definitely to see with the eyes of the spirit. We pray to have spiritual vision.

I would see Jesus. Holy Spirit, reveal Him to me while I wait.

"Come and let us return unto the Lord: for he hath torn, and he will heal us; he hath smitten, and he will bind us up." – Hosea 6:1

CHANGING OUR MINDS

We must come and return! Israel would not turn themselves and frame their movements according to God's Word. The book of Hosea graphically describes a people who are rebellious and obstinate in their refusal to heed the Lord's call. If we will be restored and revived, we must come and return. We must live in His sight, in relationship to the Lord.

If we will, we will know how to live. If we follow on to know, by learning of Him, we can be assured, certain, for He is stable. He is as sure as the sunrise.

Job 5:18 tells us it is God who strikes the final blow to annihilate us and to separate us from the old way. It is a decisive, lethal blow done by God, Himself, that He might raise us up and make us whole.

Jeremiah 30:17 speaks of a wound as a blow, a slaughter or a defeat. Then God says I will restore you, raise you up, lift you up, bring you up, lead you up. As the day star rises in our hearts, God will be exalted. First, we have to turn.

Father, in all these scriptures, we understand healing, health, and wholeness is your goal for us. We have put together some strange thoughts and ideas to live by that lead us away from, instead of toward, you. Now, as we change our mind and turn toward you, we allow you to remove and replace these false securities. In their place, you establish a strong concept of yourself. We know we cannot do this ourselves, we yield to the work of the Holy Spirit in our life.

I turn away from the old way and I set myself to be healed by God's power.

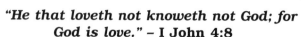
"He that loveth not knoweth not God; for God is love." – I John 4:8

HEALING BEGINS

God's love is not based on anything but Himself. God has to love, because love is what He is. He created man so He would have someone to love. We love Him because He first loved us. Love is a cycle, like rain. It waters the earth and is drawn back up into the heavens, where it fills the clouds full and then releases back to earth.

Basic to healing is the belief that God is love. If God made us to lavish His love upon, we are impoverished if we do not receive that love. We are twisted, bent, broken and mal-adjusted to live in the kingdom of God, when we are first born-again. The love of God gives an atmosphere for us to grow, develop and become nourished and whole.

Now we receive the kind of love that is pure, whole and healing. It is agape love that gives and doesn't take. Every other love takes something; agape only gives, never subtracts, always leaves you complete, whole.

Father, we know that only your love, as given to us by your Holy Spirit, has the power to change us, heal us and make us whole. This is a life long process. Thank you for placing us in churches and families where we don't give up, but keep growing.

We love you Father and we thank you.

"Behold, I stand at the door, and knock: if any man hear my voice, and open the door, I will come in to him, and will sup with him, and he with me." – **Revelation 3:20**

INVITE JESUS TO COME IN

Jesus comes where He is welcomed. The following is a list of some places He came. You will think of others.

Jesus came to be born of Mary, Luke 1:31, 38. The innkeeper made what he had available, Luke 2:6, 7. The doctors in the temple heard Him teach, Luke 2:46, 47. Mary and Martha made their home available, Luke 10:38. The tax collector invited Him to his house, Luke 19:5, 6. The merchant made the upper room available, Luke 22:10-12. Joseph, of Aramethea, made his tomb available, Luke 23:50-53.

Why have we shared the stories of these anxious souls who so readily accepted and made room for Jesus? To bring an important truth home to our hearts today. Jesus comes where He is invited and He makes a difference when He does.

Several times, recently, I have prayed for people who have asked for prayer and, in the same place, prayed for those who did not ask for prayer. As you can expect, those who asked for prayer received a touch from the Lord, while many of those not asking did not. What am I saying? I am saying, "Ask." This welcomes Him to come in.

Father, in many places, we are told to ask and to receive. We are encouraged to believe when we ask. These are all forms of invitation to Jesus to come into our life and make it different. We see clearly that we have not because we do not ask. Thank you for your sensitivity to our right to privacy, so to speak. You come only when invited.

I invite Jesus to help Himself to anything in my life today. It is all at His disposal.

"The thief cometh not, but for to steal, and to kill and to destroy: I am come that they might have life, and that they might have it more abundantly." – John 10:10

TWO PLANS

The thief's ultimate goal is to steal, kill and destroy. He wants to wipe out the image of God in a human being, to mar that likeness, so he doesn't have to be reminded every time he looks at you that he is looking into the eyes of the one who defeated him. He had a plan, to be <u>like</u> God, to be <u>God</u>-like, to be God!

God had a plan, to redeem the object of His love, to bring him back to relationship. If you love someone, you want to be with them. Isaiah 53:13-15 gives a graphic description of Jesus' appearance as He hung on the cross, with all the sin that Satan could ever think up to mar the human race, on His own precious human frame. It says His visage was so marred, He was unrecognizable. Jesus, who said in John 10:10, "I came that you might have a life that is abundant," made it possible. Two plans in the universe, one for harm, one for good. Thank God, love found a way!

Father God, our hearts are overflowing with our responses as we think about the plans you have for us. How different things would have been, if it had been Satan who had the last Word. Thank you that Jesus overcame the world, the flesh and the devil, and we live in that victory. We live on the resurrection side of the cross.

I want God's plan for my life 100%. I am in agreement with all He has for me.

"For I know the thoughts that I think toward you, saith the Lord, thoughts of peace, and not of evil, to give you an expected end."
Jeremiah 29:11

REJECTION SEPARATES

That spirit stands outside defenseless people and shoots in arrows to make them feel rejected.

Borders, or boundaries, are defenses to keep bad stuff out. These walls have gates that let the good stuff in. We have to guard against rejection, which would make us keep our gates locked and deprive our lives of God's blessings.

We need to be walled cities, against the wiles (these are methods or roads of travel), devices (this is a scheming of the mind), and deceptions (to deceive with a purpose, to bait). These are the strategies the enemy of our soul uses to keep us defeated and feeling like losers. II Corinthians 10:4, 5 clearly tells us to cast down imaginations and every high thing that would exalt itself above the knowledge of God. We are also told to bring into captivity every thought, to the obedience of Christ. It is a good thing to recognize an attack of the enemy and thereby disarm him.

Father, we know that rejection is a stronghold that lodges in our mind and our emotions. As we take every thought captive to the mind of Christ, we are reclaiming areas of our life, out of the enemy's hands.

I refuse feelings or thoughts of rejection. I know I am accepted in the beloved.

"How art thou fallen from heaven, O Lucifer, son of the morning! how art thou cut down to the ground, which didst weaken the nations." – Isaiah 14:12

LUCIFER IS HIS NAME!

It is not my intent to give undue attention to Lucifer, but rather to take these few words to identify him, his deeds, and his end. We need not to be ignorant of our enemy or his ways. Lucifer is his name. All the other titles are descriptive of what he does.

Because God used Israel for His purposes, they will yet be rewarded. God owes no man. He is just, gracious, rewarding and giving. He will pay Israel for the years of misuse and abuse because they carried His name (Isaiah 14:1,3). The oppressor will be destroyed and the awful plan dismantled. After it is all over, the earth can rest quietly from the striving and suffering. The earth shall see and witness the bringing down of the oppressor.

Lucifer has weakened the nations, made the earth to tremble, shook kingdoms, made the world a wilderness, destroyed the cities and opened not the house of his prisoners. "Vengeance is mine saith the Lord!" One has need to read Revelation 20:10 to see the end of the story.

Father God, it goes against our nature to even take up time and space to describe the work of the enemy of our souls. We do feel, though, it is important, within the pages of this little book, to make a declaration of who that enemy is. We thank you that he was defeated on Calvary's cross, and that the very plan he had to kill Jesus, was used, by you, to work his ultimate defeat! Jesus ravaged hell before He was resurrected!

I am so glad I am on Jesus' side and I know the end of the story.

*"And I saw heaven opened, and behold a
white horse; and he that sat upon him was
called Faithful and True, and in
righteousness he doth judge and make war."*
Revelation 19:11

THE SWORD

We defend our borders with the Sword of the Spirit. Supernaturally empowered words withstand the mental, emotional, spiritual and physical attacks of the enemy. Our borders are who we are in Christ Jesus, our personhood. The weapons of our warfare are not carnal. We surrender our borders at any point we get into carnality, or the flesh, to defend ourselves. Our borders have to be guarded (defended) against sniper attacks. Boundaries, what we set up to defend our borders, outline who we are. They are the expressions of our five senses.

In Genesis, when Adam and Eve transgressed their borders, God had to send them out of the garden. Genesis 3:24 tells us He set an angel with a flaming sword to keep the borders of the garden safe from interlopers. You see, God knows very well who He is and expresses what the boundaries are to relationship with Him. We could follow the Word of God as a sword all the way to Revelation. In Chapter 1:16 and 2:12, Jesus is described as He who has a double edged sword in his mouth. You see, Revelation is a picture of borders being restored.

Father, we see by these scriptures that the words we use are expressing the boundaries of our borders, where we will and will not go, what we will and will not do. We establish this border by our words. If we want our borders to be easily recognized and well defined, we must communicate this to those we are in contact with.

**May the words of my mouth and the meditations of
my heart be acceptable unto God.**

"For the Word of God is quick, and powerful, and sharper than any twoedged sword, piercing even to the dividing asunder of soul and spirit, and of the joints and marrow, and is a discerner of the thoughts and intents of the heart." – **Hebrews 4:12**

TWO IN AGREEMENT

Two-edged here, and other places in the Bible, refers to two as one-mouthed – God's mouth and your mouth speaking the same thing, two being in agreement as one. When the knowledge of the Lord God covers the earth like the waters cover the seas, then the dynamos of the dams can begin to function at full power. What a sight to behold when you stand on a dam and hear the dynamos start to pump and see the water surge in great power! When this happens, then God's people will be strong and do exploits.

Isaiah 11:2 and 9 and Habakkuk 2:14 speak of this glorious time on the earth. A time when Jesus, who has been made the wisdom and knowledge of God, is released in a people who will allow Him full control so that He might accomplish all things, through them, to bring culmination to the plans and purposes of God. We need to be very diligent during these days, to apply our hearts to coming into full agreement with Jesus, as He works the works of His Father.

Our Lord and our God, there is only one thing left to be said. Yes, Lord! Have your way in me, so that you may have your way through me.

Come Spirit of God and pour over me, in the power and might of God.

*"And the Lord spake unto Moses and Aaron,
Because ye believed me not, to sanctify me in
the eyes of the children of Israel, therefore ye
shall not bring this congregation into the land
which I have given them." –* **Numbers 20:12**

DON'T STRIKE THE ROCK

Anger, frustration, and impatience causes us to strike out. Since Calvary has done its work in us, we are to speak to the rock. Let's follow this example in Numbers 20:1-13, the children of Israel were in the desert and there was no water. They were angry and turned that frustration toward Moses, God's chosen leader. God had become an adversary and they weren't taking it very well. Isaiah 63:10 tells us because they rebelled and vexed God's Spirit, He turned to be an enemy. We don't need a lightening bolt to give us understanding on this matter!

Our focus is not on Israel here, but their leaders. They prayed and God gave the specific instructions that would alleviate the problem. Because of Moses' frustration, at the rebellion of the people, brought about by their whining, ingratitude and selfishness, He reverted to a lower form of action and struck the rock God had told him to speak to. You see, God wanted to be modeled in the presence of His people, and His leaders were required to do that. The lack of water, the need for a miracle, was all of God, that He might be sanctified in them.

Oh God, how easy it is to do a foolish thing! Some foolish things can never be undone and cause irreparable harm. It was so serious to you that Moses could no longer lead. Oh God, your Spirit has been sent to manifest the fruit of Godliness, in and through our lives. We sin terribly when we yield to the works of the flesh and model (display) awful deeds before people you desire to be sanctified in. Please forgive us.

**I will, by the Grace of God, cease to
entertain the works of the flesh and allow
the fruit of the Spirit to grow in me.**

December 5

*"While we look not at the things which are
seen, but at the things which are not seen:
for the things which are seen are temporal;
but the things which are not seen are
eternal." – II Corinthians 4:18*

IS IT REAL OR ACTUAL?

We have what may seem like a puzzle, but it is not. Pray to understand this, for it will keep you sane in an insane world. <u>Actual</u> is what we come in contact with by our five senses. <u>Real</u> is that which lies behind, that which we can't get at by our senses. You might say the actual is temporal and the real, eternal. A fanatic sees only the real and a materialist sees only the actual.

The only sane being was Jesus. In Him the actual and the real were one. Can we begin to see the need here? Jesus Christ, God's only son, stands first in the real world. Now we have a vehicle, through which we can <u>see</u> the real in the actual, that vehicle is prayer. Prayer is a method of focusing in on the thing that is happening, at any given moment, to perceive what is behind the scenes that we are missing with our senses. Now the admonition, in Philippians 4:6, to pray about everything to the intent of the peace of God reigning in your mind.

Oh God, the world is rushing at break neck speed toward destruction. We have lost the ability to live in sanity and orderliness, as we try to keep up. We <u>must</u> come aside and focus in on Jesus, the only reality in our world of illusion. Thank you for giving Jesus for us, to give us the way of escape. The way back, to life in harmony with you and all around us, is seeing through actuality to reality.

**Whenever my world begins to spin, I will
pull away and find Jesus!**

"Which hope we have as an anchor of the soul, both sure and steadfast, and which entereth into that within the veil;" – **Hebrews 6:19**

STEPPING STONES OF FAITH

Beginning in Hebrews 6:13, we have another account of Abraham and his relationship with God. Verse 15 speaks of faithfulness, through patience. We are told Abraham inherited the promises. He was triumphant in endurance and is called the father of all who walk in the steps of faith. What are these steps of faith? Can we picture them as stepping stones, on a pathway? The first stone says, "separate from the world." The second one says, "take the place of a stranger and a pilgrim." The third stone tells us to "patiently endure under severe trials and testings." These stones lead us to a doorway marked "possession of that which you have sought for on this pathway."

Christ, our anchor, has entered into our lives. Our security lies completely outside ourselves, therefore, the need to hold on to Christ. These stepping stones of faith surely take us down a pathway we cannot see the end of. A pathway foreign to all that is familiar to us. We could never go there, without the sure knowledge Jesus is holding fast.

Lord, our God, we will need to live our lives in the same manner Abraham did, if we are to be children of faith. The one thing we recall most vividly about him is that he went out, not knowing where. By your grace, we will live the life of faith, whereby you will be honored, others helped, and ourselves contented and assured.

I see the life of faith is the most freeing thing I can think of.

"And Elijah the Tishbite, who was of the inhabitants of Gilead, <u>said</u> unto Ahab, As the Lord God of Israel liveth, before whom I stand, there shall not be dew nor rain these years, but according to my Word." – I Kings 17:1

AVAILABILITY

Gilead, the place Elijah came from, means place of promise. In Genesis 31:21, when Jacob ran from Laban, he ran toward Mt. Gilead, toward God's promise. Elijah came to remind Israel of God's promises. He was an outsider. He came from the "other side of the Jordan." From the outside, you can "see" the problem more clearly. Israel was in apostasy under Ahab and Jezebel.

At some point in Elijah's relationship with God, he took up God's concern for Israel. You see, until he did, God would not have sent him to Ahab to speak a Word for Him!

Who is Israel to me? Who does Almighty God have a message for that He wants to use my mouth to deliver? God's eternal plan and purpose is to redeem and restore the world unto Himself (John 3:16). Elijah, out of relationship, became an instrument for God to use for His purpose, to bring about His plan of redemption. If I am not being sent to someone yet, I need to work on my relationship with God!

Father God, Gilead was a rocky place. It stands to reason it was not easy for Elijah to go to Israel. If we wait until it gets easy, Father, we will never go! Jesus came forth as a root out of dry ground. Help us understand, it is availability you need. We just need to get into the right place with you!

Like Isaiah said long ago, "Here I am Lord, send me,"

"And the word of the Lord came unto him,
saying," — I Kings 17:2

THE MESSAGE, NOT THE MESSENGER

Fifty-eight years after Solomon's death, Israel sank into apostasy. Seven kings had reigned, each one worse than the other. Apostasy started with the corrupting of the priesthood, installing men into divine service that were not called by God (I Kings 16:30-33). There was no sign left of pure worship of Jehovah.

On this scene, came Elijah. He came into darkness and degradation with dramatic suddenness! There is no genealogy given, his past was behind him, he was not limited by his heritage or his environment. He had come through with God, not crippled by his past failures or successes. He had come there to stand before God and to stand for God. This lone man was coming to confront an idolatrous, back-slidden nation. His heritage had made him what he was for God, a tough, strong, quiet individual. His name, Elijah, means Jehovah my God and Tishbite, the stranger here. The word itself came with dramatic suddenness and with exceeding boldness. He came unannounced, unattended, a plain man, dressed in humble clothes.

Father God, we sense, in our spirit, a drawing from you, away from the messenger and onto the message. We have perfected how we package the messenger, and have neglected to spend the time needed to hear the Word of the Lord you want delivered. We believe this is a day of plain things, so that the plain truth may come through.

I will not go forth and show myself until I
have the sure Word of the Lord.

"So he went and did according unto the word of the Lord: for he went and dwelt by the brook Cherith, that is before Jordan." – I Kings 17:5

GOING BATHED IN PRAYER

Elijah prayed six months before he went to Ahab. They were well into drought by the time he went. We must always go forth in the knowledge of prayer, of God and of His purpose. Immediately after he delivered God's message, he was hidden away. There would be no chance for further communication on the Word of the Lord. They were shut up to God's judgement, without chance of change.

The leadings and guidings of God defy sense or reason. Elijah was led from the brook to Sidon, the home place of Jezebel, who sought his life. The land of her tribute concealed her prey. Can we say the safest place to be for a child of God is in the center of His will? The leadings of God seem to be toward destruction, instead of away from. So often, we are told to fear not, only believe.

One Sidonian woman breathing fire and death, another offering safety and peace. We see it is not gender or nationality, it is the spirit controlling the individual. We cannot let one bad experience shut us off from an avenue of blessing.

Our Father, we come once again to see that prayer brings the knowledge from you, like a beam of light, directing our path as we go out. We are helpless without the Word from you. We must depend on that sure Word for direction. But we are not to sit like stranded baby birds in a nest with our mouth's open. Rather, we are called upon to pray and to seek your face and to hear from heaven.

To pray will be my recourse today. To pray until I know the will of my Father.

"He that dwelleth in the secret place of the most High shall abide under the shadow of the Almighty." – Psalm 91:1

THE SECRET PLACE

Psalm 91:1 and 2 speaks of a secret place under the wings of the Almighty. Psalm 61:4 speaks also of those wings as a covering, a protection. Psalm 32:7 goes on to speak of God as a hiding place, with Psalm 31:20 telling of God hiding them in the secret of His presence, and keeping them in a pavilion of safety.

I would like to paraphrase Hosea 2:14-16 for developing our thought for today: God, Himself, allured me and brought me to this place. With the shadow of His hand, He has concealed me, to press me from my present position into Himself. It appears to be dark here, therefore, I feel uncomfortable. It is really only the shadow of His hand that I am in. Here in the darkness, He has made my mouth like a sharp sword. With the shadow of His hand, He hath made me a polished shaft, hidden in His quiver (Psalm 45:5).

Father, Psalm 18:11 tells me your pavilion around me is as dark waters. I understand now the only way to get to the secret place is to be brought by you. I also understand it takes courage, stamina and faith to move into the secret place. I have none of these. You, in your providential care and concern, have furnished all of them.

I draw on you Father. Take me into your secret place.

December 11

**"So shall the King greatly desire thy beauty:
for he is thy Lord; and worship thou him."
Psalm 45:11**

WORSHIP THE LORD

Worship sets free the minds of men to go on to experience higher levels with God. Worship brings release. A worshipper is one who lives with an eye on God. True worship is always focused on God. The purpose of the church is to worship God. In the old covenant, there were 38,000 Levites set aside to minister unto the Lord. Their duty was to carry the presence of the Lord and to minister unto Him.

When men, women and children are free to worship God, He comes down to see. When God comes down, things happen. We need leaders in charge who see and hear the Spirit of God and what the Spirit is doing, and let it happen! The guidelines are set after the fact, not before. They develop when you perceive the direction the Spirit is taking. It doesn't need to be orchestrated. If we will just go into worship, the Holy Spirit will come. He is here to prepare us, He is here to enlarge us and get us ready for the Lord's appearing.

Father, we have been guilty of praising you and stopping short of going on into worship. We have done half of the thing and gone away feeling empty. It is in the worship of you that we are filled and that we are visited by you. Your Word tells us that you inhabit the praise and worship of your people. Thank you for coming to us, as we worship, before your throne.

Praise empties me out...worship fils me back up!

"... Not by might, nor by power, but by my spirit, saith the Lord of hosts." – Zechariah 4:6b

SANCTUARY

In Revelation 18:11-13, we find a list of commodities that merchants will be trading in at the close of this age. Down at the bottom of that list, in verse 13, is listed the souls of men. This is a sobering, as well as horrifying, revelation; that in our time because of greed, men are making merchandise of mens souls, for gain. If we will pause and think on this, it is very easy to see.

Unfortunately, the church of the Living God has fallen prey to the same wickedness. For whatever reason, and we could list several, the church is using many of the same techniques and gimmicks to manipulate people. What we have moved into is a whole lot of soul power being released, as counterfeit spiritual power, and it is warring with the genuine move of God!

A good definition of soul power is, if man can do it without God, it is not Spirit! Zechariah 4:6 expresses it best, Souls of men are in the balance. When the spirit (God given) and the body (God-formed) were joined, man became a living soul. Soul is personality, it is the meeting place with God and man, our point of union. God has such high regard and respect for the soul He formed, that it is a terrible offense to Him to misuse it. Great judgement is coming, in and out of the church, toward those who have abused or misused another person.

God, forgive us, as your people, for allowing the plans and maneuvers of Satan to be employed in your house. Your house is to be a place of prayer, where people can find sanctuary and be safe from the wiles of the devil. Oh God, have mercy on us, and send a revival of your love into our hearts, before we perish.

God being my helper, I will be a sanctuary for the hurting people seeking God.

"And herein do I exercise myself, to have always a conscience void of offense toward God, and toward men." – Acts 24:16

A CLEAR CONSCIENCE

Conscience is the faculty of the soul whereby we apprehend the Will of God. Christ's death on the cross purged our conscience once and for all. We now are free to be carnal, fleshly or spiritual, based on our decisions. What you partake of feeds your conscience (eating from the tree of good and evil).

By drawing near to God, you make your conscience tender. Our new born (purged) conscience functions by the mystery of faith. Faith guides the conscience into making spiritual decisions.

Fear is the result of a warped conscience. It is the ministry of the Holy Spirit to shed the love of God into our hearts, that we may cease to fear and live openly and freely in relationship with a loving God. Our conscience is washed and cleansed by the washing of the Word of God. As the truths of God's Word begin to pour over our awareness, we see things as they really are.

Father God, I yield my conscience to your law concerning relationships and I choose to yield to your judgements, thereby, having a conscience devoid of offense toward God and man. I choose to honor those you place before me, according to the law of God. I will be aware of others and accept my responsibility not to let my liberty be a stumbling block to my brother.

I am free unto God but bound by service unto my fellow man.

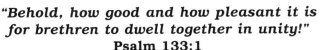

December 14

**"Behold, how good and how pleasant it is
for brethren to dwell together in unity!"
Psalm 133:1**

OFFENSE KILLS REVIVAL

Revival comes when God's people have prayed and repented of sins and come together as one. Matthew 24:10 gives strong warning against a revival killer that will surely come. There are six areas where we must be on guard and strive to avoid the spirit of offense. 1.) Do not take offense. 2.) Do not give offense. 3.) Do not offend the Holy Spirit. 4.) Do not be offended at God when things don't work out the way you wanted. 5.) Don't offend ourselves, by sinning against our own conscience. 6.) Don't be offended by the truth. Verse 12, of Matthew 24, tells us that cold love is the result of beginning with an offense. The church has laughingly been referred to as the "frozen chosen." Could that be an observation of cold love?

Perhaps we need to define offense, to help us understand what it is. It is anything that a man finds in his way, that may occasion him to stumble or fall, whether physically or morally. Another definition is a sin or trespass. For the body of Christ to come into perfection, to be the bride of Christ, it must indeed be devoid of offense.

Father, we know many places in your Word warn us against being a stumbling block or falling over one ourselves. An offense can be that thing that causes us to stumble. Thank you for warning us and helping us, by your Spirit.

God being my helper, I will not give offense, take offense, or cause offense by sin.

"Charity (agape) never faileth: but whether there be prophecies, they shall fail; whether there be tongues, they shall cease; whether there be knowledge, it shall vanish away." – I Corinthians 13:8

REAL LOVE

I have made a discovery about love. Real love is not reciprocal. It pours forth from the heart, where it has been shed, by God's Spirit. It loves in the face of all things; it neither depends on nor relies on anything to be. It just is. Real love (which is God's agape love), is an action, not a response. It comes out of a relationship of security in God. It is never threatened by another's aggression, weakness or failure to respond in like manner. It is independent of another's response. A reading of I Corinthians 13, in several translations, can prove very enlightening. In the first verse, "charity", in the King James Version, is reference to agape.

If we are to minister and to serve in the kingdom of God, we must not be hurt or wounded when those we are sent to serve lash out and attack. The picture of a wounded animal always flashes before me. They will bite the one who desperately seeks to help them. Do not draw back. You are inoculated by the Spirit of God, with His baptism of love, to go into hard places and rescue the perishing.

Father God, we are reminded of the beautiful story of love in Hosea – a picture of your everlasting striving with mankind, to accept your offer of healing and wholeness, brought by Jesus Christ, on the cross. Help us be part of the solution, not the problem.

I am not afraid to go where Jesus sends me, to pull a soul out of destruction.

"But the God of all grace, who hath called us unto his eternal glory by Christ Jesus, after that ye have suffered a while, make you perfect, stablish, strengthen, settle you."
I Peter 5:10

WHO, ME SUFFER?

Settling down means making character, by forming habits on the basis of the new life in us. It is learning to live in the kingdom by having our senses exercised, through circumstances. I cannot live what is required of me. I cannot, but if I choose to, all the grace of God is behind my obedience. Between the call of God and the settling and establishing, is a Word we don't like to hear and certainly don't want applied to us personally! That small Word, so avoided, is suffering! Suffering can take different forms for different people. I see suffering as tailor-made circumstances, taking away control of my life and casting me out into the deep, like Jonah. Interestingly enough, it has been said if it gets too rocky in the boat, we can walk on the water!

It has also been stated that the suffering is in the resisting, not in the doing, of the Will of God. If we can bring ourselves early on in our relationship with God, to give up our rights to our lives, it will make for a smoother, quicker transition in character.

Father, we hear those words echoing through our minds again, "do you have any faith? Then let go and trust me." Peter spoke of you in our passage today as the God of all Grace. This is how he came to know you as he moved, through suffering, to being established.

I can believe him. He experienced the grace of God for himself.

"For our light affliction, which is but for a moment, worketh for us a far more exceeding and eternal weight of glory;"
II Corinthians 4:17

THE GLORY WAY

If Christ is dwelling in my heart, through faith, I have the foundation of an incorruptible life, which will eventually emerge in the fullness of glory. Faith apprehends that for which it was apprehended, the glorified humanity of Jesus. For this cause we are being conformed. He is our model, pattern, representation of God's intention for all who believe in our Lord Jesus. Faith takes hold of Him now and says, He is like He is, because God wants me like that.

The Spirit of Glory is operating for me on a daily basis, to make me like Him; to transform me that I might be transfigured, and to conform me to His image (Ephesians 4:13). The meaning of all the activities and methods of the Spirit of God, in my life, is to lay a foundation of Glory.

Keep on the Glory line
Get in the way of the Glory
Keep in the way of the Glory
For you are called unto Glory (I Peter 5:10)

Father of Glory, we find ourselves breathless in the revelation that we are called to Glory. We see the insignificance of our existence, as defined by the mind of man. Yet, you tell us we are being transformed by the renewing of our minds and that we are, even now, partakers of your Glory. We are also reminded that it does not yet appear what we are going to be. Glory is embraced by faith, not vision at this time. One day it will be revealed. Oh, Glorious day!

I will keep on the Glory line by saying the same thing God says about me.

"Blessed are the peacemakers: for they shall be called the children of God." – Matthew 5:9

MAKERS OF PEACE

Peacemaker, as used in today's text, is defined only here, in this way: The one who makes peace in others, having first received the peace of God in his own heart, not simply one who makes peace between two parties. Could we say they create peace out of the peace that they themselves have received and hold in their own heart? What a joy to be around a person who can give you the peace of God. The text says, "they shall be called the children of God."

This peace-bringing one, gives evidence of the dignity of their relationship and likeness to God's character. They are easily recognized as sons of God, like Jesus. We are to impart the peace of God into others. The scriptures say that in the last days, men's hearts will fail them for fear of what is coming upon the earth. What a need for peacemakers to come forth! The peace of God passes understanding, but it is a fruit of the Spirit of God and we can receive it. Now what should we do with it when it comes? Like every other gift from God, give it away!

Father, we receive your peace, as a fruit of the Spirit, given to make us look like you. We will let your peace rule in our heart and our mind, as we live in relationship with you.

Peace has a price. It costs us trust. What do we hold in our trust account?

*"Then the Lord answered Job out of the
whirlwind, and said, Who is this that
darkeneth counsel by words without
knowledge?" – Job 38:1,2*

ARE YOU THE ONE?

God had been addressing Elihu, when abruptly, in
Job 38, He turned His attention to Job. If you will allow me,
I'd like to walk us through some interesting conversation
between Job and God Almighty. In Chapter 40, verse 8,
God asked, "Will you also question my judgement?" Self-
righteousness questions God's judgement. If I choose outside
of God's judgement, I condemn Him as wrong and myself
right. The last half of verse 8 says, "Will you condemn me,
that you may be right?" This is exactly what Satan did in
heaven and then in the garden with Eve. Verses 9-14 go on
to say, 'if you can carry out the judgements of God in a
moral universe, then you can save yourself!'

God calls Job's attention to Behemoth, in verses 15-
24, telling him that He (God) made him and that He is the
one who can destroy him (verse 19). Chapter 41 goes on to
describe an unconquerable enemy, stronger than man. God
asked Job, 'Who do you think you are? Are you the one?'
Pride and self-righteousness always makes us think we
are the one!

*Father God, when we consider your descriptions in the
book of Job, we see ourselves as very small, without strength
or understanding. No wonder you have counseled us to buy
from you all that we need. We are indeed completely destitute
without you. We are naked and blind, until you clothe us with
garments of your righteousness and give us sight. Thank you
for being a God who understands our frame and deals with
us according to your knowledge of us.*

**Pride will truly bring us down and humble
us before our maker.**

"And thou shalt remember all the way which the Lord thy God led thee these forty years in the wilderness, to humble thee, and to prove thee, to know what was in thine heart, whether thou wouldest keep his commandments, or no." – Deuteronomy 8:2

HE'LL DO IT AGAIN!

In Exodus 15:19-21, Miriam led the women of Israel in song and dance, to praise God for all His help and provision - For the drowning of Pharaoh and his pursuing army, how He moved on their behalf, establishing His great power, protection and provision for Israel. In Deuteronomy 11:4, we see the recalling of the great acts of God, on their behalf.

You will never get out of the new crisis, unless you remember the old and how God brought you out! Past experiences are the seed bed of faith for new experiences. In the dark, shadows look different from the actual object. A chair can look like a dragon, with an active imagination, stirred by fear. Events in our past (sub-conscious) can loom as destruction to our actual thought processes, casting distortions on our life at that moment, making it look different than it is. This is why we remember God in those past situations, and place them in the right perspective. In II Kings 6:17, Elisha prayed and asked God to open his servant's eyes, to see as it really was.

Father, we all have memories that make things appear harder or bigger or more dangerous than they really are. We need to be free of these "skeletons," that jump out in the dark and say, boo! We need to recall all the way you have led us and how you really brought us, through those past experiences, to where we are today. We need to think on all the things you have done for us and how you have preserved our life.

I will call on the God I know, who has led me all the way.

"If iniquity be in thine hand, put it far away,
and let not wickedness dwell in thy
tabernacles." – Job 11:14

BE DONE WITH SIN!

Job 11:13-15 is a call, from the Word of God, for men to come and put their hearts right. If there is sin, to get rid of it. If iniquity, put it away, be done with it. Then you can walk steadily toward God, without fear; standing firm and unafraid, a man of iron knowing no fear. Verse 16 says that you will forget your trouble and remember it as floodwaters that pass by. The promise of verse 17 is, then your age will be clearer than noonday, cloudless, and you will shine forth. Verse 18 talks of being full of hope, living securely and with courage. It goes on to say that you will dig about and take your rest in safety, speaking of work and rest, the rythmn of life.

One of the most beautiful promises is this passage in verse 19, "you shall lie down and no one will make you afraid. Many will seek your company and ask you for help." Casting our eyes back to the start of this wonderful Word we see the proverbial condition – come and put your heart right!

Jehovah God, we feel the pull of your Spirit to do business with you, at the altar of our heart, to rid ourselves of every sin, shortcoming and transgression, ask forgiveness, put iniquity away from us, and walk with clean hands and pure hearts, before our God.

I cannot have peace from God, and sin in my heart.

*"Come, my beloved, let us go forth into the
field; let us lodge in the villages."*
Song of Solomon 7:11

LAST DAYS SERVANTHOOD

Looking in Song of Solomon 7, we have a description of the king's wife. She is said, in verse 8, to have fresh breath as apples. I believe there is goodness coming forth from her lips. Verse 9 says her mouth is like wine. In the Bible, wine is symbolic of joy, She is full of the joy of the Lord. She desires that the wine go straight to the king. We see a picture here of praises given with the lips and worship from the heart.

Go on with me, in verse 12, to discover how she longs to go forth and check on the king's possessions, to see how things are coming along. She is willing to make necessary adjustments, so that the fruit matures and gives glory to the king. There, in the vineyards, in the field of service, she can release all she has stored up for the king, both old and new (verse 13).

Can you see here a picture of last day servanthood? It is the one who has progressed through the steps of maturity after salvation, and is now ready to go forth into service with the king of Glory.

Father God, in many areas, we are hearing the call going out to workers for the harvest. We are admonished to pray for these workers to be raised up. We give our hearts here, to pray that very prayer. Process us, Oh Spirit of God, until we are indeed ready to go forth, riding into the fields with the King of Glory.

**I am applying myself to getting ready to go.
I yield myself to the Spirit of God.**

December 23

"The Lord make his face shine upon thee, and be gracious unto thee: The Lord lift up his countenance upon thee, and give thee peace. And they shall put my name upon the children of Israel; and I will bless them." – **Numbers 6:25-27**

GIVING BLESSINGS

In Genesis 1:27-28, we are told that God created man in His own image and blessed him. We see, by this, that God was in the blessing business from the very beginning. We move on through the Word of God to the New Testament and the life of our Lord Jesus. He taught on blessing, even to the point of blessing our enemies in Matthew 5:44. It was His desire that everyone be blessed, from the smallest child, to the most undesirable enemy. He gave His very life so we can be blessed. Galatians 3:13-14 states that cursed is everyone who hangs on a tree and Christ, Himself, redeemed us from the curse of the law, that the blessing of Abraham might come upon the Gentiles.

If we make a study of blessing in the New Testament, we see that Christians are called to a lifestyle of blessing. There are several definitions of blessing: to make holy or whole by the spoken Word; to ask favor for; to wish a person well; to make prosperous and to make happy or glad. There are three things we can apply blessing to: situations, people and God. What an adventure we can have, as we set our hearts to be a blessing.

Father, I don't believe I have ever had such an awareness of the mandate to bless, as I have today. I move to bless you with my praise and my worship, and Lord I want to begin to bless everywhere I go. Help me.

Blessing will release me into a relationship of intimacy with the Father. I'll be doing what He does.

"Art not thou our God, who didst drive out the inhabitants of this land before thy people Israel, and gavest it to the seed of Abraham thy friend for ever?"
II Chronicles 20:7

FRIENDS FOREVER

To be friends, in Hebrew, means to love, to desire, delight, be beloved, close ties of friendship. It suggests desire to possess, or be in the presence of. Look with me, today, at the life of a man referred to as the friend of God (James 2:23). He was called, by God, into this lifelong relationship, in Genesis 11. He walked with God a long time before the dark night of the soul passed. Chapter 12 gives account of his entering into the separated life. God unfolded His plan for Abraham on a need to know basis. We who would seek to follow Abraham, in the walk of faith, must settle this, before we will release control of our lives to God.

Abraham was a man, just as you and I. He had a strong self-life. The reasoning of the expedient need before him spurred him into erroneous action more than once! It always boils down to two roads of action, trust (God's way) or mistrust (I'll do it!). In the long night spent in prayer, God first revealed His covenant name, El Shaddai, I am the God who is more than enough. Abraham was old and frail when God commissioned him to walk before him. It is a life long friendship we are speaking of. It never ends.

Father God, Genesis 15:6 says it all! Abraham "<u>believed</u> in the Lord," and you counted that belief to him as righteousness. We have to understand this relationship goes beyond the law, it goes to want to, not have to. It goes to no greater love than this, that a man (Jesus) would lay down His life for a friend (me). It is truly a love that is stronger than life itself.

Oh Hallelujah, what a Savior! And He is my friend forever and ever. Amen!

"And they came with haste, and found Mary, and Joseph, and the babe lying in a manger." – Luke 2:16 "And he bearing his cross went forth into a place called the place of a skull, which is called in the Hebrew Golgotha:" – John 19:17

THE MANGER AND THE CROSS

It is the time of celebration of the birth of Jesus. His entrance into the human race as a man, flesh, blood, reality. As the demons fought that first advent, so they move in to oppose even the mention of it. It made the cross possible. Without the manger, there would be no cross. The cross and the manger were cut from the same piece of wood. It's all a part of the total picture.

Jesus Christ has to be birthed in your spirit man and laid, so to speak, in your manger. Then He walks out His earthly life in you, growing and maturing, and then moving out into service. You are launched out, for a time, and then the cross looms directly in front of you. Will you die to family, friends, abilities, the ministry He has given you? Will you lay it all down? In exchange, pick up the cross and come and walk as He did, as He wishes to continue walking in you.

If you accept the baby Jesus into your manger, then you sign up for the whole package, including the cross.

Father, in the very midst of the joy, the bells and the angel voices, we have cause to behold the shadow of the cross over the manger. Yes, it is necessary to complete the journey we start with Jesus, and it does take us up Calvary's hill. But even in this, we know you are with us and because Jesus died, there we will never taste death. Hallelujah!

I move to embrace the cross of Christ, as I behold this tiny baby in the manger.

"For God so loved the world, that he gave his only begotten Son, that whosoever believeth in him should not perish, but have everlasting life." – John 3:16

HELD BY THE LOVE OF GOD

It has been established that December 25 is not the real day on which Jesus was born. Neither is the day I partake of the bread and wine the exact day Jesus did in the Upper Room. To discount and have no participation in the celebration of the birth of Jesus can cut us off from the flow of love that comes from many devoted loved ones. It is an exchange of love, and love overpowering the forces of evil, as we direct our appreciation toward heaven.

For our consideration, today, I would like to list several scriptures on love, and ask you to find a quiet place, and allow the Spirit of God to soak you in His love: Romans 8:35-39; Ephesians 3:19; I John 3:16; 1 John 4:19; Jude 21; I John 4:18. To sin against love is much more terrible than to sin against the law. Hebrews 10:20 tells us Jesus made a way into the presence of God, by giving his own life to save us from the curse of the law. Can we see ourselves along with the apostle Paul, being constrained by the love of God?

Heavenly Father, we are persuaded that you love us with an everlasting love. We will spend more and more time in your presence, so that we may perceive more and more of the love you have for us. Thank you for making us super conquerors through your love.

I will not sin against love by turning away from God, but will set myself to receive more and more.

"For the love of Christ constraineth us; because we thus judge, that if one died for all, then were all dead:" – II Corinthians 5:14

THE AWL REQUIRES OUR ALL!

Paul goes on, in verses 15-21, in explaining why he acted and reacted as he did; that because Jesus had died for him, out of love, that love held him fast in relationship to Christ. All that was done by God, through Jesus, on Calvary, was done out of His love for mankind. In other words, Paul was saying, 'I do what I do because I am nailed to the cross by love.'

In Deuteronomy 15, we have the picture of a servant that had served his time out and was free to go his way. In verses 16 and 17, we have the breathtaking response of the servants to the more than generous offer of this master to leave. He prefers, out of the relationship of love that has developed, to stay and serve willingly, not out of bondage. God instructs the master to give a sign to the servant and all who see him, that he is there because he wants to be there. He lays his ear on the door post and the master thrusts the awl through and pierces his ear. He is then a servant – forever!

Oh God, we know Jesus' death on the cross paid our debt and set us free. We can go out with blessing and provision or we can turn to you and see your look of love and say to you, our Master, "pierce my ear through, that I might be your servant forever!"

Where could I go but here? You, my Lord, have the words of life.

"If thou hast run with the footmen, and they have wearied thee, then how canst thou contend with horses? and if in the land of peace, wherein thou trustedst, they wearied thee, then how wilt thou do in the swelling of Jordan?" – **Jeremiah 12:5**

LIFE AND DEATH IN THE JORDAN

The name Jordan means "descending." It is a wonderful, fast-flowing river in Palestine. The course of the river is about a hundred miles, from sixty to eighty feet wide and ten to twelve feet deep. It discharges approximately six million and ninety thousand tons of water every day. It has double banks but the usual channel is within the inner banks. At certain seasons of the year, it overflows the inner banks and is embraced by the outer ones. In the space between, there is an immense thicket wherein wild beasts conceal themselves, but the overflowings of the river dislodges them. Jeremiah used this analogy (Jeremiah 49:19) to describe Israel's enemies.

It was during the flood season that the Israelites passed over the Jordan. This enhances the wonder of this miracle, some say beyond that of the Red Sea crossing. It was made to stand upon a heap, until the children of Israel all passed over and then resumed its course.

I said all this to say that there are times, in all of our lives, that the river overflows its inner banks and dislodges the evil lurking in the shadows. Our scripture today calls us to soberly consider our walk with the Lord, in the quiet times; to prepare our hearts with the Word of the Lord, that we will not panic when the floods come.

Father God, our confidence is in you. In peace time or in havoc, you are always the same. Our confidence is in the Word that says the waters stood up, until all the children of Israel were across. In Joshua 5:1, it tells us the rulers in the new land shook and quivered at the awesome display of God on behalf of His children.

The God that split the sea and stood the river up like a mountain is my God!

"Thou that dwellest in the gardens, the companions hearken to thy voice: cause me to hear it." – Song of Solomon 8:13

THREE GARDENS

We will consider three gardens in our time today, the Garden of Eden, Gethsemane and the King's Garden. Genesis 2:8 tells us God planted a garden and there He placed the man He had formed. What a glorious thought to have been Adam and walked in paradise, without stress, sweat and torment. We would think so, but chances are Adam didn't last a day! We know the story: he blew it, got kicked out, and it was rough from then on.

Until we consider garden number two. Gethsemane is described as a place to rest in the shade. We believe Jesus took His disciples here often, to rest and reflect, but we are considering one visit. The night before Jesus was crucified, He went to the garden to pray through, to accept the horror of sin. Matthew 26:36-46 gives us an account of the agony of soul Jesus passed through that night, before He opened the way for us to again enter the garden of God.

Which brings us to the references in Song of Solomon, of the king's garden. Chapter 5:1 throws open the invitation to come, and eat and drink. Jesus came to the garden so that we might enter again into paradise. Paradise is where God is!

Our Lord and our God, we have always delighted in gardens. To go apart and gaze upon the beauty of a well-ordered garden brings such joy and rest to our souls. Song of Solomon 1:4 is a wonderful prayer for us to pray to you. Oh Lord, draw us, by your Spirit, and we will to respond, to run after you.

To come away with you and sup with you is my heart's desire.

"O come, let us worship and bow down: let us kneel before the Lord our Maker." **Psalm 95:6**

DON'T SAY HOW TO HIM – BOW TO HIM!

In Luke 1:34, we have Mary's response when the angel informed her she was chosen to be the mother of Jesus. "How shall this be, seeing I know not a man?" The first thing we want to do is figure out a way to carry out the command of the Lord. The angel quickly gave Mary the answer to her puzzle. "The Holy Ghost shall come upon you." Mary responded as every one of us is required to respond. Before she knew the hows, whys or wherefores, she said, "Be it unto me, according to thy Word," (verse 38). This is what is meant by bowing to the command of the Lord, that makes known His Will. Yes, Lord!

Song of Solomon 8:4 warns the daughters of Jerusalem not to stir things before time. Take heed to these words! If a thing desired and commanded by God is stirred up before time, it will contort and mutate and hybrid and turn grotesque! Let it come awake in response to the bridegroom. Let the Holy Ghost come upon it and bring it forth.

Father God, no man knoweth the heart but God. Down through the pages of your Word, we see men and women after your own heart, who you used to do exploits and to change the course of history. Mary was one of these! You knew, when you called her, she had a heart that would respond to you. Father God, by your Spirit, do a work in our hearts, that we would quickly bow down and say "yes," not "how!"

I want to respond to the call of God quickly and not question the outcome.

"For the kingdom of God is not meat and drink; but righteousness, and peace, and joy in the Holy Ghost." – Romans 14:17

WINE NOT WHINE!

Whose finger is God using to crush your grapes? We are clusters of grapes, growing in the king's vineyard. When these grapes are squeezed and test out sweet, ripe and mature, it's time to go to the winepress!

Now, the grapes do not get to choose which winepress! We don't drink grapes, do we? We drink wine at celebrations, wine that has been made from lots of grapes, coming together to make the wine.

At the wedding in Cana, Jesus' first miracle, He made wine! It was the best wine the host had ever drunk. You see, dear ones, we must grow in the king's vineyard to become ready to be made poured out wine, to bring joy to the heart of God. When the Lord inspects His vineyard and squeezes a grape; if it is green it whines; if it is ripe, it's wine! Wine will get the whine out of us!

Dear Savior, make me all you prayed I'd be; body, soul and spirit, by thyself, made free. Take this bread and break it; broken bread I'd be, and poured-out wine, before Thee.

This, my humble plea. Amen.

(This closing prayer was taken from "A Dwelling Place for God," by Ruth Specter LaScelle.)

If you would like Edith to minister to
your group or church, please write or call:

Edith Jackson
Bread of Heaven Ministries
4365 Sunscape Lane
Raleigh, NC 27613
(919) 571-4671
e-mail: breadofheavenmin@prodigy.net